A Passion For Pens

"SWAN"
REMPLISSAGE AUTOMATIQUE
FABRIQUE PAR MABIE TODD & C⁰ LTD LONDRES

MARQUE DE FABRIQUE

PARIS

"Scriptor" Pen

STYLOTO

"THE SELECT" Porte-Plume Réservo
PLUME PLAQUÉE OR

Plume "IVA BIEN"   Plume "ELVA BIEN"

MADE IN ENGLAND   THE "ERIC" PEN   18 CT SOLID
   NIBS
IRIDIUM T

SELF FILLING PEN 5/-
FOREIGN

Porte-Plume "BLACKBIRD"
PRODUIT DES

REMPLISSAGE AUTOMATIQUE
FABRICANTS DU STYLO "SWAN"

3 3

IRIDIUM TIPPED 14 or 18 ct GOLD NIB
Bermond pen
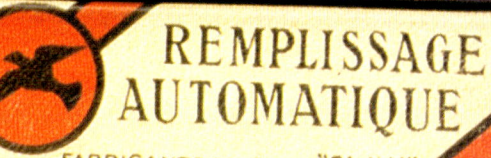

L'ONOTO
A REMPLISSAGE INSTANTANÉ ET AUTOMATIQUE (FABRIQUE PAR T.D.L.R & C⁰...

GOLD STARRY
MANUF⁻ FRANÇAISE GOLD STARRY

- fine -

The Imperial Safety Fountain P

SWELL" Pen
MARQUE DÉPOSÉE
RATS - POINTE IRIDIUM

THE EXCELSIOR SAFETY
Fountain Pen

RODO

ZODIAC
PORTE-PLUME RESERVOIR FRANÇAIS

TRADE MARK   The "Pelican" Self-Feeding Pen   PATENTED   PELICA
PELICAN   MANUFACTURED BY THOS. DE LA RUE & C⁰ LTD   PEN
BUNHILL ROW, LONDON, ENGLAND.

Waterman Co.   173, Broadway New York USA
terman's   Ideal   Fountain Pen
Sole European   Representatives
RDTMUTH. LTD Koh-I-Noor   House, Kingsway, London WC

Safety Fountain Pen   Pebeco

With 14 ct go

XCELSIOR

MANUFACTURE FRANÇAISE d'ARMES & CYCLES

Pierre Haury & Jean-Pierre Lacroux

A Passion For Pens

Translated by Fred Gorstein, M.D.

GREENTREE
PUBLICATIONS

A Geneviève H.

P.H.

A Eliane G. et Alexandre C.

J.P.L.

The outstanding contributions of Pierre Haury and
Jean-Pierre Lacroux are acknowledged with gratitude
by the translator and publisher of the English
version of this volume.

Special appreciation to Anne Echerd for coordinating
the translation and editorial review and to Edward
Fingerman and Boris Rice for their advice and review
of the text

Photography:

Charlie Abad,

Jean Castel,

and Karine Berthelin

Artistic Direction

and Editing:

Camille Scalabre

Layout: Studio Tract

Sketches and diagrams:

Jean-Pierre Lacroux

© Editions Seghers/Editions Quintette, Paris, 1990

ISBN: 0-9637887-01
© For the English Translation Greentree Publications, 1993

Greentree Publications
P.O. BOX 1154
Ridgefield, CT 06877

TABLE OF CONTENTS

FOREWORD

THE FOUNTAIN PEN is both an attractive and practical object about which few writers remain indifferent. Emotions range from a casual attraction to unbridled passion, with every variation in between. Although the reasons for such intense attachment vary, the feeling is universal. What is it that makes this small cylindrical object so irresistible?

The fountain pen is, of course, a writing instrument, but then so is the felt-tip pen, the pencil, the ball-point pen, the stylus, the reed pen, the point, chalk...the list is too long to enumerate. The difference is obvious - the fountain pen is not merely a writing instrument, but something more.

It can be adorned with gold, silver, or lacquer; it can be encrusted with diamonds or inlaid with floral or geometric designs. For some, such ornamentation is where its attraction lies. Originally, the pen and the automatic pencil were similarly decorated. Today, the ball-point pen or felt-tip pen may be likewise enhanced, yet they are hardly equivalent.

The splendor of the overlay may be a sign of wealth or social status for those who, as a rule, do not wear ornamental jewelry. For such individuals, the external signs of wealth are, in many cases, replaced by the ostentation of specific objects, such as a cigarette lighter or a fast car.

Still, in keeping with the type of explanation proposed by psychologists, the fountain pen can be a means to assert one's social standing. It might be inferred that a superb pen reflects the material and intellectual status of its owner. We are familiar with the image of the senior reporter distractedly wielding his sceptor to edit the poorly written lines of his junior colleagues. Never mind...disregard the jokes meant to explain the social role of the instrument only in the context of the behavior of occasional users.

None of these theories nor the meaningless studies that would attempt to explain the fountain pen's social role hold any water. The unique character of the fountain pen owes

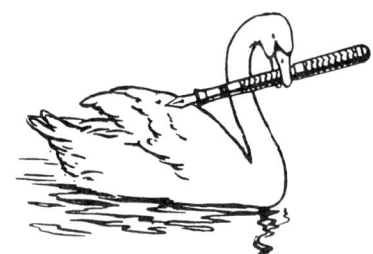

nothing to the beliefs of the economic or political elite who see in the gold nib affixed to a plastic tube filled with ink, a clear symbol of their authority.

People may buy fountain pens for themselves; they are often given as presents, a token of affection or love. But after all, the same can be said of ties...there must be something more to it.

Many children and teenagers have received a fountain pen to mark a milestone in their lives. Over the years it has become one of the accoutrements of our religious and lay rites of passage: first Communion, entry into secondary school, a reward for passing a test.

The fountain pen quickly becomes an intensely personal object, familiar to the hand. Although millions may be produced, each is unique. Only in rare circumstances should it be loaned, even to a close friend. In a matter of a few weeks a fountain pen is irrevocably altered by the user's hand. This is one of the characteristics of the instrument, that it is

friendly to one person's hand but not so to another's.

In summary, the fountain pen is a beautiful writing instrument as well as a personalized token. Nevertheless, this is only one part of the story; there is still something missing - an essential ingredient that fully defines the fountain pen and sets it apart.

The missing ingredient is simple. In most languages, it is expressed by the name of the instrument, although this is no guarantee of clarity. In French, it may be found in the complete dictionary definition.

Developed slightly over a century ago, the fountain pen is the last in a long line of writing instruments, the most important in the Western World, the one with a split nib. It is the great-grandson of the reed pen, the grandson of the quill, and the son of the steel nib. The fountain pen is simply a pen with a fountain. Even though it took centuries to reach this point, the modern pen works on the same principle as the one used by 11th century scribes. It is the pen of our time. All else is secondary, anecdotal, and unimportant.

The fountain pen has no heir apparent, and although it almost fell into disuse at one time, it continues to offer a priceless heritage. Without this legacy, the children of the next millenium would have every reason to believe that writing was merely a haphazard assemblage of arbitrary signs. No one would be able to criticize them for writing even more poorly than the current ball-point and felt-tip pen generations, an unlikely possibility.

Not so long ago, the fountain pen was nearly extinct, destined to survive only among nostalgia freaks or as a trendy gadget. In recent years, the situation has improved and the fountain pen has earned countless new admirers and users. In addition to the numerous personal motives, such as childhood memories, love of that which is beautiful or unique, the desire for acquisition or speculation, and the thirst for knowledge (all of which are equally shared by collectors of cheese labels or Sevres porcelain), the interest, attachment, and passion elicited by the fountain pen are based on a rare phenomenon - we feel that without it a bridge would collapse behind us in the terrifying silence of our distorted memories.

Many books have been written about fountain pens, most of them in English since this instrument was developed in the United States. These books, however, tend to give the impression that fountain pens are, above all, collectors' items whose value is expressed in dollars and cents. In leafing through or even reading these books carefully, one tends to forget that these small cylinders were created for writing. While it does not add to their monetary value, it remains an essential detail.

This volume does not contain exhaustive lists of the revelations of some obscure manufacturer in Cincinnati or Nuremberg nor of the minute detail found on the band of a certain cap of a certain model in a certain year of a certain brand of pen. Such information is sought after by and important to collectors;

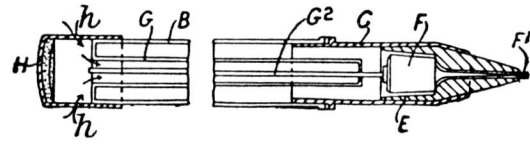

Stylographic Pens
Like the originators of the fountain pen with a nib, the pioneers of the stylographic pen with a needle were American. In 1875, Duncan MacKinnon invented an instrument equipped with a floating needle that slid in a tube which was fitted with a valve blocking the reservoir. When writing, the pressure of the needle on the paper released the valve and permitted a small amount of ink to flow. In 1878, Alonzo Townsend Cross improved the concept by adding a spring, and christened the instrument with a name that stuck: stylographic pen.

however, they have at their disposal other sources to quench their thirst for knowledge. The goal of this book is to show what a fountain pen is.

After a rapid overview of its ancestors, *A Passion For Pens* will attempt to explain how the fountain pen was developed during the 1880s in the United States and to identify its ancestors. It is the story of men, not brand names. It chronicles the first appearance of the fountain pen in France. It then examines the fountain pen as a writing instrument, describes its mechanism of operation, offers advice to beginning collectors, and lists major manufacturers in the appendix. The principal goal of this volume is to cause these small extensions of our hands to be loved, so that they will be collected, of course, but above all, so that they will continue to write for a long time to come.

A Note About Terminology

The question of terminology needs to be addressed. The instrument under discussion is known by several names in the French language (with none being totally satisfactory): **stylo, stylographe, stylo à plume, porte-plume à réservoir, P.P.R., porte-plume**...

The term **fountain pen** (*stylo* in French), commonly used today, is the abbreviated form of **stylographic** pen, from the Greek *stulos*, from which is derived the Latin *stilus*: **writing tip**. The *Petit Robert* lists the first appearance of the French word in 1902, from the English word **stylograph**, which was coined in the 19th century. In 1877, Alonzo Townsend Cross was the first to call a writing instrument a **stylographic** pen. In 1848, a Parisian jeweler called his own invention of a pen with a reservoir a *stylographe* (patent no. 7007, filed January 3, 1848 by a Mr. Valory). This word was derived from the term *stylographie*, which had been coined 2 years earlier to designate a process of reproduction perfected by the Danes.

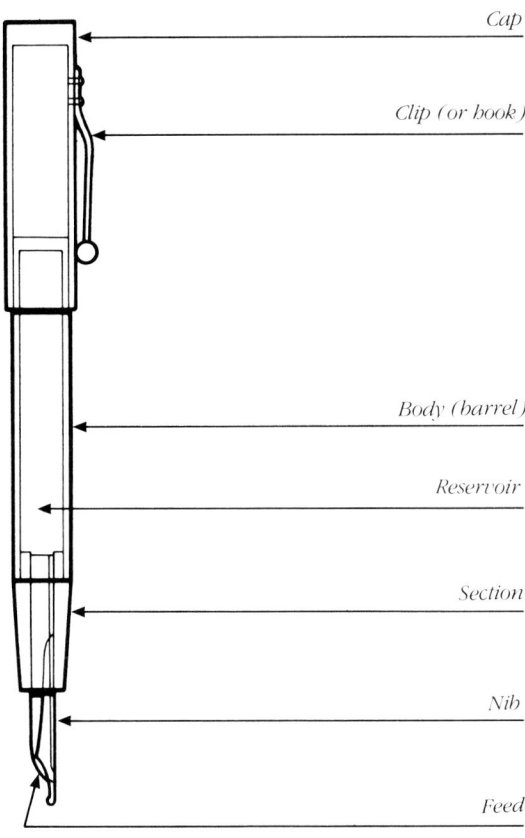

Cap

Clip (or hook)

Body (barrel)

Reservoir

Section

Nib

Feed

Between 1880 and 1900, the English term **stylographic pen** came into common use, but designated only those pens with a tubular tip of the type used almost exclusively for drawing today. These needle-shaped tips produce a line comparable to that of the stylus rather than the fine line of the quill. To speak of the *stylo à plume* is at the same time a redundancy and a *non sequitur*. The ball-point pen (*stylo à bille*), which scribes an even line, is aptly named. To designate the French *stylo*, in English the term **fountain pen** is used, which is the counterpart of the French *porte-plume à réservoir*, an awkward, outdated term no longer in use, but which had the merit of being accurate. Such a practical instrument could not carry so cumbersome a name for long. Some collectors still use the initials **P.P.R.**. French-speaking Belgians use the term *porte-plume*. Although the old *porte-plume* has almost been forgotten, the term still creates some confusion.

There is no single correct term; however, common usage seems to have settled the dispute. Since **fountain pen** (*stylo* in French) has been the most frequently employed term, that is the English word commonly used to designate all writing instruments with nibs. **Stylographic** pen will serve to designate those with tubular tips.

Just for fun, we have included a list of some of the diverse names proposed in the 19th century by inventors and merchants passionately interested in either applied etymology or commercial rhetoric: *aérophore, atmocleide, syphoïde, polygraphe* (versatile author), *mictographe, sanographe, capillographe, crayon-plume* (pencil-pen), *plume-source* (pen with a fountain), *encro-pompe* (ink pump), *encrivore, plume-encrier* (inkwell pen), *plume-écritoire* (writing case pen), *plume perpétuelle* (eternal pen), *intarissable* (inexhaustible pen), *plume à courant d'encre* (flowing ink pen), *plume sans arrêt* (endless pen), *plume alimentée* (feeding pen), *porte-plume alimentaire* (feeding penholder)... clearly we had a narrow escape.

Experts generally refer to the early fountain pen models as *régulier* (standard). However, this terminology is hardly satisfactory. *Régulier* is a bad translation of **regular**, which in English means usual or common. Here again, we struggle with common English usage, and the successors to these early models fared no better. The term **safety** is likewise ambiguous. It has been used to designate all standard models equipped with a screw cap as well as those with retractable nibs. In this volume, the term **security** is used for standard models equipped with a screw cap and not for those with a retractable nib.

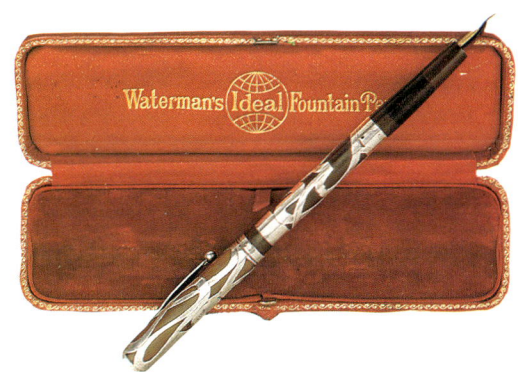

Beautiful example

of a standard Waterman

fountain pen with

an 0.999 fine silver filigree body,

very rare (1905).

SECTION I

A Long Awaited Birth

Man has been writing for 5,000 years.

The fountain pen has been available only since yesterday.

An old dream finally come true,

The "eternal pen" has its future before it.

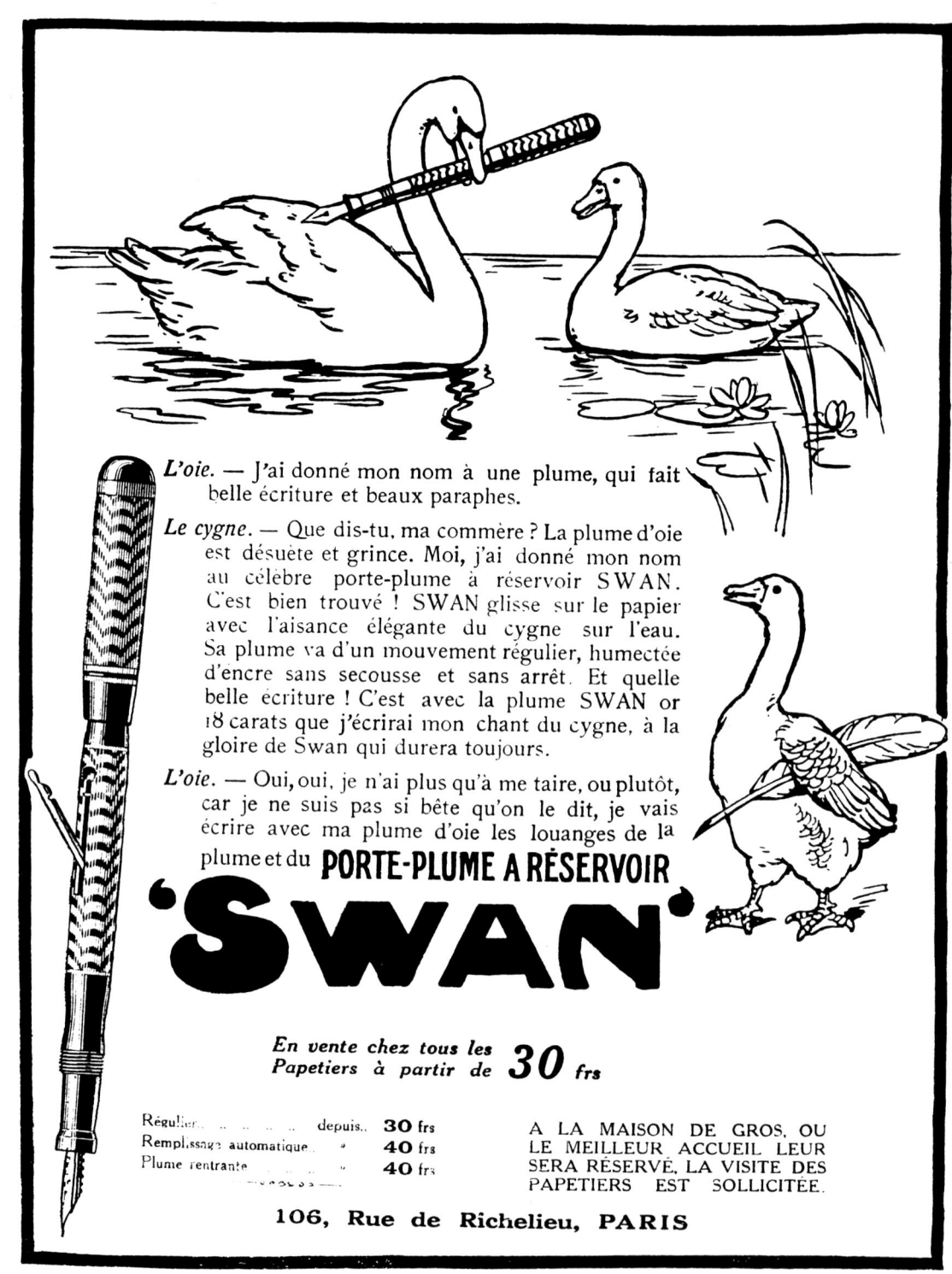
Family Portrait

In order to appreciate the contribution of the fountain pen, we must consider its place in the larger family of writing instruments. The following is not a detailed study of each member, but rather a brief overview. Since the dawn of time, when man drew on cave walls with pieces of rock or charred wood, only two basic types of writing tool have been available - that is, until the present-day invention of tape recorders, computers, and the like made possible a new type of communication. It is a long story...one in which the descendants of the piece of charred wood have not yet written their final word.

Nous ne donnons plus d'encre, tous nos Clients possèdent une Waterman! Monsieur veut-il que je lui prête la mienne?

Du quartier Latin à l'Académie, il n'y a qu'un pas, grâce au "Waterman"

A writer or an artist can either carve or scratch a surface with a hard object, or he can apply a substance of a different color or texture onto a surface.

The **chisel**, the **point**, and the **stylus** belong to the first category. Although their use as writing instruments in the present day has been more or less limited to tombstone engravers, their usefulness should not be underestimated. The Mesopotamians, who invented the alphabet more than 5,000 years ago, used the point. Our upper case letters still bear the imprint of the Roman chisel. All civilizations have used the stylus at one time or another, and some still do.

Tools that apply a substance onto the writing surface can be divided into two groups of unequal importance. The first group includes those that leave traces of their substance on the surface. The **chalk** and graphite **pencils** we use today are descendants of those fragments of limestone and charred wood. There is also the group of instruments that apply a third substance to the writing surface. They are filled with pigmented substances, usually ink for writing. This is the most common type of instrument: **pencils, nibs, fountain pens, ball-point pens, and felt-tip pens**. Almost all writing instruments in use today belong to this second category.

By shredding and exposing the tip of a hollow stemmed rush, the Egyptian scribes devised a rudimentary **pencil**. But it was the Chinese who, 3,000 years ago, invented the pencil as we know it. The **felt-tip** could be considered its direct descendent, providing a certain continuity, since the Japanese use it for writing today.

In the West, the history of writing is closely related to another type of writing instrument, the **split nib**. Its ancestor was the **reed pen**, a simple stem sharpened to a point and then split. From Palestine to the Columns of Hercules, the reed pen was used throughout the Mediterranean basin. In the Middle Ages, it was seriously threatened by the **feather quill**, which eventually prevailed, except among the Muslims who refused to write with an animal product and continued to use the stem of a plant.

The **feather quill** is more flexible than the reed pen and easier to sharpen, as well as less likely to break from the pressure of the writer's hand. Besides, there were geese nearly everywhere, each providing at least 10 usable quill feathers that only required cleaning and sharpening to make a wonderful writing instrument. These qualities made the quill a favorite for nearly 1,000 years, and it was used to record

CH. LEMONNIER 265

René Ravo

Edacoto 87

Le stylo de France Noel 46

23

NE PARTEZ PAS EN VOYAGE
SANS
PORTE-PLUME RESERVOIR
ONOTO

Ehrmann

almost all early Western literature. The drawbacks were the time and effort it took to sharpen the quill and the speed with which the tip wore down, necessitating frequent touchups. Metal, of course, could have solved these minor problems, but not until the middle of the 19th century was the charm of the organic material replaced by the advantages of a metal.

The concept of a metal nib was not new. The Egyptians had thought of it, and the Romans rolled sheets of bronze to form conical reed pens. From the time of the Barbarian invasions of Europe until the middle of the 19th century, people were motivated in their choice of writing instruments by various considerations. First, there was the desire not to use the instrument of the masses, even if only to scrawl an illiterate signature. A prince or a powerful leader deserved to use an instrument other than the piece of bird's wing used by a monk to

copy the gospel of St. John. Nibs or reed pens of gold or silver were designed for this purpose. They did not write as well as their organic counterparts, but that did not matter. Utility was not their attraction.

Other inventors worked with copper, brass, steel, silver, and gold in the hope of creating a durable, permanently sharpened nib that would withstand changes in humidity. By the end of the 17th century, considerable progress had been made, but despite triumphant announcements, the results were less than convincing. Yes, the nibs did last longer; however, they had a distressing tendency to tear the paper. When it was humid, unlike the quill that became only temporarily weakened, the metal

nib became rusty. This was in addition to the damage caused by the acidity of the ink used. Only gold and silver could be used to create satisfactory instruments, yet even these nibs were inferior to a well sharpened quill. They were well-made, but little used. Their price did not make them a bargain either. One mediocre metal nib was far more expensive than a fistful of high-quality feather quills.

It was not craftsmanship but rather the Industrial Revolution that would replace geese. With the advent of the latter in the 19th century, steam engines proliferated and manufacturing facilities were developed, creating a need for factories and office workers. Society was changing and becoming more urban. Governments required more civil servants. While it was advantageous to keep the peasants and even the proletariat class illiterate, civil servants and office workers needed to write. Schools were created. In addition, post-1815 Europe had been shaken by revolutions. Education was now a right as well as a necessity. An industrialized Europe needed pens in many hands and a democratic Europe wanted them in all hands.

By the end of the 18th century, the first steam engines had appeared in England. Into this cradle of industry the steel nib was born. It

The covers of metal nib boxes were offered in a variety of imaginative colors. Unfortunately, the dip pens to which these nibs were affixed did not always exhibit a similar use of color and design.

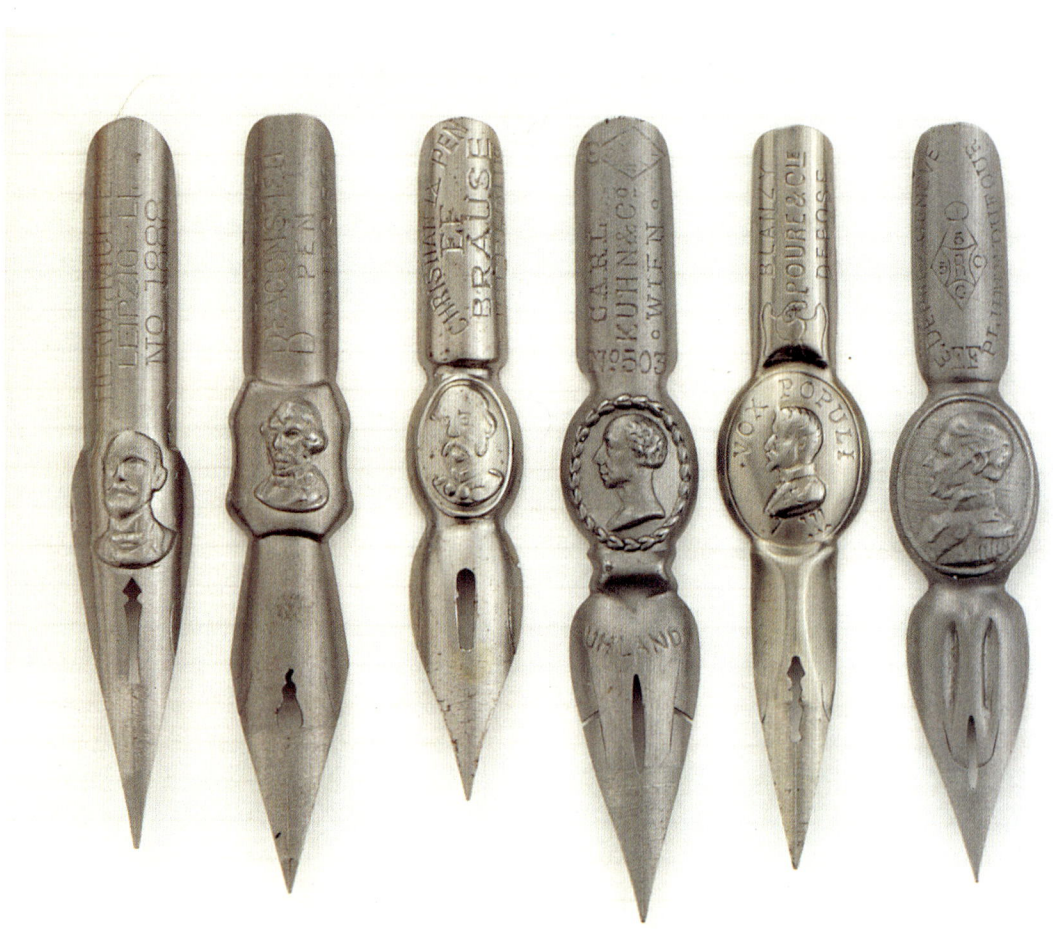

Fine examples of steel nibs with figurine bust engravings.

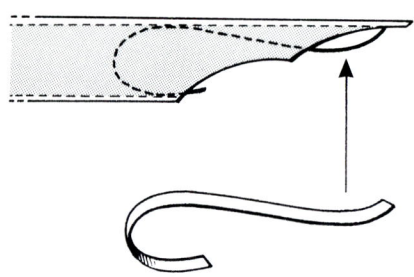

One patent among thousands, demonstrating a reservoir chamber for a metal nib. This one, designed by C.F. Clarke, dates from 1919 and represents a futile attempt to compete with the increasing popularity of the fountain pen.

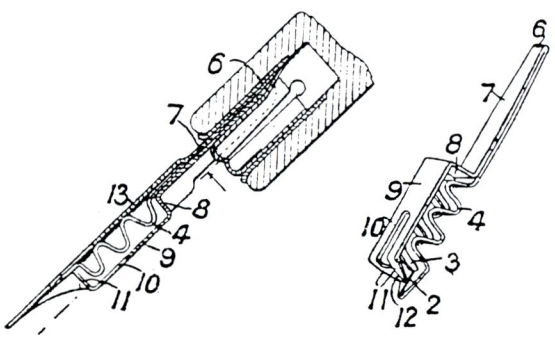

first appeared in Birmingham, England around 1820. Its creators were Joseph Gillott, John and William Mitchell, and Josiah Mason. These men were apprentices to craftsmen who produced, among other things, metal nibs. Gillott worked in the Sheffield workshop of the cutler John Skinner, the Mitchells worked for Spittle, and Mason worked for Samuel Harrison in Birmingham.

James Perry was another type of pioneer - a financier. With Josiah Mason's help, his company became prosperous. Between 1820 and 1840, patent after patent was filed as improvements continued to be made to the nib. Flexibility of the nib was increased by adding slits, a hole, and incisions. Tubular nibs using a large amount of steel were gradually replaced by models with shanks. The metal nib became a quality instrument whose price continued to drop. The feather quill was doomed to extinction. In 1846, the French, with the aid of some specialists from Birmingham, created a

flourishing industry at Boulogne-sur-Mer. The Germans followed suit. Thousands of different nibs were produced, some of them marvelous. The steel nib conquered Europe and would become the weapon with which the battle for democracy in writing would be won. For more than a century, it was used to make the civilized art of writing a reality for the majority of people.

Throughout the 19th century, new companies were created, many of which remained in business until the middle of the 20th century before being acquired, more or less successfully. For those who learned to write with a steel nib, the major names will evoke memories of the gentle rustling of pen on graph paper, of the mastering of downstrokes and upstrokes, of the odor of ink, and of blotches. The important names in order of their appearance are: Gillott (1820), John Mitchell (1822), Perry (1824), William Mitchell (1825), Hinks & Wells (1839), Myers (1842), Blanzy-Poure (1846), Heintze & Blankertz (1849), Baignol & Farjon (Sau-

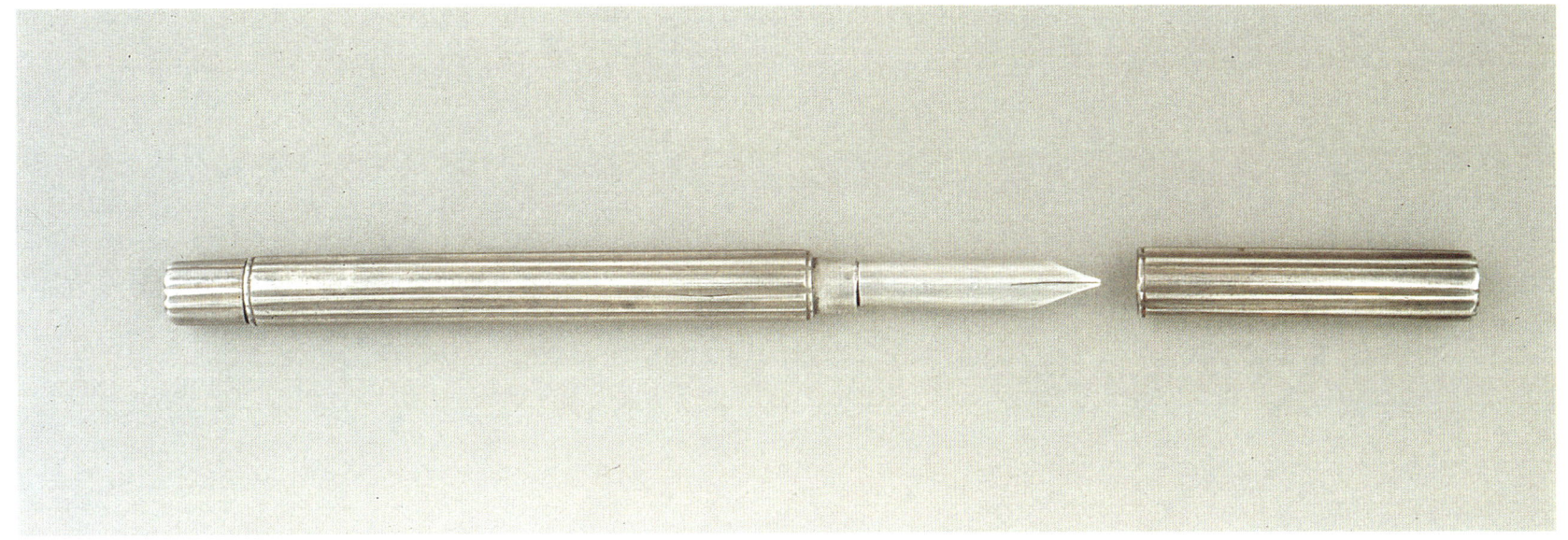

vage 1850, Lebeau 1856), Leonardt (1856), Brandauer (1862), G.-W. Hughes (1865), Soennecken (1875), and the Compagnie Française (Delpierre 1880).

It is difficult to obtain a clear picture of an industry that has virtually disappeared today, but a few figures might help. At the end of the 19th century, 5,000 people were employed in Birmingham and 1,600 in Boulogne-sur-Mer. Annual production reached 2,800 million nibs: 1,800 million destined for England, 500 million for France, and 500 million for the rest of the world. Between 1830 and 1900, estimated total production was 125,000 million nibs. Business was good. In Birmingham and Boulogne-sur-Mer, everyone was convinced it would go on forever. The future was bright but had crossed the Atlantic with no warning. The steel nib would die, but not until a descendant had been born.

The Pen and The Ink Well

The following does not really belong to the history of the fountain pen, but rather to its prehistory. No fountain pen worthy of the name was manufactured before the 1880s. Nevertheless, the first true fountain pens did not appear out of the blue. A long series of more or less successful attempts paved the way.

While it may be an exaggeration to claim that the Egyptian reed pen filled with dried ink was a real fountain pen, it is evident that the idea of creating a reserve of ink inside the pen is as old as the pen itself. From the reed stem to the feather quill, the pen was always envisioned as an independent tool, not tied to the ink well (that tyrannical watering trough manacling the very instrument that in its greatest days would write of liberty). Its freedom was slow in coming. Nevertheless, numerous well-intentioned inventors had tried to free the pen. Two different goals were pursued throughout the centuries and are described here.

The first goal was to supply the pen with a sufficient reserve of ink so as to permit it to write without interruption and frequent refills. In ancient times, reed pens were filled with ink-soaked fibers and, later, the same method was tried with the shafts of goose feathers. A simpler and more efficient method was to insert a small metal nib under the tip of the quill. The nib retained enough ink to write long sentences. In the 17th century, many artisans of varying ability tackled the problem and customized metal nibs with ink reservoirs. The products of their imagination have, for the most part, disappeared; the only traces left are the descriptions of these "eternal pens" found in specialized journals and newsletters. According to such articles, these "eternal pens" were amazing instruments. Nevertheless, they all

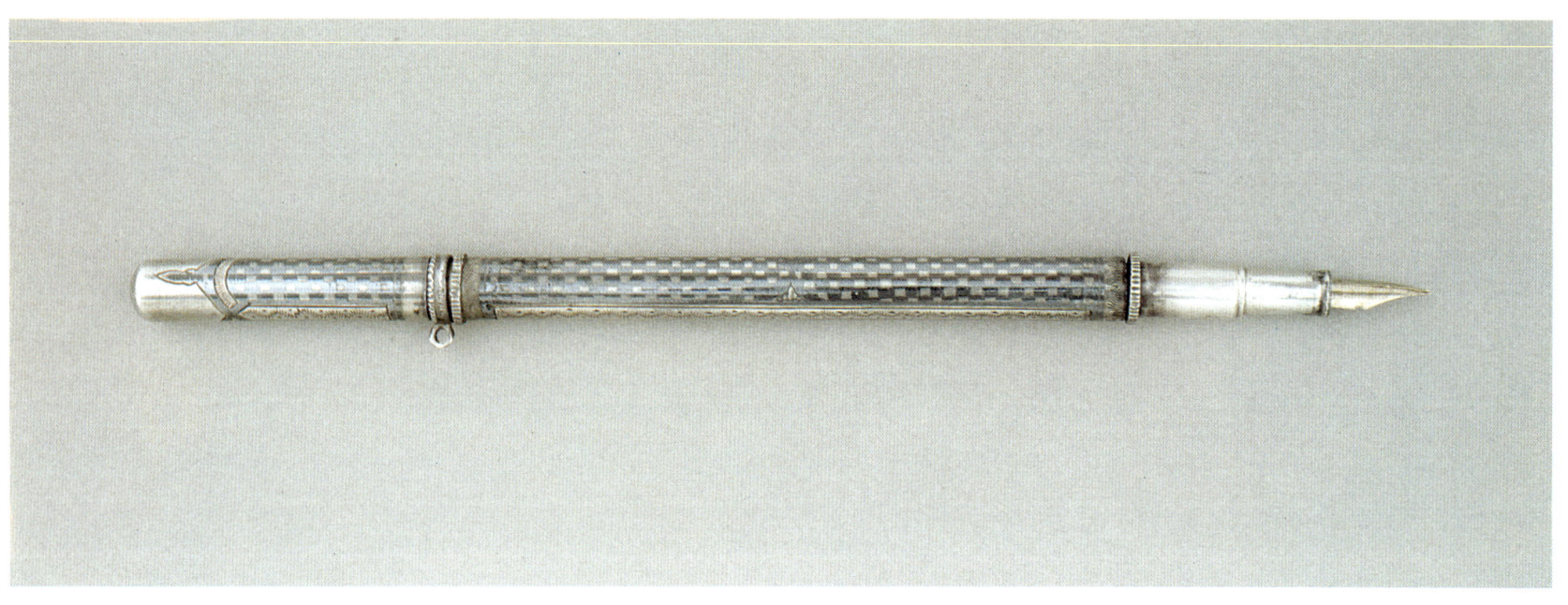

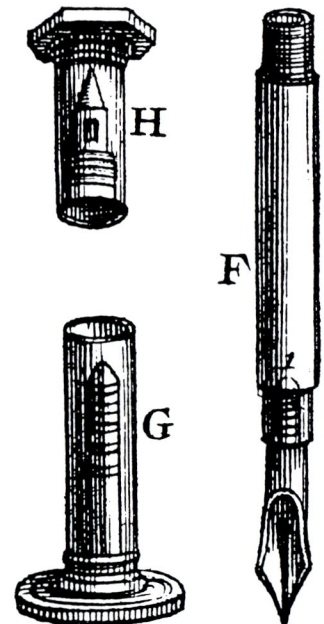

The Syphoïde

The Syphoïde *was designed by Jean Benoît Mallat (1864). Not quite a real fountain pen, but one of its rare mass-produced ancestors. The pen worked in a conventional manner...on the condition that the instructions were followed very carefully (C.P.).*

Patent for the "eternal pen" of Nicolas Bion (1707).

must have had major flaws since they appear to have been completely disdained by quill users. In 1657, in Paris, there were pens with reservoirs that could be used to write more than half a quire of paper, or 12 to 13 pages. Few were sold. In 1707, Nicolas Bion, the "King's Engineer for Mathematical Instruments," developed a perpetual needle for compasses. In England, Germany, and Italy, there was similar activity but no success. Diderot and d'Alembert's *Encyclopédie* mentions "a sort of pen made so that it contains a quantity of ink that flows little by little, allowing one to continue writing without a refill." An annotated note written in the margin of the page reads "poor instrument." Those people really knew what writing meant.

In the 19th century, the quest continued and intensified. Hundreds of patents were filed. Watchmakers, cutlers, mechanics, pharmacists, metalworkers, jewelers, gunsmiths, physicians, and teachers all tried. The instruments that were created began to resemble what we would today call a fountain pen, but only in appearance. Aside from their questionable designs, most had a metal body, often brass, which the ink corroded. This caused the composition of the ink to be altered. The feeds were poorly conceived. Some were as simple as shaking the pen to cause the ink to flow downwards, but nothing prevented the user from being splattered.

Wiser from such an experience, inventors thought to fill the body with a spongy or fibrous material to slow down the flow, but nothing provided a steady flow. Finally, there were patents inspired by plumbing or hydraulic systems with valves and faucets, one faucet for ink and another for air. Among these largely useless ideas, two techniques were actually noteworthy. The first involved applying pressure with one's finger to a diaphragm or rubber sac. The other method involved a piston. While it is true that both of these techniques worked on the same principle as a faucet, they did contain the seeds of what would become excellent systems of filling the pen reservoir.

In 1905, James P. Maginnis made a list of all the patents for pens filed in the civilized world, that is to say, the Anglo-Saxon world. More than 50 pages of the *Journal of the Society of Arts* were filled with this incomplete and one-sided list, which ever since has been considered by many to be a definitive and exhaustive source document on early fountain pens. In 1911, Georges Sénéchal produced the same type of list, citing only those patents filed in France. He did, however, inform the reader of the limitations of his book. Patents were filed in countries by inventors who were not nationals of the country in which the patent was filed. Both Maginnis' and Sénéchal's lists contain some of the most important patents, including

PLUME

et

PORTE-PLUME SIPHOÏDE

GARANTIS INALTÉRABLES

Contenant assez d'encre pour écrire pendant deux jours

De J. B. MALLAT

BREVETÉ S. G. D. G.

Instruction

Le trou qui est dans la tête de la clé indique la direction du trou intérieur qui sert au passage de l'encre; il faut donc pour ouvrir tourner la clé en travers, et en long pour fermer.

Pour remplir le Porte-Plume, il faut tenir la Plume plongée dans l'encre pendant qu'on desserre la vis, et, tout naturellement, serrer la vis pour donner de l'encre à la Plume.

Quand on a cessé d'écrire et qu'on veut le mettre dans son portefeuille, il faut avoir soin de desserrer la vis pour faire rentrer l'encre qui est en dehors de la clé; ensuite vous tournez la clé en long, afin que l'encre ne puisse plus communiquer à la Plume, et vous recouvrez la Plume avec le dé que vous retirez de l'extrémité du Porte-Plume.

Paris. — Typ. Morris et Comp., 64, rue Amelot.

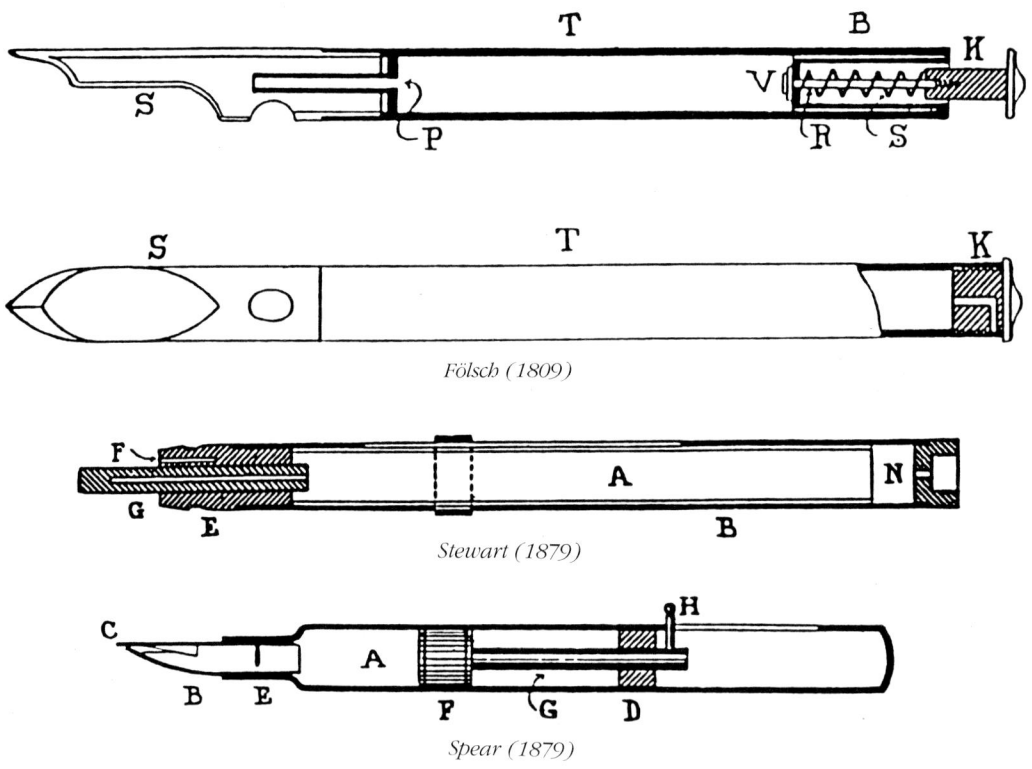

Fölsch (1809)

Stewart (1879)

Spear (1879)

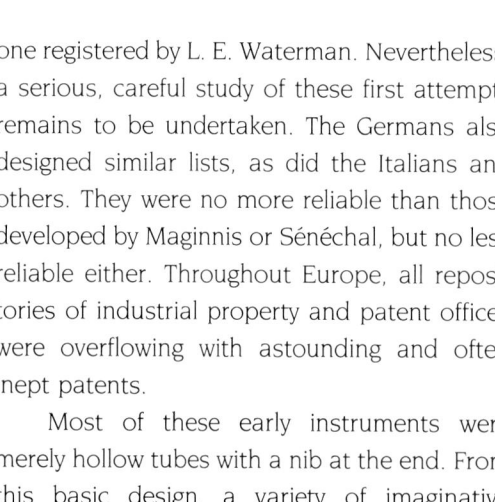

one registered by L. E. Waterman. Nevertheless, a serious, careful study of these first attempts remains to be undertaken. The Germans also designed similar lists, as did the Italians and others. They were no more reliable than those developed by Maginnis or Sénéchal, but no less reliable either. Throughout Europe, all repositories of industrial property and patent offices were overflowing with astounding and often inept patents.

Most of these early instruments were merely hollow tubes with a nib at the end. From this basic design, a variety of imaginative methods of filling pens and controlling ink flow were possible, using faucets, pistons, valves, springs, siphons, bulbs, and sponges. It is amazing that even after 1890, some would-be inventors desperately continued to propose the same types of systems that clearly had been proven unworkable decades earlier. For over two centuries, all attempts to add a reasonably sized reservoir to the nib failed. The initial goal was too ambitious. However, ultimately a nib containing a small reservoir did become a

reliable adjunct. Many inventors filed hundreds of useless patents, whereas the major manufacturers offered remarkable models with hollows, ridges, tabs, covers, small receptacles, and fixed or removable reservoirs. The best of these enabled an individual to write several pages with a safe, even flow of ink.

The desire to escape incessant trips back and forth between the page and the ink well seems to be the principal reason for the success of the fountain pen. Its importance should not be overstated. "Incessant" is not a completely accurate term. A well-sharpened quill or a good steel nib allowed an individual to write a sentence longer than the grammatical capacity of most people. Only someone who has never used a quill would think it necessary to return to the ink well after writing only five or six words. Besides, as we have seen, there were nibs with a reservoir that held enough ink for even the most verbose writers. Of course, one might consider the need for even infrequent refills to be a hindrance, an annoyance, or an impediment to the written expression of the ideas of a

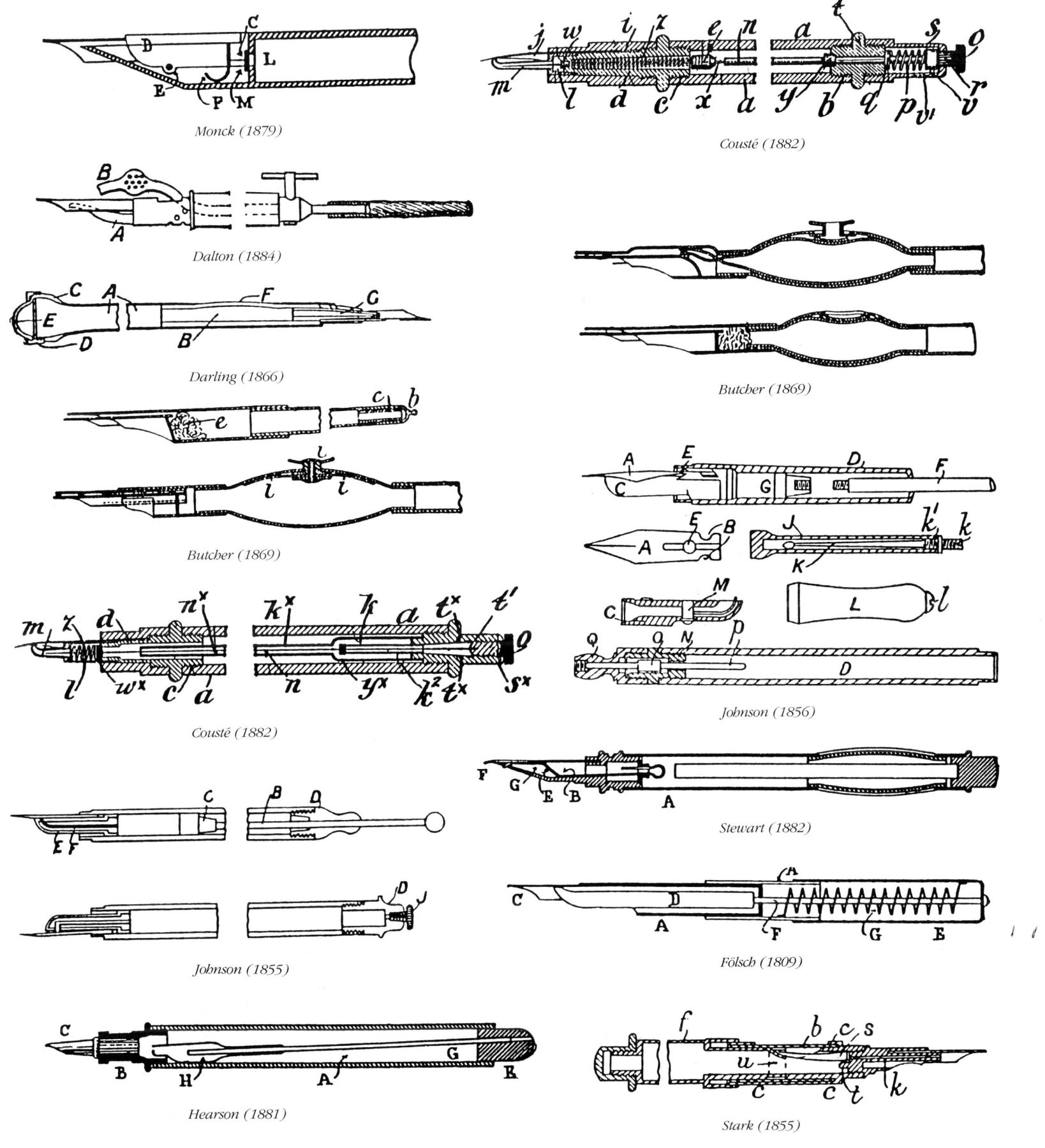

Monck (1879)

Cousté (1882)

Dalton (1884)

Darling (1866)

Butcher (1869)

Butcher (1869)

Johnson (1856)

Cousté (1882)

Stewart (1882)

Johnson (1855)

Fölsch (1809)

Hearson (1881)

Stark (1855)

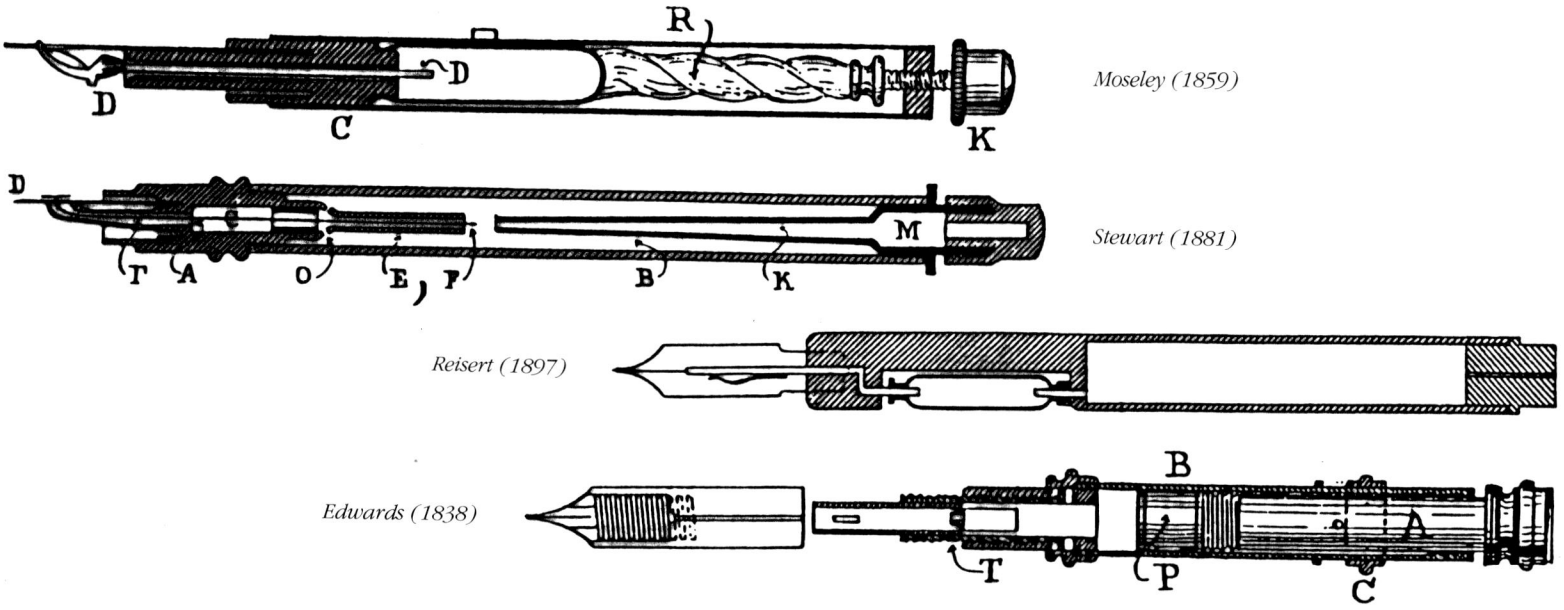

Moseley (1859)

Stewart (1881)

Reisert (1897)

Edwards (1838)

quick mind. It is debatable. Many writers, even very good ones, hesitated to give up the quill or steel nib for a gold fountain pen. These short, yet obligatory, interruptions were apparently beneficial at times. Rather than slowing productivity, they provided the writer with an opportunity to reorient his thoughts. The interruption afforded the writer an opportunity to rethink an awkward turn of phrase, thus gaining time for him in the long run by avoiding the need to make corrections. Admittedly, this attitude masked, in part, a difficulty in accepting that which was new. Furthermore, the need to dip a pen in ink may be one explanation, but it is not the only one.

People tend to write everywhere, not only seated at a table or desk near an ink well. They also stand up and even leave the room. In doing so, the need to write continues, either for pleasure or for professional reasons. That is where the difficulty begins for the bucolic poet, the tax collector, the salesman, or the policeman. A pen is easily transported, but ink is not. Inkstands and portable ink wells in various forms have long accompanied traveling writers throughout all parts of the world where ink is used. But despite many clever gimmicks designed to prevent leaks, these devices were not very practical and spills were frequent. As soon as a fountain pen capable of functioning in a

satisfactory manner was developed, it rendered them obsolete. The disappearance of the desk ink well was not as rapid as that of the portable ink well; the elimination of the latter assured the success of the fountain pen as soon as it functioned properly. This took place in the United States at the end of the last century and marked the end of the fountain pen's prehistory.

The New World

The United States at the End of the 19th Century

The history of new technology offers at least one source of amusement - a collection of various claims of "undisputed paternity." The modes of transportation and countless applications of electricity are rich in contradictory and "unshakable" claims still maintained today. Writing instruments have also been the subject of similar outrageous claims printed in scientific reviews with the utmost sincerity, but which today seem like delirious ravings. If we make an exception for the shameless advertisement copy writers and incompetent specialists, it is very difficult to maintain the claims that the pencil is unquestionably an

American invention and the metal nib is a French invention, and that the origin of the fountain pen or of the typewriter is...and here you should open your atlas or consult the list of member countries of the United Nations.

The stylus can be attributed to the whole of mankind, the reed pen to the Old World, the feather quill to Europe, and the pencil and paper to China. In fact, the pencil owes much to the Frenchman Nicolas Conté and the industrial metal nib was born in Birmingham, England, the fruit of the intellects of Joseph Gillott and James Perry. Finally, the fountain pen is American by birth, and without Lewis Edson Waterman, it likely would have remained for some time little more than an absurd tube outfitted with a nib, releasing ink at flow levels ranging from a trickle to a torrent.

Although it is true that the inventive genius of one individual can be a determining factor, rare are the occasions when that genius survives the test of time. Conté conceived the admixture of clay with graphite, not just because he was intelligent, but because the Crown and the British Government had imposed a blockade on the young French Republic, thus depriving its writers of Borrowdale's graphite. Gillot began the industrial production of steel nibs in Birmingham around 1820, because he was at the heart of the first Industrial Revolution, at a time when the United States was only a limited, agricultural society populated with semi-literate people who dreamed of wide open spaces. At that time, thanks to the needs of an industrialized society and to democratic aspirations, Europe was learning how to write, while the United States was getting ready to conquer the Indians. Thus, the requirements of society and feathers were really at different levels.

Fifty years later, the situation had changed considerably. In Europe, the pioneers of the steel nib had died and their successors, sitting on considerable fortunes, were preoccupied only with making more money; there was no longer a premium on imagination. In contrast, in the United States, the surviving Indians were on reservations, and the eastern part of the country was becoming industrialized. Times were hard, but creative.

To manufacture a pen requires a lot of know-how. To produce them at a reasonable price requires specialized equipment and even more know-how. The small craftsmen were no longer needed. As a viable artisan class, they died out around 1830, crushed under the presses of Gillott, Perry, and others. However, any tinkerer was capable of fitting one of these marvelous nibs onto a wooden cylinder.

By the second half of the 19th century, there were very few manufacturers of steel nibs in the United States, while there were scores of small pen companies that purchased metal nibs to be mounted onto more or less ornate, complex holders. In a fountain pen, two things are of critical importance: the nib and the feed system. Before 1884, the latter did not exist.

Hence, it was the nib that was all important. Even if the pen "manufacturer" merely assembled parts and did not make the nibs, nothing prevented him from advertising his wares extolling the advantages of his particular pen.

Most pen manufacturers at this time had a very localized distribution and only limited production, and some had a very fleeting existence. Only a few authentic pioneers are worthy of note - Paul Wirt, John Holland, Warren Lancaster. Brief notes on these men are found in the appendix of this volume.

There were also the four great fountain pen manufacturers - Waterman, Parker, Sheaffer, and Wahl-Eversharp. This group of four made its place in history on one major basis, namely, production capability. These four manufacturers have one thing in common - they dominated the market for half a century because they supplied the world with fountain pens of excellent quality. This fact is the chief rationale for their place in history.

Waterman, Parker, and Sheaffer were not only names of companies or trademarks. They were also the names of individuals who played a crucial role in the history of the fountain pen. Such was not the case with Wahl-Eversharp. In this volume, emphasis is placed on the importance of the men, more so than on their companies.

Lewis Edson Waterman (1837-1901)

Lewis Edson Waterman was an insurance broker in New York who, like his peers, pursued contracts with unreliable writing implements. A few bold souls adopted the first fountain pens, but Waterman remained faithful to his old steel nib and its indispensable companion, the ink well. Without belittling the merits of the steel nib, one must admit that it could never be the instrument of choice for a traveling writer, whether he be a mailman, salesman, or policeman. Leakage from the ink wells could cause, at any time, minor mishaps, such as stained suits, soaked traveling cases, and splattered documents. This constant problem was frustrating and Waterman wondered if the time had finally

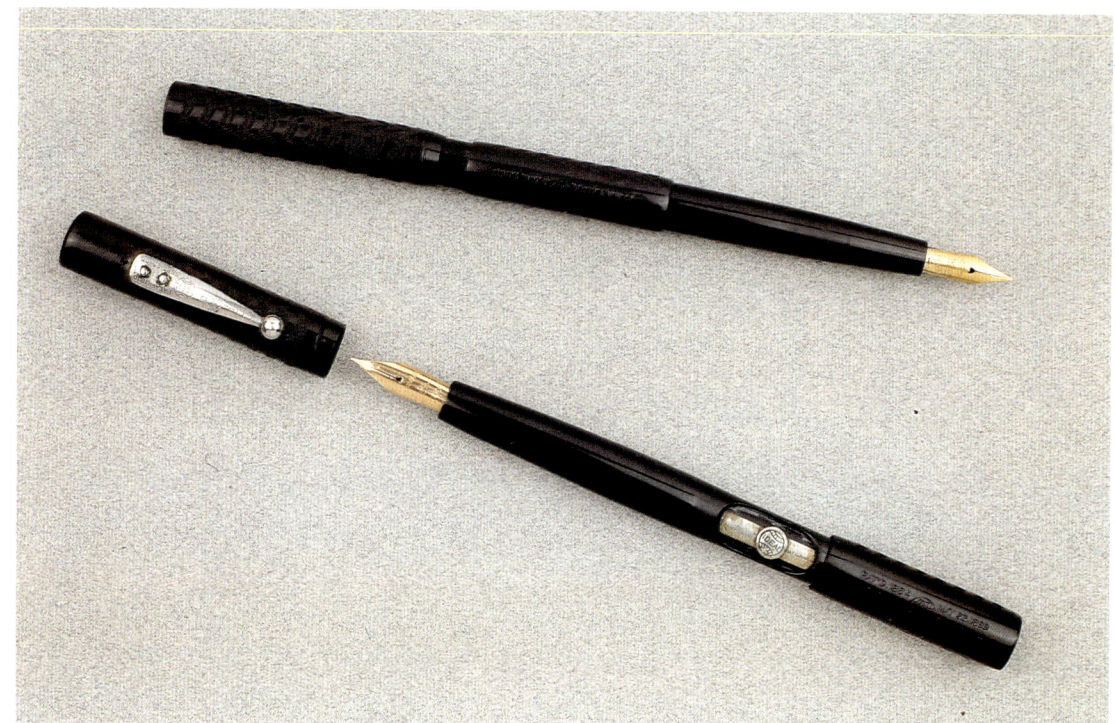

come to acquire the latest modern instrument, a fountain pen.

Folklore has it that Waterman, having done his research with skill and diligence, was lucky enough to have the opportunity to obtain a sizeable insurance contract, the type of contract that happens once in a lifetime, a contract with a substantial commission, a windfall. So he took the opportunity to acquire a brand new fountain pen, not wishing to leave anything to chance. He sat behind his desk, filled his new-fangled fountain pen, carefully prepared the contract documents, filled out the names, the addresses, and all pertinent information, correct in every way. The fountain pen was really great; the only thing that was missing was the client's signature, a mere formality. The client, a contractor, had asked Waterman to meet him on a construction site. With a light heart and a bouncy step, Waterman arrived at his meeting and handed over the contract with his new fountain pen for his client to sign. As the client put the pen to the paper, nothing happened. He shook the wonder of modern technology and a drop of ink fell on the document...a nuisance, but nothing serious. He tried again and still nothing happened. The client shook the pen once again. All the facts are not completely clear, but at this point a few epithets may have escaped from Waterman's lips, because instead of the long awaited signature, a black puddle of ink appeared on the contract and spread, swallowing provision after provision. The pen was emptying all over the contract...a bad omen for a life insurance policy.

Supposedly after recovering his lost composure, Waterman returned to his office and prepared a new contract only to find, when he returned to the construction site, that a competitor had beaten him to it and had obtained the coveted signature. Waterman did not let this setback defeat him. He swore that his career would never again depend on so precarious a circumstance. Having some mechanical aptitude, he undertook to invent, purely for his own use, a reliable instrument that would deliver ink evenly, without caprice...a fountain pen worthy of the name.

He studied most of the models that were currently available on the market and came to the inescapable conclusion that none had solved the essential problem, namely the regulation of ink flow. Although many of these models had very sophisticated ink distribution systems, all the instruments dispensed ink erratically. Their designers had not grasped an

*Historical meeting on a construction site
of an insurance broker, a businessman,
and a capricious fountain pen.*

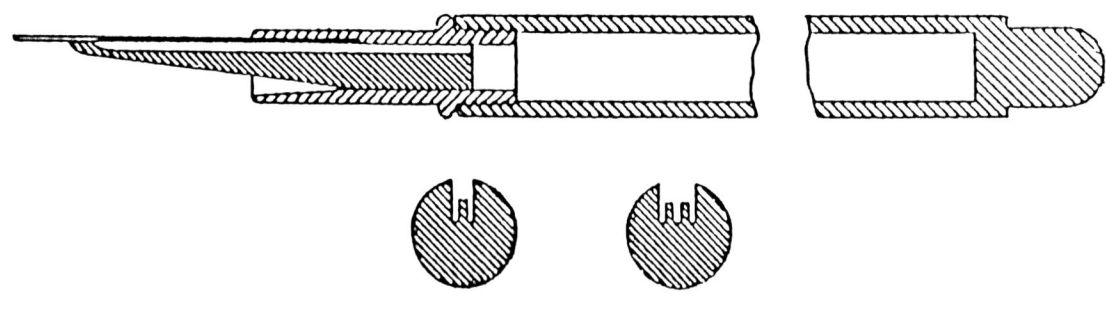

*Patent for the feed of Lewis Edson Waterman -
an excellent example of efficient simplicity.*

understanding of the complexity of the principle of capillary attraction combined with the effects of atmospheric pressure. If the body of the fountain pen is compared to an ink bottle, then the feed must play the role of a flow regulator. Waterman directed his efforts to that end, and he quickly realized that a conduit allowing simultaneous air and ink passage would be the solution. There still remained the challenges of manufacturing and testing. At this point, he went to see his brother Elijah, a wheelmaker in Kankakee, a small town to the south of Chicago. Legend has it that Elijah Waterman manufactured a fountain pen out of a spoke salvaged from an old wheel. With a saw, a rasp, and a pocket knife as his only tools, Lewis Edson Waterman began carving and shaping small wooden and black hard rubber rods. The first attempts were disappointing, but knowing that he was headed in the right direction, he continued designing and testing his ink conduits. Finally, he succeeded in building a working model - a cylinder with a canal having a square cross section and two thin grooves located at the bottom. It worked, but later Waterman wanted to perfect his invention and added a third groove in the middle of the canal. It was with this system that he registered his patent on February 12, 1884, a historical date because it is without question this event that marks the birth of the fountain pen as we know it today. All feed systems with which pens were subsequently equipped were based on this same principle. Nothing in Lewis Edson Waterman's life could have predicted this success. Born in 1837 in Decatur, Otsego County, New York State, he had only a minimal education. At the age of 16, he moved to Illinois with his parents. During the summer months, he worked as a carpenter. He became, in turn, a publishing agent, a stenography teacher, and finally found his calling in insurance sales. Nothing he had done up to this point demonstrated any scientific gift nor was he a skilled mechanic, but

INSTRUCTIONS POUR L'USAGE
de Watermans "IDEAL" Pomp-filling Pen

Ce porte-plume à **Remplissage automatique** est établi sur un principe nouveau qui n'a jamais été appliqué aux porte-plume à reservoir. Il est le plus simple et le plus ancien de tous les systèmes à remplissage automatique, rien ne peut s'y déranger et il permet de s'assurer que le remplissage est complet.

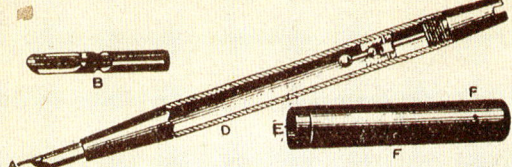

Les instructions suivantes sont à observer pour le maniement de ce porte-plume :

1. - Le porter dans la poche pointe en haut ; le déposer la plume légèrement relevée.

2. - Ouvrir les trous d'air du capuchon, si le porte-plume est destiné à être porté dans la poche ; les boucher à la cire au contraire, si celui-ci doit rester sur un bureau ou pupitre, autrement l'encre sécherait et la plume n'écrirait pas de suite.

3. - Pour enlever le capuchon, lui donner un léger coup de gauche à droite ; pour le remettre un tour de droite à gauche. Si le capuchon était sale à l'intérieur, *l'essuyer soigneusement*, autrement on salirait l'autre bout du porte-plume et ensuite les doigts.

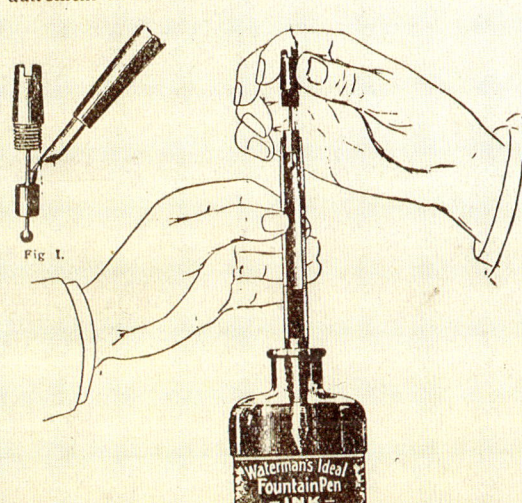

Fig. I.

Le remplissage se fait automatiquement dans ce porte-plume par un petit système de pompe très ingénieux. Pour y procéder, enlever le capuchon, tremper la plume entière et une petite partie du réservoir (1 à 2 $^{m/m}$) dans l'encre, dévissez le bout opposé de la plume avec les doigts ou avec une pièce de monnaie et humecter préalablement la petite pompe pour établir l'adhésion si le porte-plume n'avait pas encore servi.

Faire actionner ensuite la petite pompe par un mouvement rapide de va-et-vient dans le réservoir sans toutefois le retirer entièrement de celui-ci. Quand on voit arriver l'encre au-dessus de la petite pompe on arrête le mouve-ment et on revisse rapidement le tampon sans retirer la plume de l'encre. Seulement lorsque cette partie est vissée à bloc, le porte-plume tiendra l'encre et pourra être retiré. Après un petit essuyage de la plume et de la jonction, la plume est prête à écrire. Le petit tampon ne doit jamais être dévissé sans que la plume se trouve trempée dans la bouteille ou tenue au-dessus d'un récipient quelconque autrement le réservoir se viderait, comme il est facile à comprendre, et un accident pourrait s'en suivre.

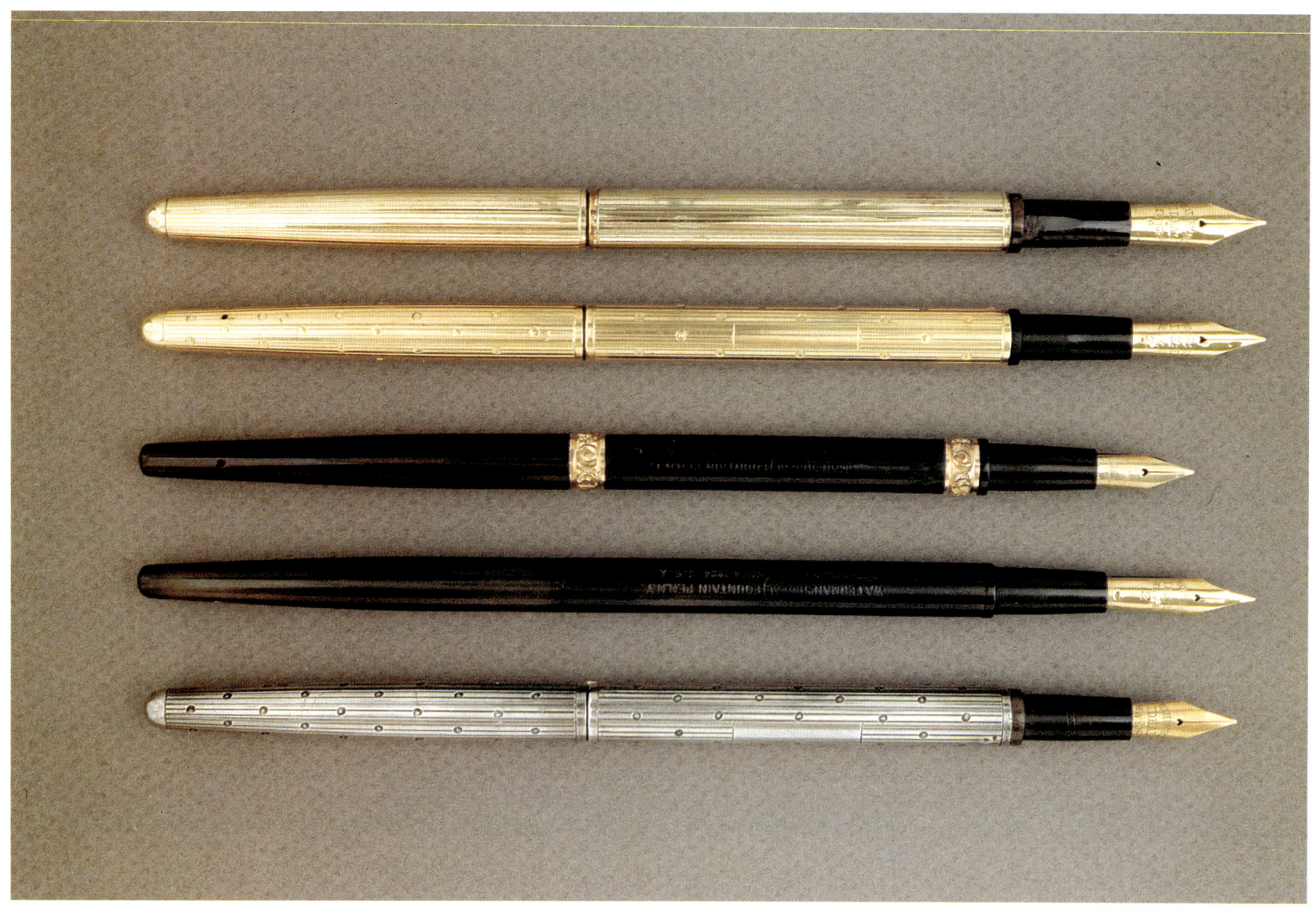

Standard Waterman Taper Cap, French and American bodies (circa 1904).

Banded Pens
Retractable pen by Waterman in red and black hard rubber (1907-1920), with plain bands and French clips, ornate American bands. Very simple yet elegant bodies. The bands were used to personalize the pen and could be engraved with the name or the initials of its owner.

rather a self-taught jack-of-all-trades. It might be said that to have created a few grooves and a canal in a segment of black rubber was not a terribly complicated process. This may be true, but the fact remains that no one had conceived of it before. Hundreds of intellects, some sharper than Waterman's, had for centuries pondered the question, but with no success. Mechanisms both more and less complex had been invented by brilliant scientific minds, but millions of ink blots had also been produced. The most striking thing about Waterman's early pens was their incredible simplicity - the beauty of just five components. There was no complex mechanism, merely a closed tube as a cap, another to hold the ink, a feed, a nib, and a shank to keep the whole thing together.

Lewis Edson Waterman built his first fountain pen for himself in order to have an instrument that would allow him to pursue his career as an insurance broker without mishaps, leaks, ill-timed ink blots, and ruined contracts. The first "Waterman" worked so well, at least so much better than any of its predecessors, that it would have been a shame, even unethical, to deprive the rest of humanity of its benefits. Close friends, colleagues, and clients all wanted to have a Waterman fountain pen. It was difficult to deny them; hence, Waterman's career as a door-to-door insurance agent came to an end and, as a consequence, a new industry was born.

Waterman opened a shop on Fulton Street, located behind a cigar store, with a sign

Top: "Knock on Wood". Hard rubber and wood talismans were given away as advertising gimmicks.

Right: Standard Waterman fountain pens with screw caps, called "securities" (circa 1913). This pen became the P.S.F. (Pocket Self-Filler), Waterman's first lever filler, with the addition of a rubber sac and a lever.

Filigree
From 1900 to 1925, this type of trim was very popular. Most manufacturers offered several models in their catalogs, in gold, gold-plate, or silver. They are beautiful but erroneously named. Filigree is an English term that means assembled with metal wires, which has nothing to do with the cut-out metal designs shown here.

that read: "**Waterman's Ideal Fountain Pen - Guaranteed for 5 Years**". In his first year of business, he made 200 black hard rubber fountain pens on his kitchen table; in the second year, 500. Although he sold all that he produced, profits were lean. The pen, at least initially, proved to be less profitable than insurance policies. Fortunately for him, his landlady advanced him credit.

The third year was decisive. Advertising came into play through the efforts of a very shrewd salesman named E.T. Howard, who offered Waterman a quarter page advertisement in a well known magazine at a rate of $62.00 per issue...a mere trifle, but too much for the impoverished Lewis Edson. So Howard did something rather unusual, even for those days. He financed the advertisement himself, asking to be paid only if it was successful. Orders flocked in beyond expectations. The first phase was ending but another one was beginning. Waterman had to move to larger premises, he had to find factory facilites that would enable him to meet the demand. As a result, the Waterman Pen Company was founded, and

Lewis Edson Waterman managed it until his death in 1901.

Waterman had given the company its foundation and impetus so that it could survive without him and dominate the world of fountain pens for three decades, while at the same time remaining a family business. In 1901, his nephew Frank D. Waterman succeeded him. In the early 1930s, the chief management officers were: President, Frank D. Waterman; Vice-President, L.E. Waterman, Jr.; General Secretary, Fred S. Waterman; Treasurer, Frank D. Waterman, Jr.; Sales Manager, Clyde H. Waterman. Unfortunately, genius is not hereditary, which partially explains the decline of the Waterman Company in the United States. Today, the Waterman name is still inscribed on fountain pens, but on the other side of the Atlantic, in Paris. But that is another story.

Standard Waterman, hard rubber overlay, (from top to bottom) gold-plated, gold-filled, solid gold (circa 1900).

Thin line Waterman Secretary pens in marbled and black hard rubber, American made bodies, silver and gold-filled (1908-1916).

Cone Cap

This style first appeared in 1893, but was called the Cone Cap only from 1898 on. The ends of the body and of the section are truncated, which allows for better handling and an improved fit for the cap. This illustration shows several sizes, from 12 1/2 to 18, and one large size 20.

Retractable nib (safety) Waterman, 42 1/2 v. Among many American and European models (gold, silver, and gold-filled), three silver lacquered French models are shown. The "coquille d'oeuf" (circa 1930) and two models designed for export to French Indochina are also shown.

Standard Waterman pens, black hard rubber, silver (English and French), gold-filled (French). The tip of the cap is embellished with semi-precious stones, which could be engraved and used as seals (1906-1908).

Ladies Pens
Retractable nib Waterman pens (42 1/2 v.) in black hard rubber and red marbled. They were manufactured in the United States from 1908 until 1929 and in France until World War II. French models in gold, silver, and gold-filled. These pens cover two periods. Until 1930, threading for the cap was short and protuberant; in the 1930s, the threads were longer and deeply grooved.

George Parker's first patent (December 1889), registering a feed.

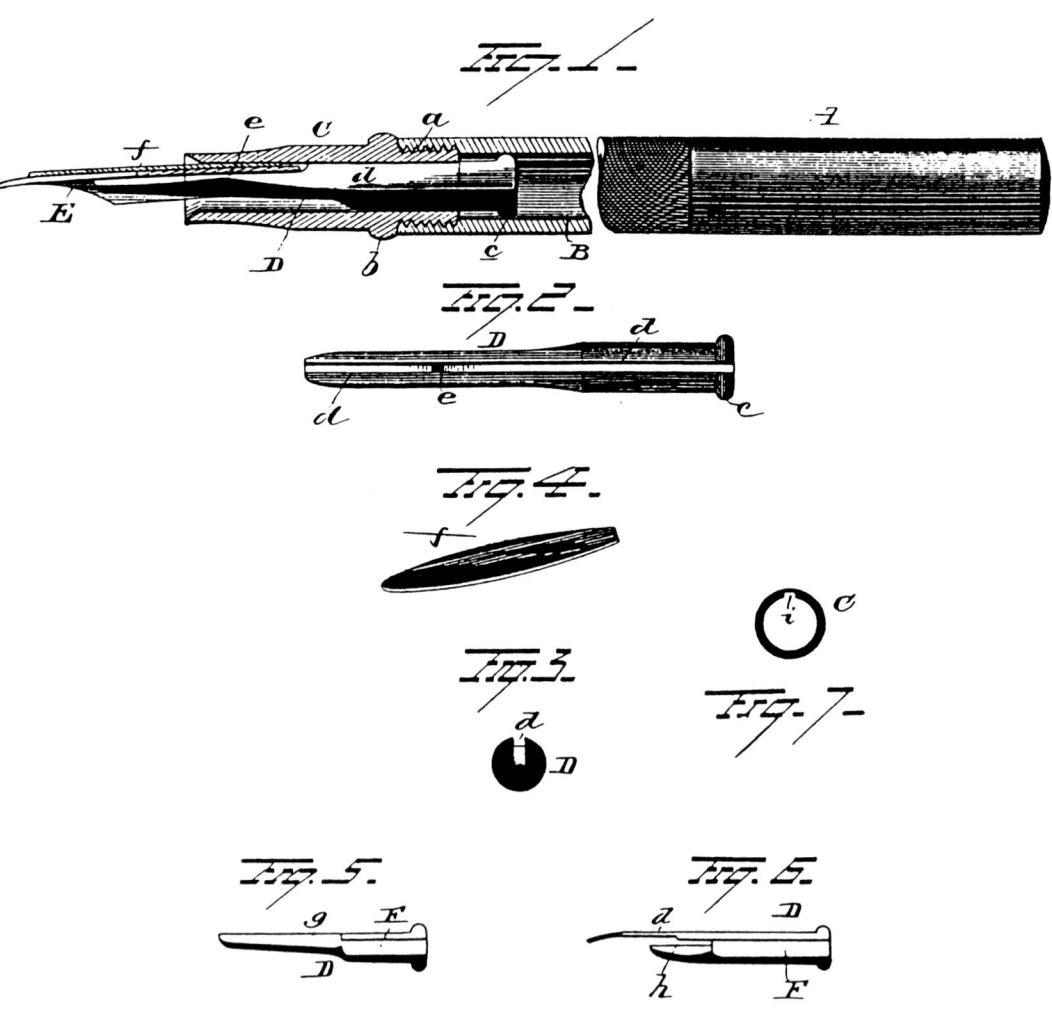

George Parker (1863-1937)

In the latter part of the 19th century at the Valentine School in Janesville, Wisconsin, there was a young teacher of telegraphy named George Parker, who, in order to supplement his meager salary, sold John Holland fountain pens to his students. These young men were demanding consumers and they brought him their pens whenever they were in need of repair. The conscientious Parker undertook the servicing of the problematic instruments. With the exception of the contemporary Waterman models, a fountain pen's ink flow was interrupted whenever air failed to enter the barrel chamber. Initially, Parker's competence with repairs was almost nil and his knowledge even sketchier. He learned on the job, by dismantling and then reassembling his students' pens. He soon became discouraged because it seemed that the more pens he sold, the more he had to

repair. Nevertheless, this vicious cycle afforded him the opportunity to acquire a thorough understanding of the mechanisms of pens used at that time. Like Waterman, with whose invention he apparently was not familiar, he sought to resolve the problem of air-ink exchange. He bought a few tools, a lathe, a chain saw, a small drill, and tinkered endlessly in his rented room.

Parker created a small feed with an air channel onto which he fitted a nib. The miracle was that it worked! He proceeded to fit John Holland pens with his system. His students were delighted, to the point where he seriously thought about making his own pens. In that way, he could see to it that they would be so well made that they would not be returned immediately to his shop for repair.

In 1889, he obtained his basic patent. He purchased black hard rubber rods and 14 karat nibs, and began manufacturing. To minimize the risk, he retained his teaching position. While

Fig. 1.

Fig. 2.

Fig. 3.

Fig. 5.

Fig. 4.

Fig. 6.

Lucky Curve
George Parker patented this feed on December 4, 1894. Its principle is simple. When the fountain pen is in a vertical position with the nib upward, gravity causes the ink to flow in a downward direction towards the reservoir but capillary attraction causes a little ink to remain in the feed. This small amount of ink is pushed upward if heat creates an increase in air pressure; when the pen is taken out of the pocket and the cap removed, a leak will almost certainly occur. In this system, the curvature of the feed is in close contact with the reservoir, thereby creating additional capillary attraction, and the ink contained in the feed flows back into the reservoir. Parker manufactured the Lucky Curve *for more than 30 years.*

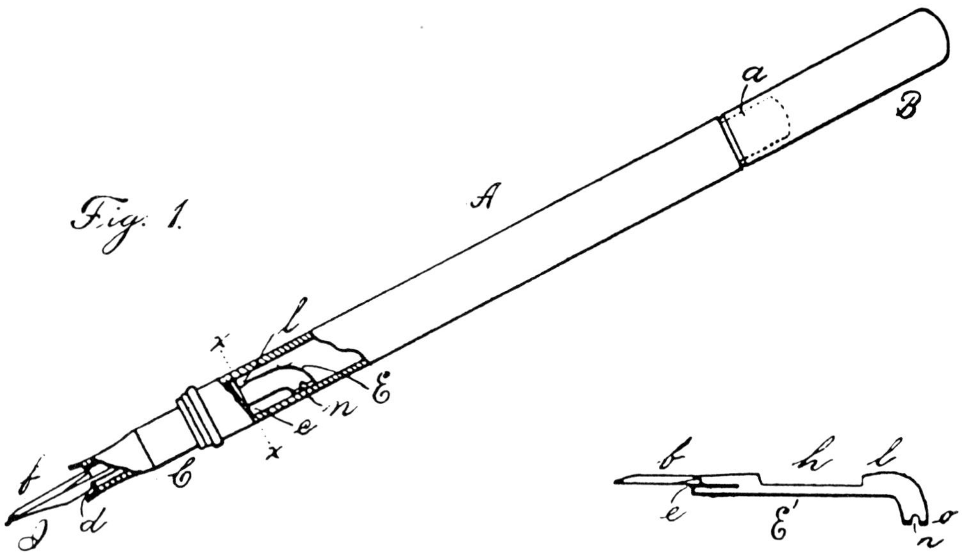

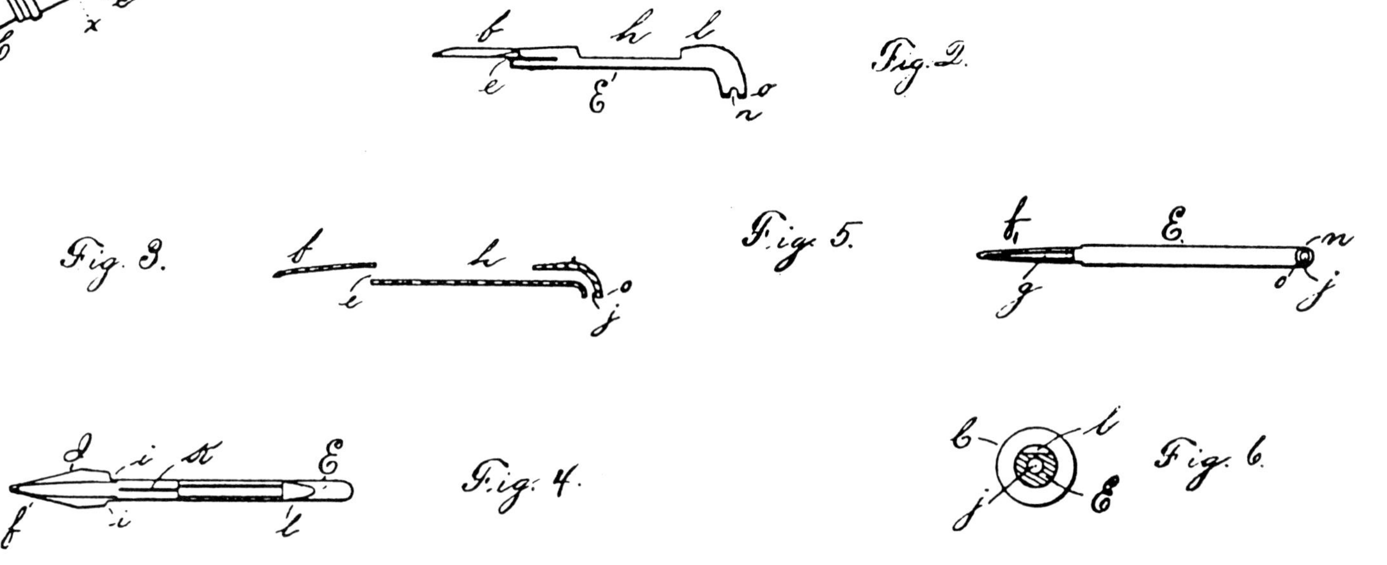

Waterman had started his business in a back alley, Parker started his in a rented room. Without financial support or a method for distribution, his future was, at best, uncertain. Competition was fierce and small manufacturers like Parker were a dime a dozen. He knew he had to find a gimmick. In those days, there were very few hotels in Janesville, Wisconsin, and the one in which Parker was lodged also housed most of the traveling salesmen of the area. Parker distributed some of his pens to a few of them. From that time on, sales accelerated at a rapid pace, but not without significant financial problems. An insurance salesman named W.F. Palmer called on Parker to sell him a policy, but poor George was too broke. So Palmer, who had a keen interest in the Parker's fountain pen, seized the opportunity to offer

Parker a partnership. Parker sold Palmer a 50% share in the business (including the patents) for $1,000. The combination of the two men's talents worked well, with Parker running the manufacturing, sales, and advertising and Palmer managing the money and the bookkeeping.

Parker registered a succession of patents during the first few years, including the **Lucky Curve** feed (1894), the **Jointless Pen** (1899), a filling system with a compression bar (1904), and the **Arrowhead** feed (1905). Subsequent new models appeared every 10 years or so, with names that reflect fountain pen history: the **Jack Knife** (1909), the **Duofold** (1921), the **Vacumatic** (1933), and the **51** (1939).

In time, George Parker involved his two sons in the management of the company:

Russell, who was the elder, in 1914 and Kenneth in 1919. In this instance, nepotism proved to be a wise move because the two sons played a very active role in the development of the company. Kenneth Parker championed the **Duofold** despite strong objections and was instrumental in fostering research that led to the development of the **Vacumatic**. George Parker travelled the world promoting his pens and opened new branches of the business.

Russell Parker died in 1932 and George Parker, who never recovered from the death of his son, died 5 years later in 1937. Kenneth Parker continued the innovative work and contributed tremendously to the success of the company, but that is another story. In 1986, the Parker Pen Company was sold to English investors, and in 1993, to the Gillette Company.

Duofold I

A significant name in the history of the fountain pen, Parker's Duofold was created in 1921. Until 1925, it was manufactured in black or red hard rubber. Thereafter, Parker produced colored models using permanite (derived from nitrocellulose). The career of the Duofold spans two periods. From 1925 to 1929, the ends (cap and push-button blind cap) were corrugated and the section had a ridge. From 1929 to 1932, its ends were smooth and truncated, and the section curved. The Duofolds shown on the opposite page are from the first period. Two examples (red) of the second period illustrate the differences.

Top: French Parker pens (in display case) and Plexor (made by Fernand Laureau).

Bottom: Ladies Duofold by Parker, green permanite, made in Canada (1930-1933).

Duofold

Duofold by Parker made in black, red, yellow, orange, burgundy, lapis blue, jade green, and moderne green permanite (1925-1932).

Fountain and ball-point pen set, Parker 51, with
"aerometric" filling mechanism (1949-1978).
Moholy-Nagy was a prolific inventor and the Bauhaus
influence is evident. The special character of the
fountain pen was no longer apparent, due to its lack of
an obvious nib.

Saved By the Vacuum
At the beginning of the 1930s, the Great Depression and
Sheaffer's Balance placed Parker in a difficult economic
situation. Kenneth Parker decided to attempt a recovery
by launching the Vacumatic in 1933. The conventional
rubber sac was eliminated and filling was
accomplished using an air column controlled by a
plunger with a diaphragm.

Conklin pen in black hard rubber with a Crescent Filler *system (circa 1920).*

Sheaffer, The Story of a Little White Dot
Top: Four Lifetime *pens with lever, jade green and black radite (1924-1929). Center right: Two pens with gold-filled trim (circa 1920). Center left: Three* Lifetime Balance *pens with lever, black radite (1930-1934), one of which is a fountain pen and mechanical pencil combination. Bottom:* Military Clip *(permitting pocket flap to be closed), brown and gold (1941-1946),* Triumph 1250 *(1942-1945),* Triumph Snorkel *(1952-1954). (P.H.-K.T.).*

Walter Sheaffer (1867-1946)

In the early part of the 20th century, in Fort Madison, Iowa, there lived a jeweler named Walter A. Sheaffer. Life in the midwest at that time was a far cry from the elegant streets of New York or Paris. Sheaffer primarily sold watches and, occasionally, a fountain pen or two to neighboring farmers. He was secure, but not wealthy, and his business flourished. Sheaffer could have spent his life selling his wares, but one fateful evening in 1907, Providence intervened in the form of a Conklin pen advertisement in a local newspaper.

At that time, most fountain pens were filled using an eye-dropper, a delicate, clumsy, and sometimes risky operation. Roy Conklin had partially solved that problem with the invention of his **Crescent Filler**.

Conklin's pens were fitted with a rubber sac that was compressed by a pressure bar fitted to a semi-circular crescent-shaped metal extension that protruded through the barrel of the pen, and broke the graceful lines of the pen. Around the pen was a circular "doughnut", which slipped through the crescent, to avoid any unintentional compression of the sac.

Walter Sheaffer felt that there must be a way to improve Conklin's system; something perhaps a little less simple, but more elegant and practical. He was able to devise a mechanism that improved upon Conklin's system. By the next day, he had come up with a brilliant idea. He planned to replace the metal crescent with a lever, which, on closing, would disappear into the body of the pen. He set to work in the small workshop of his jewelry store and, after a few unsucccessful attempts, designed a workable system. On August 25, 1908, he registered his first patent. Knowing that he was on the right track, he returned to selling watches, while still working to improve his idea. By 1912, he had registered another patent in which the lever was not directly linked to the rubber sac. He had a few samples manufactured and distributed them to his friends for testing. Everyone agreed the automatic filling system was a fine idea.

This was all well and good, but Sheaffer, who was a devoted family man already in his forties, owned a stable business and, at the time, there were already many fountain pen manufacturers in the industry. His small lever was clever, but most of his friends advised him

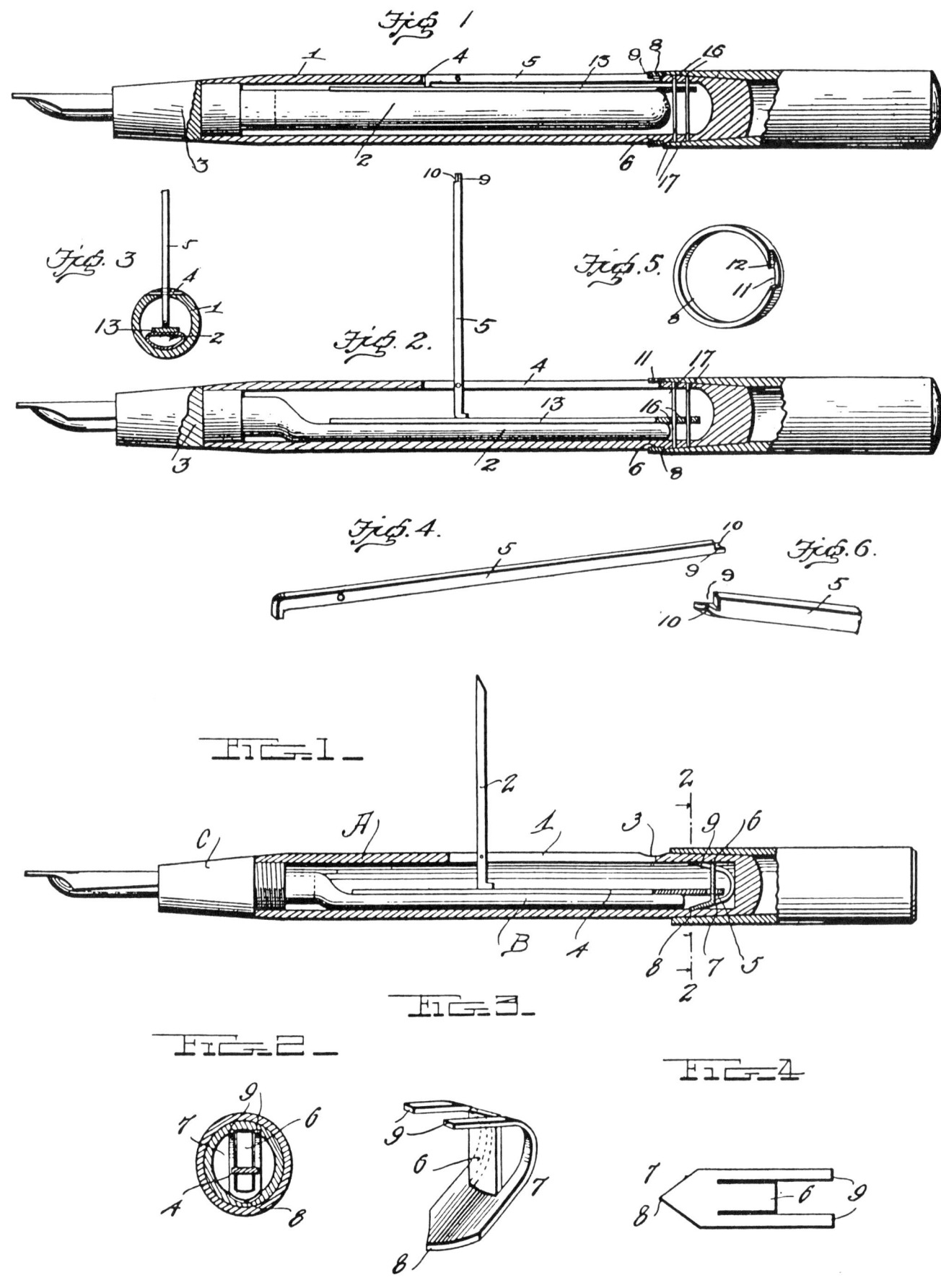

Fig. 1

Fig. 3

Fig. 2

Fig. 5

Fig. 4

Fig. 6

FIG. 1

FIG. 3

FIG. 2

FIG. 4

against doing anything rash. He knew that he was capable of manufacturing good pens, but he was not sure if he could sell them. He pondered the matter for a long time.

George Kraker and Ben Coulson, two former Conklin salesmen, assured him that they could easily sell his pens. As a result of their confidence, he turned his workshop into a factory with the help of his young son Craig and six employees. The W.A. Sheaffer Pen Company was created in January of 1913, with a sales office in Kansas City, and Kraker and Coulson as partners. The contract stipulated that Sheaffer would retain at least 51% of the shares. Later, when there was a need to increase the capital investment, Kraker and Coulson tried to take control of the company. Sheaffer was furious and threatened to dissolve the partnership. Eventually, he was able to repurchase Kraker's shares, who had subsequently left to start the Kraker Pen Company in Kansas City. In the process Kraker was able to entice Sheaffer's chief of production into quitting his job with Sheaffer and coming to work for the Kraker Pen Company. In an attempt to establish that

Sheaffer's former production chief was the actual inventor of the lever filling mechanism, Kraker initiated a lawsuit that was to last for 4 years. Every device was used; Kraker even hired a private detective to tail Sheaffer, who, at one point, lost the detective by jumping off a train just as the doors were closing. Finally, Justice prevailed, resulting in a victory for Sheaffer and the demise of the Kraker Pen Company.

Sheaffer could have monopolized the market for fountain pens with a lever filling mechanism, but, unfortunately, he made a serious error. There was an old lever patent that had been registered by a man named Barnes in Rockford, Illinois. His lever did not function and the patent was worthless, but it would have been wise to have acquired it, which was exactly what the L.E. Waterman Company did, for $100.00. Waterman succeeded in improving Barnes' lever and, by 1913, was able to compete with Sheaffer on his own ground.

None of these events prevented the Sheaffer company from prospering. In 1917, Sheaffer moved to a real factory, employing

To facilitate filling and avoid wetting the section with ink, Sheaffer invented the Snorkel. By turning the tip of the compression column counter-clockwise, a little tube appears that is dipped into the ink well without immersing the section. After the column is pulled to compress the sac, the latter is filled by pushing, while the tube is reinserted by turning the tip clockwise. A very ingenious system. Nothing complex.

Top: First patent obtained by Sheaffer in August 1908 described a lever and compression bar filling system. Bottom: The system was improved in 1912. The action of the lever is no longer linked to the rubber sac.

more than 100 people and producing over 100,000 pens in that year. In 1923, the company launched the first "colored" fountain pens, using a plastic material made of nitrocellulose manufactured by Dupont de Nemours (pyroxylin).

By 1929, the Sheaffer company had reached a landmark in the history of fountain pen production when it became the first to introduce a streamlined pen, called the **Balance**. In 1938, Sheaffer entrusted the managment of the company to his son Craig Royer Sheaffer, but Walter did not relinquish overall control prior to his death in 1946.

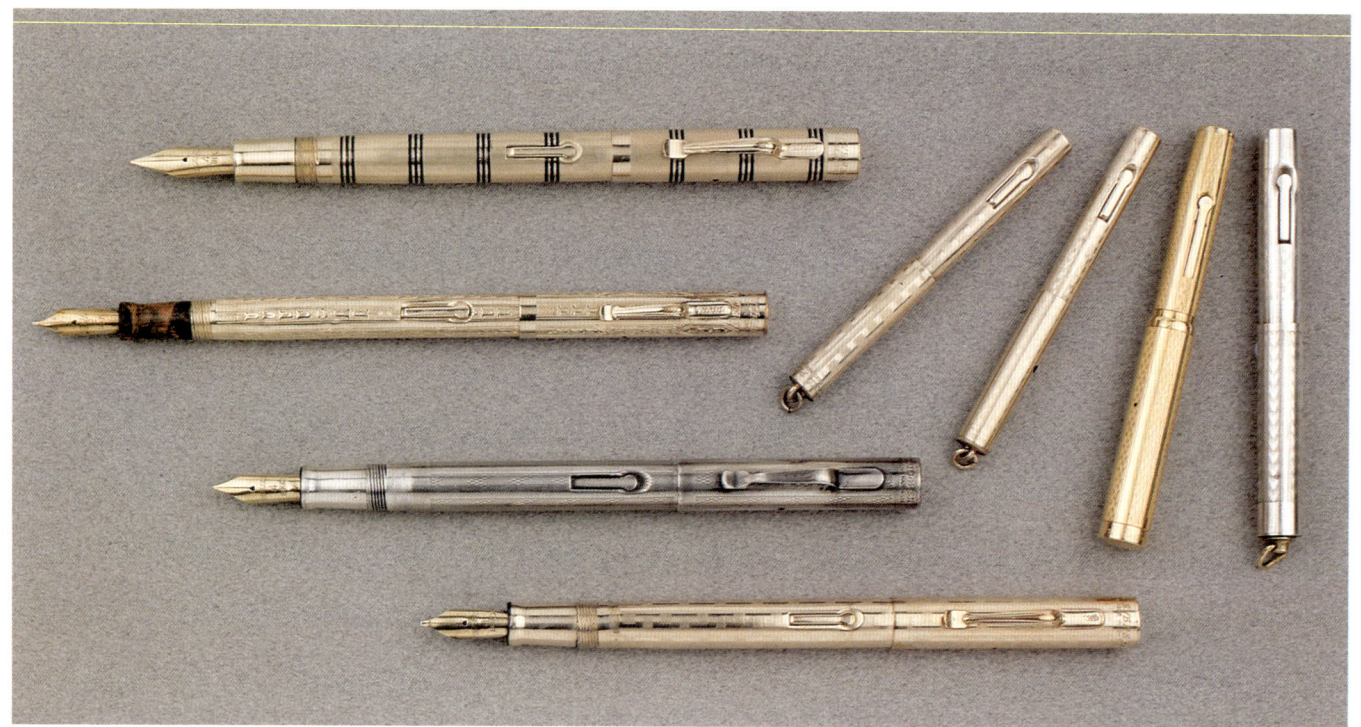

*"Cylindrical" models
by Wahl, with lever
filling system, silver,
and gold-filled (1922-1932).*

Wahl-Eversharp

Wahl-Eversharp pens are magnificent in design and of outstanding quality, and they are collected today for good reason. The **Doric** is certainly one of the best pens ever made. There was never a Mr. Eversharp, and if there was indeed a Mr. Wahl, the latter neither invented anything nor manufactured any pen with his own hands. He was not a typical pioneer like his three competitors. Nevertheless, his is still an American success story.

The Wahl Adding Machine Company was founded in 1905. Wahl was one of the major stockholders and the company manufactured adding machines. It had nothing whatsoever to do with fountain pens, an involvement which only developed much later, due to an acquisition and the resulting financial opportunity.

Around 1912, a Japanese man named Tokuji Hayakawa began manufacturing a mechanical pencil, of which he is credited as being the inventor. This is a bit of an exaggeration. His mechanical pencil worked well, but not any better than the one invented and manufactured previously by the English. He named his pencil the **Eversharp**, a great name for a mechanical pencil, and called his company, the Ever-Sharp Pencil Company. In 1914, Hayakawa began

exporting to the United States and was hugely successful. The Wahl Adding Machine Co., looking for low-risk opportunities to diversify, acquired the Japanese firm and set up manufacturing facilities in Chicago. Very rapidly, the mechanical pencils became their top selling product, with adding machines a far distant second. For his part, Hayakawa founded the Hayakawa Electric Company, renouncing forever the Ever-Sharp name after its acquisition by the Americans, which later became the Sharp Company, still in business today.

In 1917, Wahl acquired the Boston Fountain Pen Co., a company which produced fountain pens and nibs of excellent quality. The production facilities were moved to Chicago and almost overnight the Wahl company became one of the major fountain pen manufacturers in the United States. Production was well-regulated, efficient, and mechanized. The fountain pens were of excellent quality and, as a result, success quickly followed. Wahl's sales at this time were greater than any other fountain pen manufacturer's. However, the company's leadership lasted only for about two decades as innovations were needed to compete with Sheaffer, Parker, and Waterman, and these were not readily forthcoming.

In 1919, the adding machine division was

From Wahl to Eversharp
*The two upper groups illustrate the models produced at
the end of the 1920s (1925-1932). In the center, the
Doric pens were produced during the 1930s
(1931-1934 for the models with roller clips and
1935-1941 for the models with plain clips). Two of them
are equipped with adjustable nibs. The Skyline pens
(bottom) are a good example of the "aerodynamic" fad
of the 1940s (1941-1949), (P.H.-K.T.).*

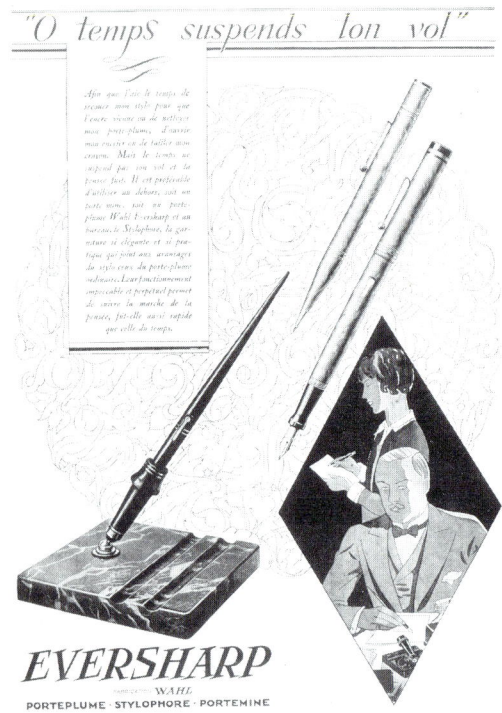

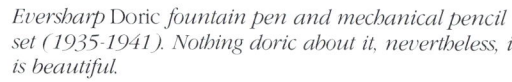

Eversharp Doric *fountain pen and mechanical pencil set (1935-1941). Nothing doric about it, nevertheless, it is beautiful.*

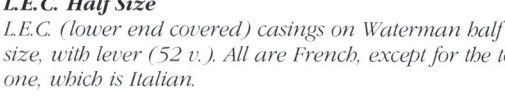

L.E.C. Half Size
L.E.C. (lower end covered) casings on Waterman half size, with lever (52 v.). All are French, except for the top one, which is Italian.

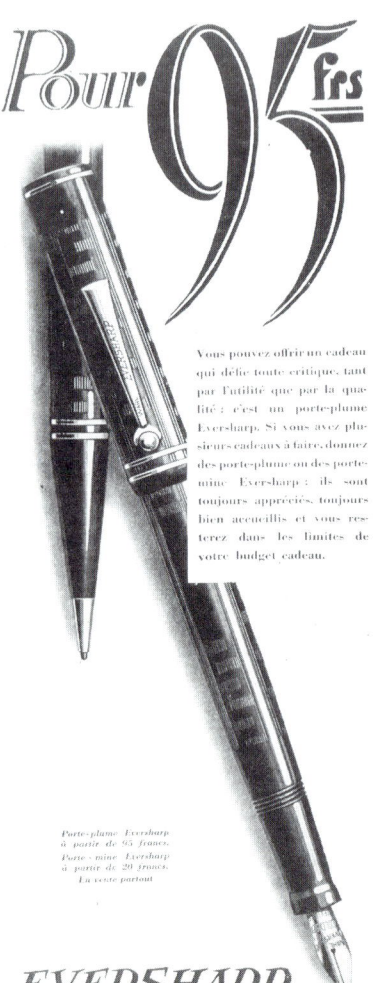

sold to Remington. Between 1925 and 1940, Wahl closely paralled the big three pen manufacturers in production. While the company's pens were generally as good and as handsome as the others' (notably the **Personal Point** in 1929 and the **Doric** in 1931), sometimes of even better quality, they were not as inventive.

In 1940, Wahl merged with its subsidiary Eversharp and new management took over. Finally, an extraordinary man, Martin Straus, was hired, who, in 1941, launched a line of fountain pens that is considered by some to be among the ugliest and the best sellers of all time. Called the **Skyline**, it had a squat cap with a line that looked like the nose of a flying fortress. After the introduction of Sheaffer's **Balance** in 1929, aerodynamic shapes were the rage, and, of course, everyone recognized that wind resistance slowed down your handwriting.

Thanks to the **Skyline**, Wahl-Eversharp briefly took the lead in the market, but could not hold it for long.

The period immediately following World War II saw the beginning of the ball-point pen hysteria. Straus joined the trend and the company lost millions of dollars. The losses continued until 1957, when Parker acquired the writing instrument division of Eversharp and converted it to the manufacture of low-end products. About a year later, the Wahl-Eversharp name was dropped and, in 1962, the company was sold.

Epilogue

Once upon a time there were three great American inventors and four great fountain pen

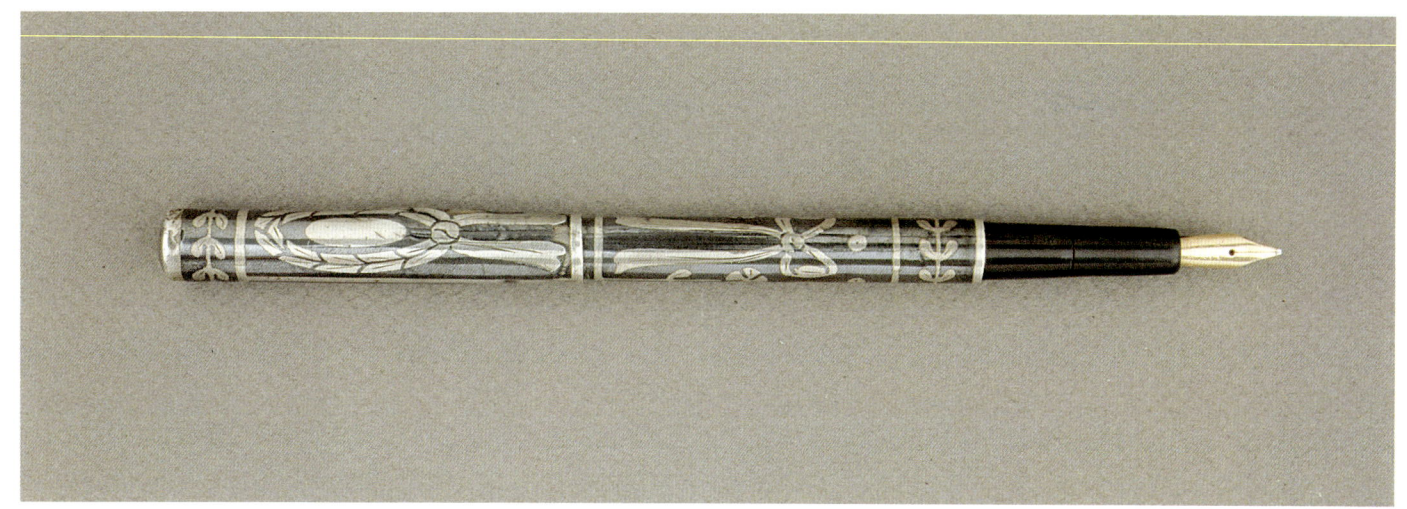

Standard model in enameled silver (circa 1905).

Gemini

Two nibs, two inks within the same pen; is that useful? Well, at any rate, it is possible. The Duocolor, *made by Unic (1932, Zerollo patent), is one of the most complicated fountain pens ever created. Its mechanism retracts one nib when the other is extended. To fill it, the lever corresponding to the extended nib is pressed through a small pin placed in the upper part of the cap. As is the case with most Unic models, the finish is extraordinary. Other manufacturers, such as Omas (circa 1925), were equally stymied by the challenge.*

Mallat and Unic

Top: Mallat: Plexigraf (1938), 150 (1943), 120 (1943), 250 (1947), 300 (1947), Plexigraf 225 (1947), Leda (1950). Bottom: Unic: (1917), (1928), (1930), (1932), (1932), (1938), (1940), Mondial (1939), Luxe (1946), (P.H-B.J.)

manufacturers. The fourth has disappeared, the third is still American, the second is now British, and the pens of the first are now entirely manufactured in France, but owned by an American corporation.

French Production

It is rather difficult to retrace the birth and first steps of the fountain pen industry in France. Whether they were made in France or abroad, many fountain pens were sold under the trade name of the retailer. Consequently, many small manufacturers, such as Sabon, Charcellay, and Laureau, have been virtually forgotten today. Their pens were of a quality comparable to those of the "big" names. Some manufacturers subcontracted for parts that they could not produce themselves. Companies specializing in the cutting and molding of metal parts supplied the levers, compression bars, push buttons, clips, etc... Others were merely pen assemblers, since they could procure the bodies, caps, and feeds from small manufacturers located in or around the environs of Paris or in the Jura area (Eastern France). They could buy the cork for the safeties and rubber sacs from those specializing in the production of such materials. However, only the major manufacturers produced nibs. As a result, it is difficult today to determine whether any given company was a manufacturer of fountain pens or merely assembled the component parts.

Bayard and Edacoto
Top: Bayard: (1920), (1930), Special 8 *(1932),* Super Luxe *(1934), (1935),* Excelsior *(1938),* Special Luxe *(1938), (1947), (1949). Bottom: Edacoto:* Edac *(1920),* Edac Cadet *(1925),* Edacoto 104 *(1932),* Jewelers *series, gold-filled (1934), (1934),* 37 Luxe *(1937),* 200 *(1938),* Super Edacoto Visible *(1939),* 33 *(1939),* 87 *(1943). (P.H.-B.J.).*

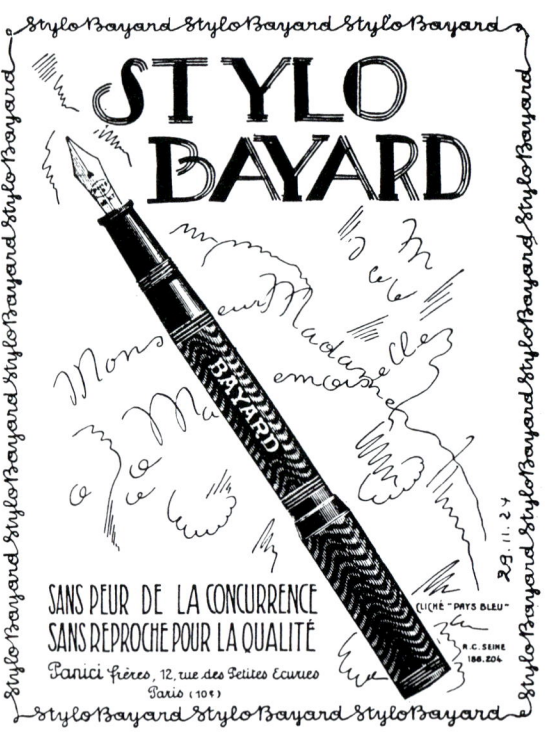

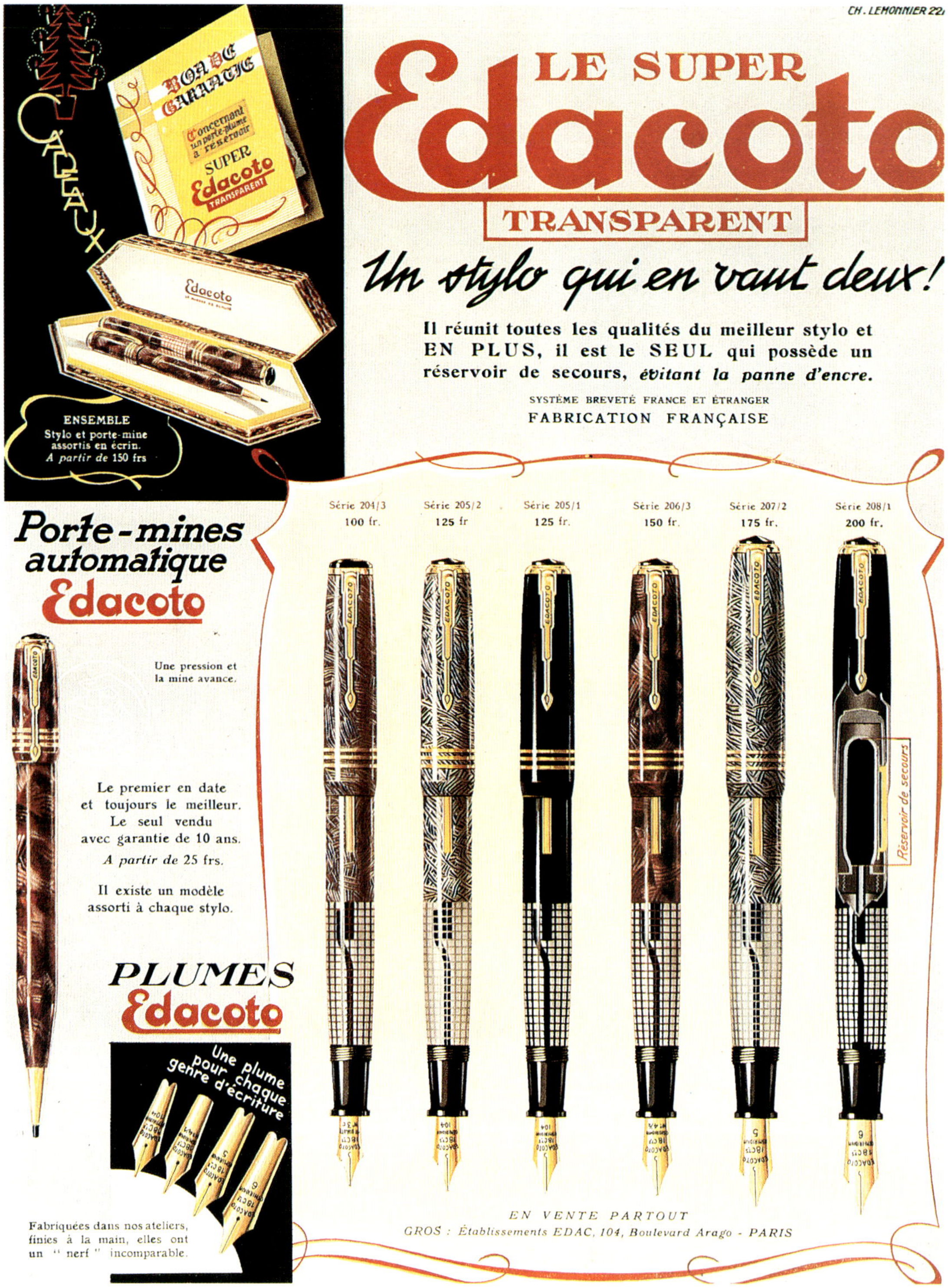

Abbreviated Chronology of the Fountain Pen in France

1864. Jean Benoît Mallat obtained a patent for his **Syphoïde**. The feed and filling (by piston) systems were not in the least revolutionary, but it was the first "instrument" with a reservoir to be mass produced and marketed. It was not quite a fountain pen, but it was the only conventional operative ancestor of the fountain pen to be sold.

From 1886 until the end of World War I, the fountain pen market was dominated by the Americans and the British. There were a few French companies but their production was limited. From 1910 on, the Germans manufactured moderately priced pens, generally in celluloid. Quality fountain pens in black hard rubber were still imported from the United States and Great Britain.

In 1887, in the Didot Bottin Almanac, under the category, **Writing Nibs (natural quills, metal nibs)**, there appeared an advertisement for a fountain pen nib, placed by the Anglo-American Co, the first exclusive licensee of the L.E. Waterman Company.

1889. During the Universal Exposition in Paris, bronze medals were awarded to L.E. Waterman & Co. and to Caw's Nib and Pen Co. At that time, Waterman's world production had reached 30,000.

1898. De La Rue (Great Britain) obtained a distributor in Paris. In the same year, E.L. Moreau started business (in 1904, E.L. Moreau changed its trade name to J.M. Paillard).

1900. L.E. Waterman, Blair, and Caw's

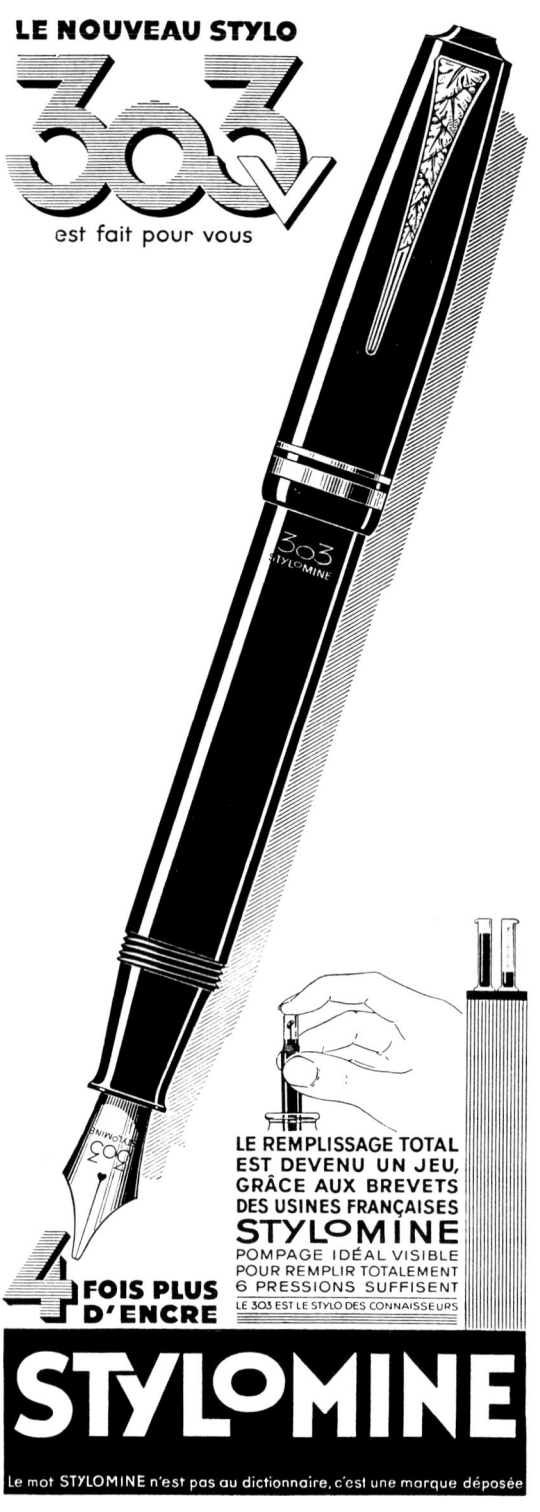
Stylomine
Top: One of the first 303s, 303B small, 303B medium, 303B large, 303B medium, 303V medium. Bottom: Three 303V large and three 303D pens. (P.H.-B.J.).

were represented in the American pavilion of the Paris Universal Exposition. Waterman was the big winner, with a gold medal for the company, a silver medal for Lewis Edson himself, and a bronze medal for William J. Ferris, the other inventive genius of the company. Caw's received a silver medal.

1904. L. and C. Hardtmuth, agents for Waterman in Europe, opened an office in Paris.

1909. Maurice Jandelle began distributing Conway Stewart (Great Britain) pens under the brand name, Gold Star. Unfortunately, this name was already registered, and the brand name was changed to Gold Starry in 1912.

1910. Charcellay founded Franco-British Pen Manufacturing.

1912. The Forbin company, already a distributor of American brands, started manu-

Triomphe, *completely metal, except for the section and the feed, which are in hard rubber, push-button filling (circa 1920).*

Right: Rool's. Unusual model with a "flattened" body and cap, transparent section. Clip and compression bar are mounted on a center rod surrounded by a spring. Made by De Soultrait in the late 1940s.

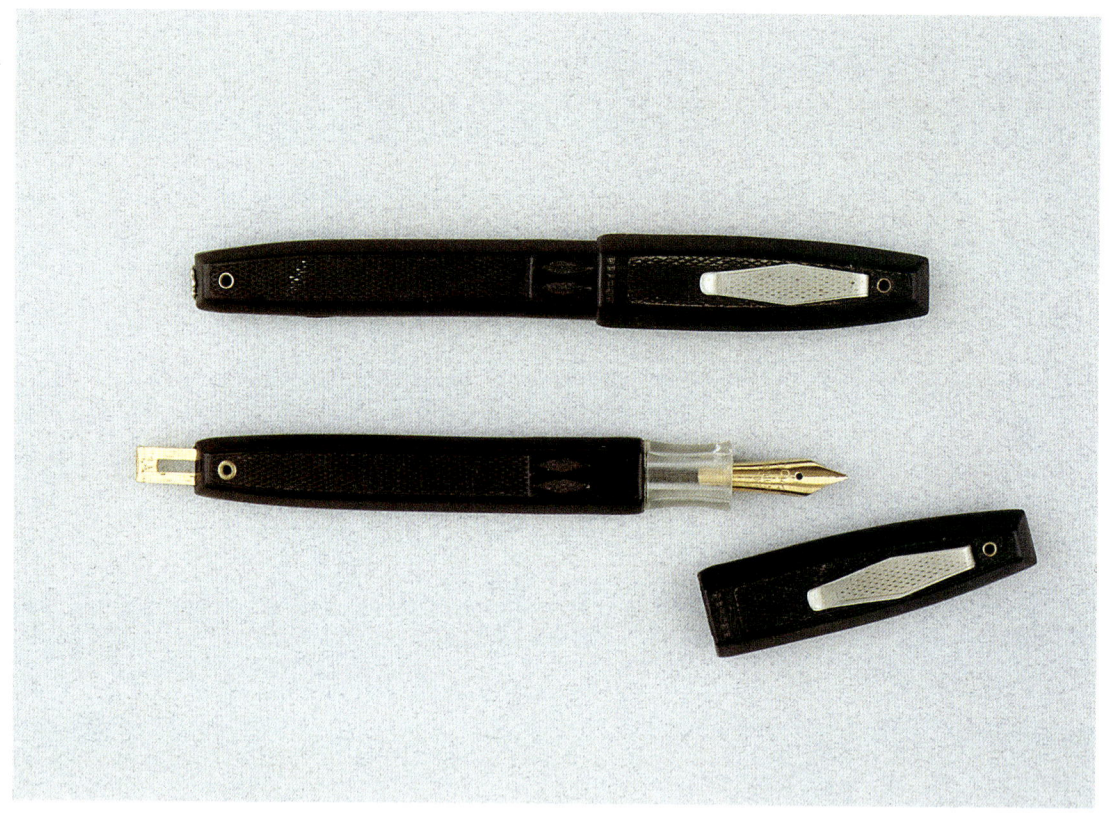

facturing its own pens under the trademark, **Bayard**.

1914. Jules Fagard became Waterman's distributor for Belgium, France, and their African and Asian colonies.

From 1915 to 1922, fountain pen development rapidly evolved. It is probable that American and British troops contributed to the introduction of an instrument that most French soldiers knew little about. After the war, a few veterans, former jewelers, went into the fountain pen industry. In Toulon, Joseph Mercier founded La Palice Company and sold his fountain pens under the trademark, **Grand Aigle**. Joseph Beaufils founded the Stellor company. Demilly and Degen created La Manufacture Parisienne de P.P.R. company, which would become La Plume d'Or and would sell pens under the brand name, Le Météore. The Mallat company reinstituted the manufacture of fountain pens. Founded in 1842, it was the oldest French company making writing instruments

(the **Syphoïde**, invented in 1864). Even so, this still was not enough to justify the company's advertisements stating that Mallat was "the oldest P.P.R. in the world" (porte-plume réservoir). Paul Janvrin and André Petit began manufacturing quality fountain pens in a Paris suburb. In 1921, they went into partnership with Maurice Jandelle, who distributed Gold Starry pens that were no longer imported, but manufactured in France. Kothe and Vannier founded the Unic company. Jacques Bonhomme opened a factory in Issy-les-Moulineaux, creating the Edac company. The Panici brothers, nephews of Étienne Joseph Forbin, acquired the Bayard name. Y.E. Zuber took the brand name, Stylomine, for its mechanical pencils, and, in 1925, started making fountain pens.

1926. Jules Fagard founded JiF, a name derived from his initials.

The 1920s and 1930s mark the golden age of the French fountain pen. For the most part, they were made of black hard rubber until 1935;

Pneumatic Pens

Top right (horizontally):

Styloplum *(1925) and* Plumoto *(1929).*

silver-plated, with filling system

based on the same principle

as that of the Stylo-Pneu *(1932)*

and the Babel *(1948).*

Brand Names
The trademarks of large or small manufacturers and retailers, and the names of the models are often the fruits of rhetoric, certainly a little old-fashioned, but charming.
The superiority of King, Emperor, *and other* Ruler(s) *is clear, as is the size or inaccessibility of* Everest, Canigou, Himalaya, Mont Blanc, Mont d'Or, Simplo...*on the other hand,* Bambin *and* Lilliput *rival the* Mignon *and the* Miniature *in their diminuitive size.*
Beginning in 1910, the Age of Aviation saw an abundance of Aviator, Aero, Aeroplane, Aeroman's, Aeronautique, *etc. models. During World War I, there was a veritable mobilization of* Glorieux, Revanche, Triomphal, Vainqueur, Victorieux *and, of course, the* Stylo des Alliés *and the* Piou-Piou. *Pens named after animals would fill a good-sized zoo:* Condor, Cygne, Eagle, Furet, Gazelle, Grand Aigle, Griffon, Hirondelle, Merle Blanc, Oiseau Bleu, Paon, Pelican *(English),* Pelican *(German),* Roitelet, Scarabée, Seal, Swallow, Swan, Zèbre, *etc.*
In addition, there are the facetious names, such as the KIHE-CRI *and its contemporary* KI-E-CRI, *as well as the* IVA BIEN *and* ELVA BIEN *set. Other models made use of all possible variations of the word* "stylo": Stylobloc, Stylochap, Stylomine, Stylophore, Styloplum, Stylopompe, Stylotube...

From Head To Toe
Waterman lever pens for men with E.C. (end covered) casing covering the part of the body opposite the nib. These models were produced from 1924 until the late 1930s, while their predecessors, without such trim, were still being sold. From top to bottom: gold, silver, gold, silver, gold-filled, and silver.

Pullman, *made by La Plume d'Or (1932). The nib can be extended or retracted using only one hand. When the rear tip of the pen is pushed, a trap opens and the nib appears. Filling is accomplished through a compression bar and push-button.*

they were subsequently made of cellulose acetate and, by 1941, of plexiglas.

World War II considerably changed the picture. An increase in demand, combined with an interruption in supply from the Allied countries, brought about the creation of many small companies. Unfortunately, the poor quality of raw materials, often made with recycled products, resulted in the production of mediocre fountain pens. There even appeared wooden fountain pens (only the feed and the section were made of plastic) and others made from aluminum that was recycled from armament factories.

Even after 1945, it was illegal to use gold in the manufacture of nibs and fountain pens, a restriction that was not lifted until 1949. In the 1950s, pre-war companies had to face dual competition, namely, newcomers in a declining market and the new ball-point pens.

In an effort to combat these unfavorable conditions, some of the oldest French companies joined forces and offered co-production models. In 1956, Stylomine, Météore, Paillard, and Unic launched the **Pulsa Pen**. In 1959, Gold Starry, Edac, Mallat, and Evergood produced the **Visor Pen**, a name that will be remembered by scores of students from the 1960s.

In 1958, Waterman went out of business in the United States. Fortunately, the JiF/Waterman partnership continued operations during rough times and survived the 1960s reasonably well. The year 1971 marks an important date in French fountain pen history. JiF/Waterman became Waterman S.A. and acquired the American name, Waterman from BiC. The following year, it acquired the English Waterman name.

From that time on, all pens bearing the name of Waterman have been and continue to be manufactured in France. Waterman is currently the second largest worldwide producer of quality fountain pens.

NÉ A PARIS
FABRIQUÉ PAR LA GRANDE
MARQUE FRANÇAISE DES
"CRAYONS CONTÉ"
LE STYLOGRAPHE
CONTÉ
EST ADOPTÉ PAR TOUS CEUX
QUI EXIGENT UN PORTEPLUME
SOLIDE ÉLÉGANT ET D'UN
FONCTIONNEMENT PARFAIT

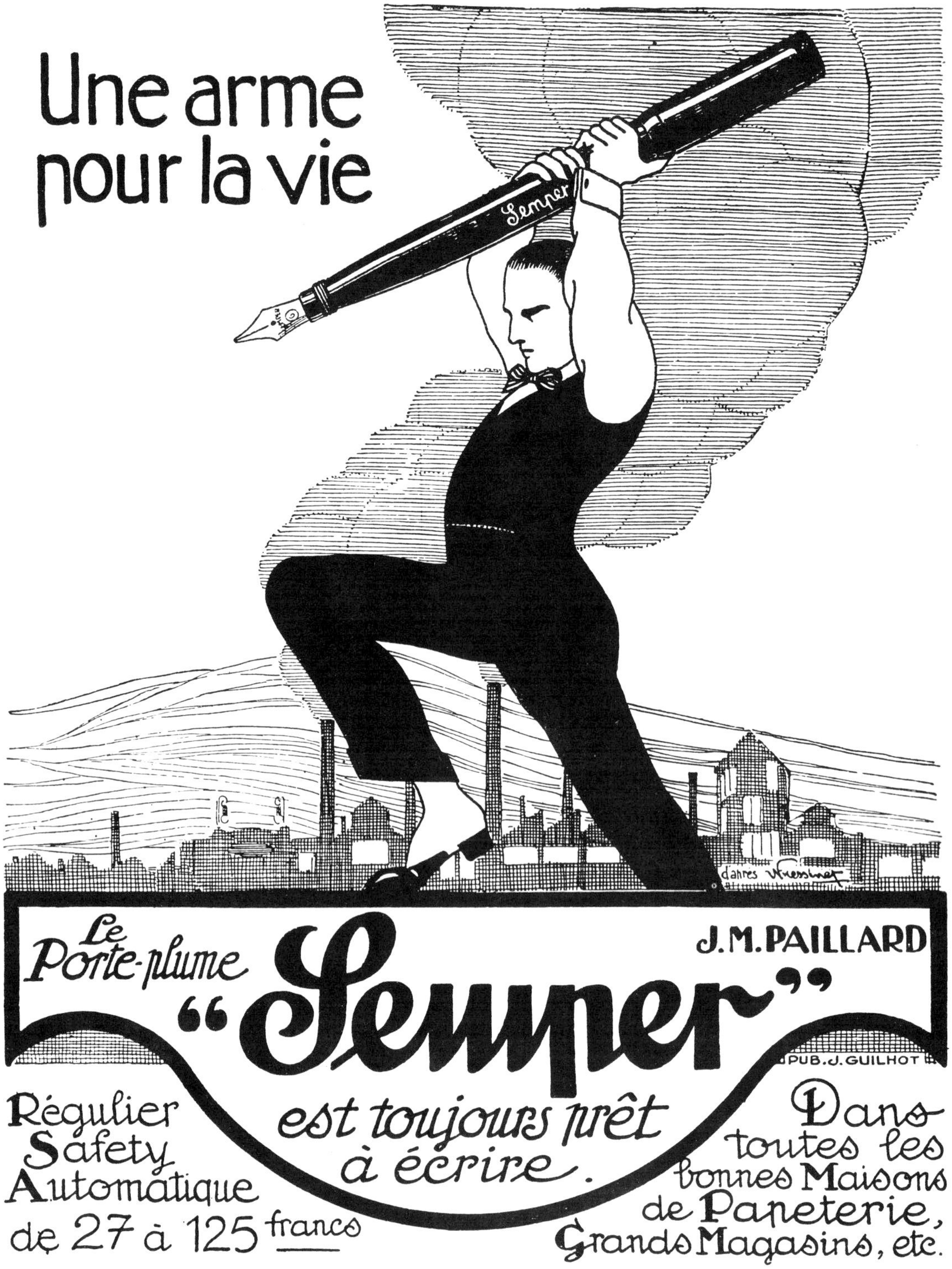
Une arme
pour la vie
Semper
d'après Vuessinet
Le Porte-plume
J.M. PAILLARD
"Semper"
PUB. J. GUILHOT
est toujours prêt
à écrire.
Régulier
Safety
Automatique
de 27 à 125 francs
Dans
toutes les
bonnes Maisons
de Papeterie,
Grands Magasins, etc.

Le Météore
90 fr. 80
Météore
DÉTAIL : Papeteries, Spécialités, Gds Magasins
GROS : Sté La Plume d'Or, 63, r. des Archives PARIS
UNIS
FRANCE

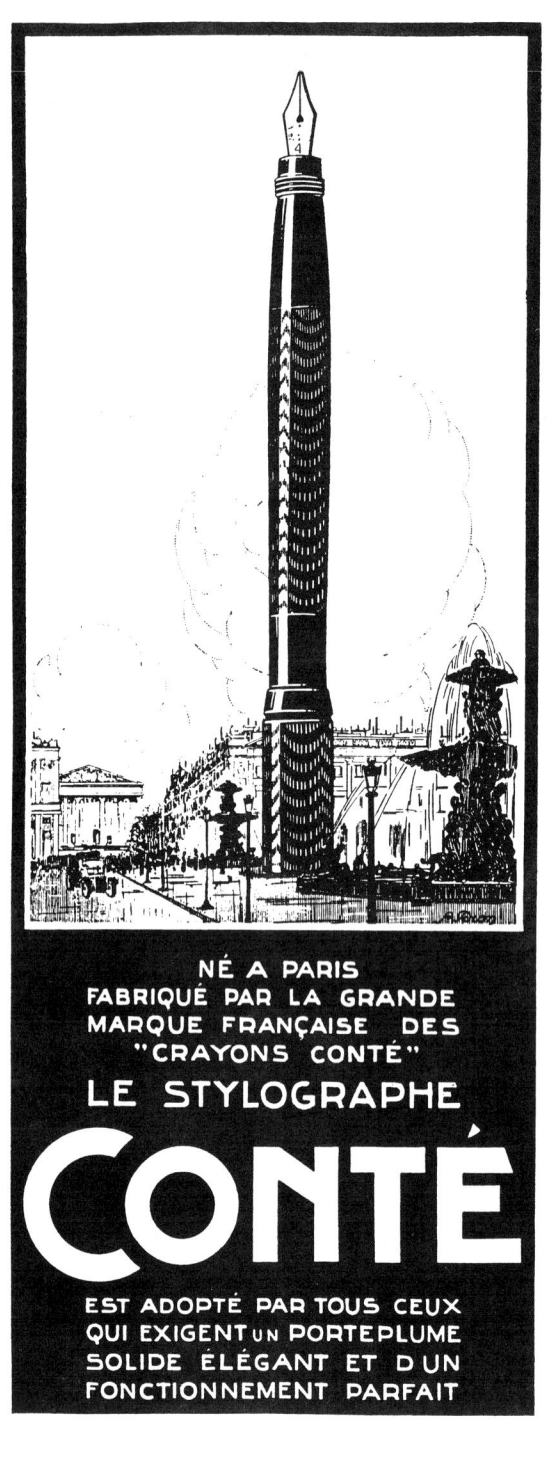

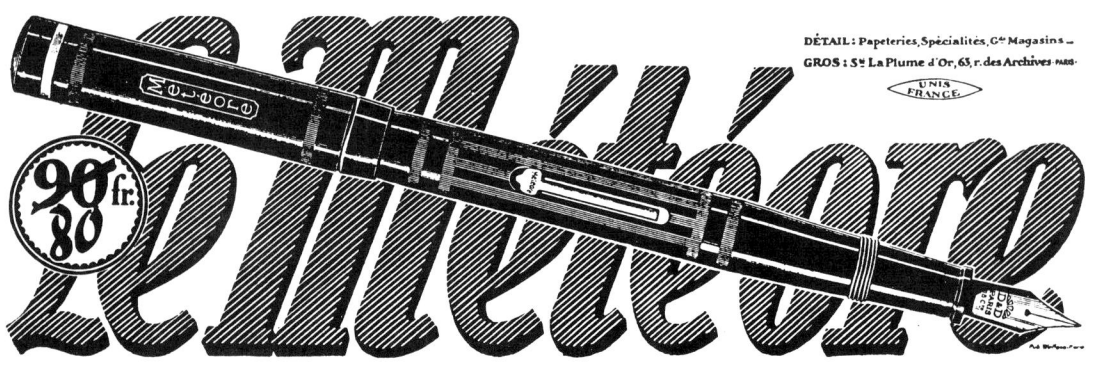

Veterans

For many soldiers in World War I, the fountain pen was a very precious companion, one of the rare civilian objects that they carried into the trenches, a small piece of hard rubber that permitted them to be heard beyond the roar of battle, by a wife, a child, a friend. In those years, the only pleasant words to be heard were those conveyed by the fountain pen. The pen did not win or lose the war, it was only used to carry a little love from a soldier under fire. Once peace was restored, some veterans threw away their fountain pens, others kept them, and today some of these pens enjoy a peaceful retirement with collectors.

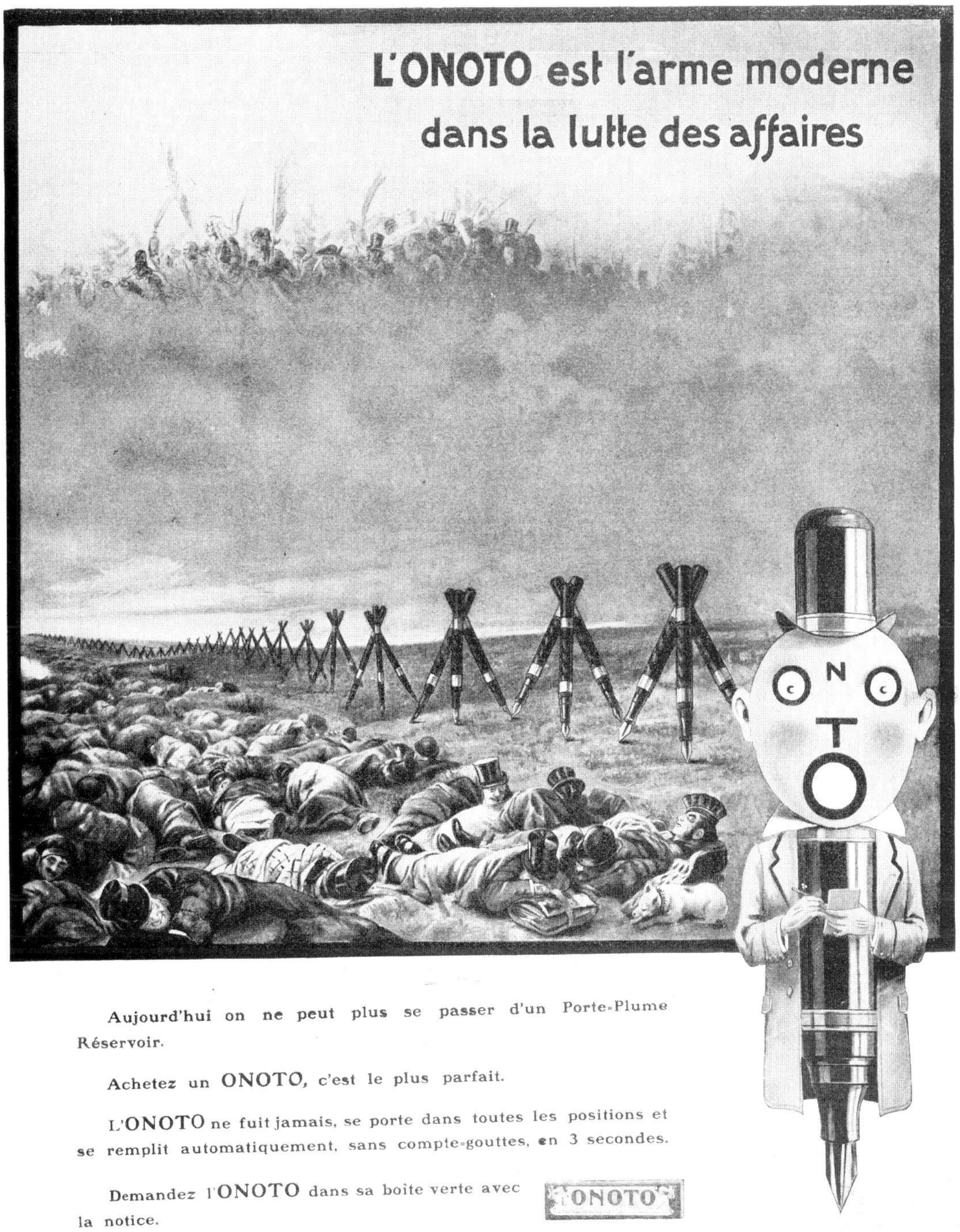
L'ONOTO est l'arme moderne
dans la lutte des affaires
O N O T O
Aujourd'hui on ne peut plus se passer d'un Porte-Plume Réservoir.
Achetez un ONOTO, c'est le plus parfait.
L'ONOTO ne fuit jamais, se porte dans toutes les positions et se remplit automatiquement, sans compte-gouttes, en 3 secondes.
Demandez l'ONOTO dans sa boite verte avec la notice.
ONOTO

INDISPENSABILI
MI SONO
IL FUCILE
E LA
Waterman's
Ideal
Fountain Pen

Porte-Plume Ideal Waterman
LE PLUS APPRÉCIÉ SUR LE FRONT
En Vente dans toutes les Bonnes Maisons et chez
KIRBY, BEARD & C° L^d
Catalogue Spécial 201 franco.
5, Rue Auber, Paris.

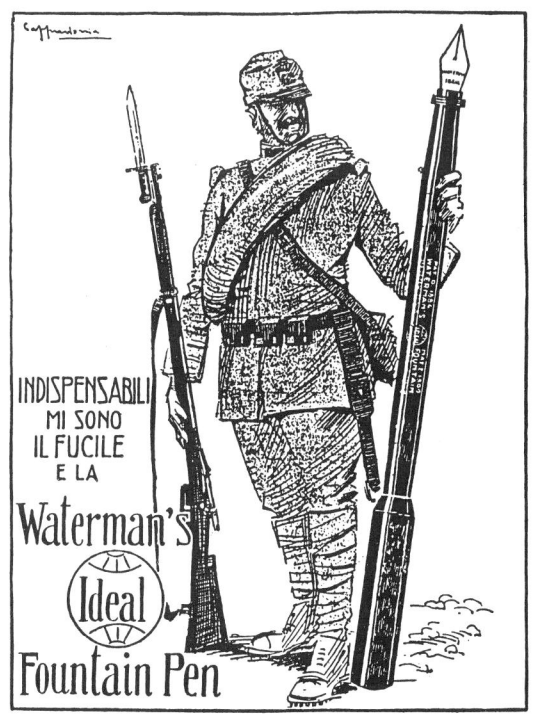

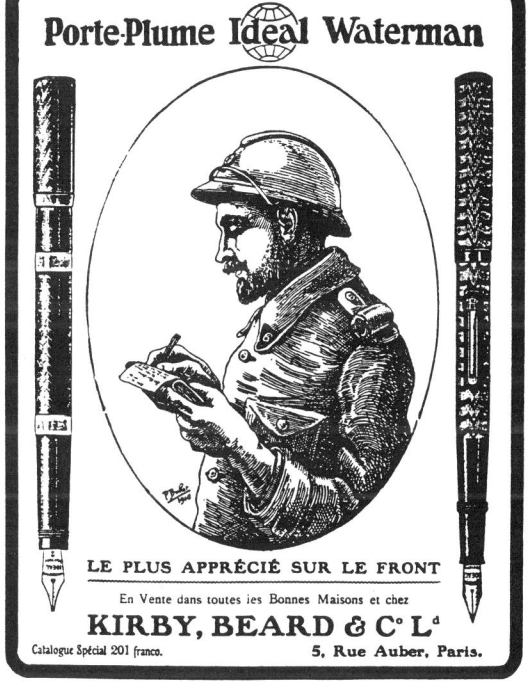

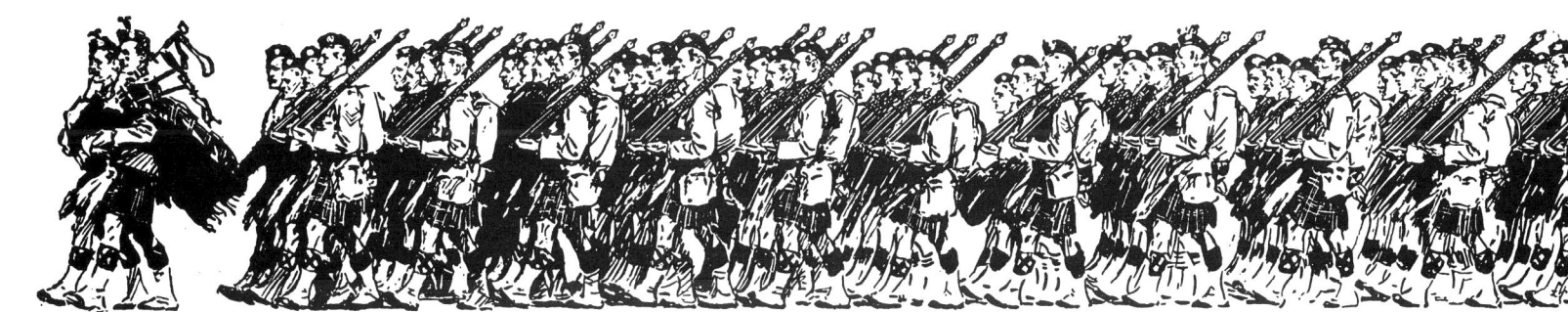

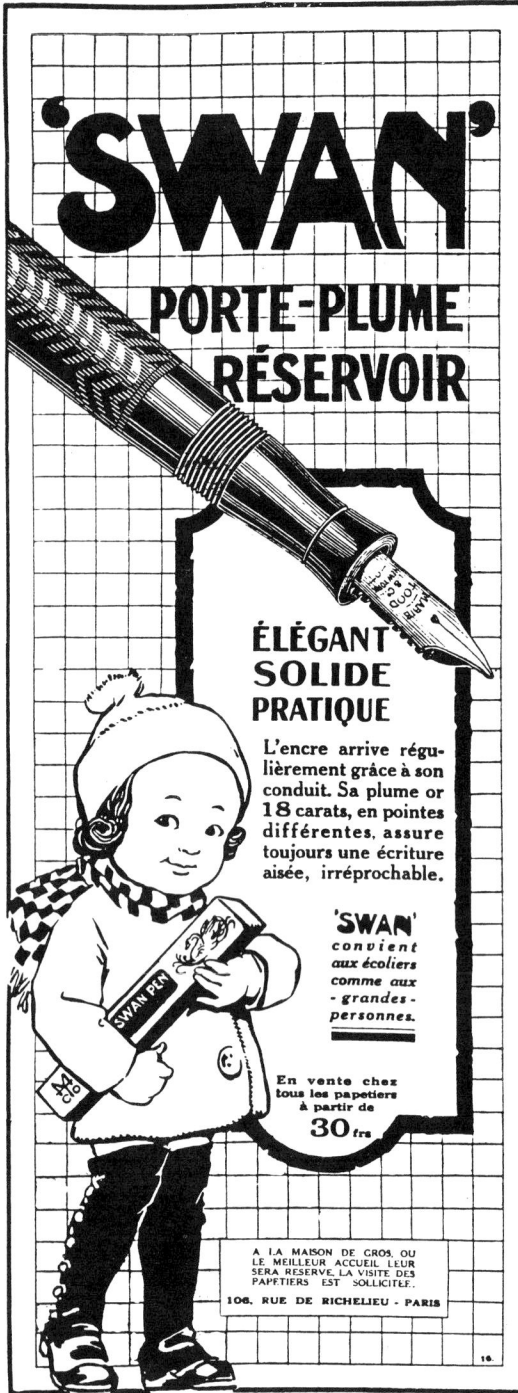

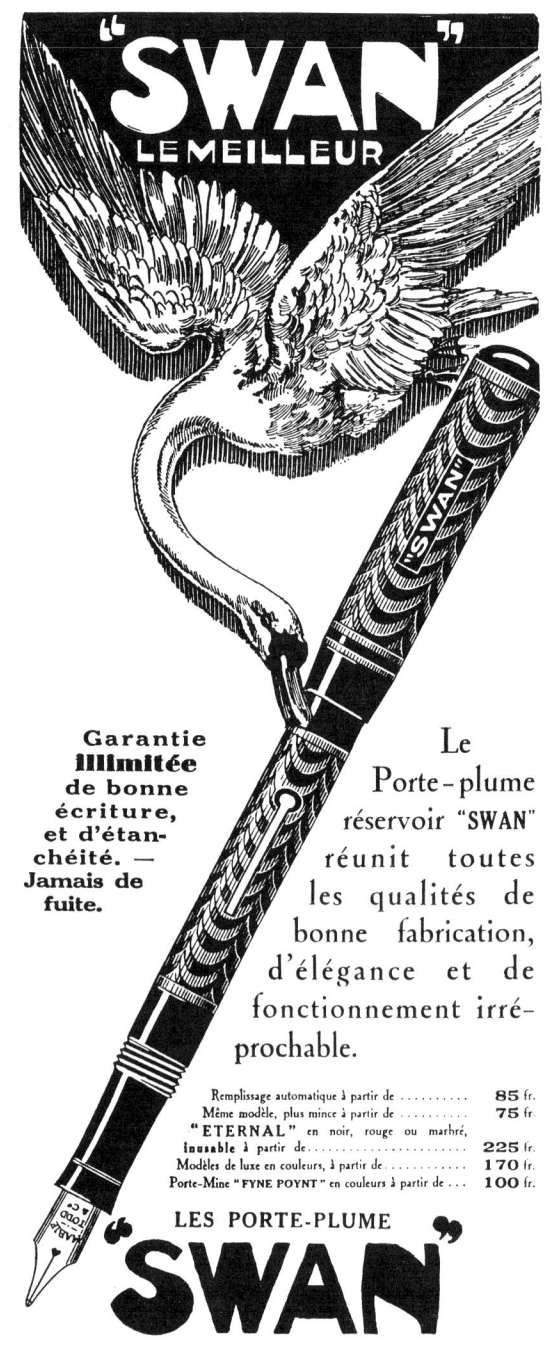

Half a Century of Swans
Swan *fountain pens manufactured by Mabie Todd. The collection on the opposite page groups together American and British made Mabie Todds (1905-1947).*

ONOTO

L'ONOTO a conquis l'univers! Tous : hommes du monde, officiers, magistrats, savants, hommes d'affaires, etc., etc., se serviront de l'**ONOTO**, ce merveilleux Porte-Plume-Réservoir qui ne fuit jamais dans la poche, quelle que soit la position où il se trouve, et se remplit automatiquement sans compte-gouttes en trois secondes.

Chez tous les Papetiers.   *Gros : DE LA RUE, PARIS.*

Onoto
de quoi écrire pour la vie!

De La Rue
With the exception of the lever filling model (1920), all of these fountain pens were made by Onoto. Filling by plunger, dual feed, black hard rubber with precious metal trim (1910-1915). Lower left: Silver (1908). Lower right: Solid gold (1910).

......ET DE DOUX RÊVES HABI-
TAIENT LEURS NUITS . ILS
VOYAIENT EN SONGE MONTER
DANS LE CIEL UNE ÉTOILE
NOUVELLE ...... C'ÉTAIT UN
PRÉSAGE . NOËL LEUR
APPORTA UN STYLO MONTBLANC
OU L'ÉTOILE ANNONCÉE APPA-
RAISSAIT AU SOMMET DU
CAPUCHON . ELLE SYMBO-
LISAIT LA FINE ÉLÉGANCE
ET L'EXCELLENCE RÉPUTÉE
DU STYLO MONTBLANC.
LE STYLO MONTBLANC
EST L'ÉTOILE DES CADEAUX

AGENTS GÉNÉRAUX
J.E. CANETTI & Cie
24, RUE DE PARADIS, PARIS, 10e

PUBL. ELVINGER

STYLO MONT BLANC

Montblanc
Top, left to right: Pen with lever, black hard rubber
(circa 1920); pen with lever, marbled (circa 1924);
pen with push-button (circa 1930); Meisterstuck in
black hard rubber, push-button filler (1931);
Meisterstuck in celluloid, marbled and black,
push-button filler (1931); Spider standard (circa 1920),
with push-button (1936), with piston (1936);
Meisterstuck 149 (1952).
Bottom, left to right: Three Red and Black safeties (1910),
Simplo-Montblanc (1911-1914), Montblanc Red and
Black (circa 1920), black hard rubber (1925), gold
(1925), hexagonal No. 1 in black hard rubber (1927),
No. 0 gold-filled (1925), (P.H.-K.T.).

Wahl Gold Seal Personal Point

lever filling pen

in lapis blue (1927-1932).

SECTION II

A Pen and a Bit of Ink

Gravity? Check.

Atmospheric pressure? Compensated.

Capillary action? Finally obtained.

Viscosity? Perfect.

Steady hand. Ready to write.

We have ink flow…

Matador with lever at the end of the body (circa 1925). Pump fountain pen with a metal pin that screws into a piston for filling. Very simple mechanism, but useless if the pin is lost.

Display box by Sabon, a Bordeaux manufacturer. *Models with push-button and lever (circa 1935). German plastic (nitrocellulose).*

How Does It Work?

General Principles

In an attempt to simplify the complex nature of the fountain pen as a writing instrument, it might be described as "a pen containing a reservoir that automatically feeds the writing point with ink" (Webster). While a dictionary may define it in this way, such a description is incomplete. For a fountain pen to function, to be able to write, there has to be a flow of ink between the feed and the nib, which is not very difficult in and of itself, but, in addition, the flow also has to be steady and regulated. The ink in a fountain pen is subject to the action of several forces. At rest, these forces must cancel each other out, regardless of the position of the fountain pen. This fragile balance must be disturbed only when the nib comes into contact with paper. Three elements must be considered - gravity, capillary attraction, and atmospheric pressure.

The first element plays an obvious role-nothing on this earth escapes the law of gravity...the fountain pen included. However, its

capillary passages have properties that somewhat modify that law. On the other hand, as ink is consumed, gravity forces the ink to the proper end of the reservoir.

A sugar cube placed in a spoon containing a small amount of coffee illustrates the principle of capillary attraction. The liquid will penetrate the porous material (the sugar cube), which is, in fact, nothing more than an extensive network of capillary chambers. Liquids are irresistibly attracted to smaller spaces. It was this subtle principle that Lewis Edson Waterman put into practice. Capillary passages function as feeds, but are they the only ones involved and do they have a defined size? Both questions may seem simplistic. Yet, there is another feed and it is as old as Time, or rather as the reed; namely, the slit that divides the point into two parts. In fact, capillary attraction has made writing possible for thousands of years. Waterman's genius was not only to have realized this, but also to have applied the principle to the feeding of the nib. The size of the "duct" thus varies with the amount of pressure applied by the hand, as does the space between the nib and the feed, thus regulating the flow of ink.

The Telescopic Fountain Pen

For a pen to fit in a ladies purse or in a vest pocket, it had to be very short. However, for it to write well, it had to be long. A clever mechanism took care of the problem. A telescopic device allowed the pen to extend to a sufficient length. It also permitted a mechanical pencil to be hidden at the other end of a fountain pen.

In a fountain pen capillary attraction is influenced by the nib in two ways, as is the case with both the reed pen and the feather quill. The first occurs via the contact between the ink and the medium on which writing takes place, and the second occurs during the feeding process. (Ink viscosity naturally has a considerable influence on both aspects.)

The mastery of ink flow should result in the end of leaks, stains, and worries. However, this is not quite so simple, since as we write the reservoir empties, creating a relative vacuum. The feed must, in addition, permit an air/ink exchange. Not only must the ink output be compensated by equal air intake, but the effects of gravity and atmospheric pressure must also be considered. Atmospheric pressure is not uniform; it varies with altitude, and the higher we climb, the lower the air pressure. However, at any given time and place, it has a specific value. Thus, it is likely that the air contained in the pen's reservoir will be exposed to an air

pressure fairly close to that of the prevailing atmospheric pressure. Assuming that the fountain pen is placed horizontally and out of the direct heat of the sun, when we write our body heat will slightly warm the air contained in the reservoir, causing some expansion. If a writer, inspired by the fresh mountain air, decides to create a poem and grabs a half empty fountain pen in his warm hand, heating the air inside the pen, the air expands and creates a pressure much higher than that of the prevailing atmospheric pressure. As a result, a virtual flood of ink will be released all over his budding masterpiece. To prevent this sort of thing from happening, most feeds are designed to contain some overflow; the ink in the slit of the nib should be exhausted before the ink in the reservoir is allowed to flow.

To this end, materials that are poor heat conductors are preferable. Black rubber has this quality, whereas most of the metals used in the fountain pen industry do not. When metal is

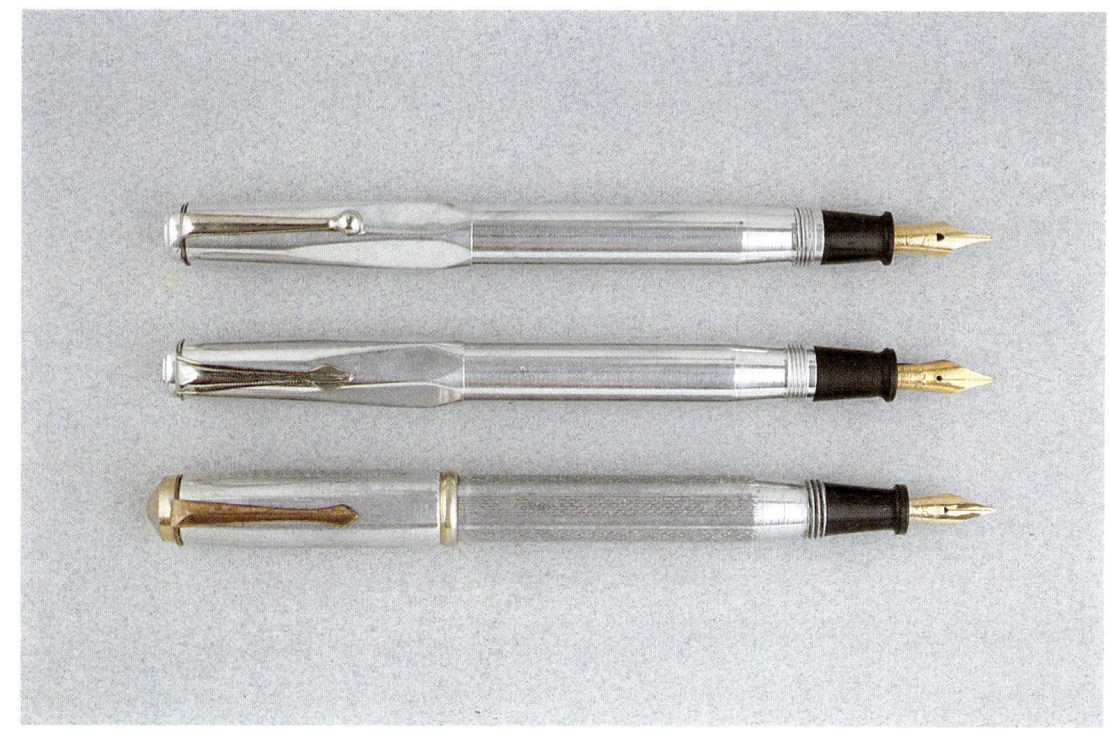

Metal pens made in France during World War II from aluminum scrap metal. The section and feed were made of hard rubber. Push-button filling system.

Bibax
Instrument made by La Plume d'Or that looks like a fountain pen, but is not really one. Launched in 1924, it can be considered the "missing link" or a very late transition between the dip pen and the fountain pen. It is filled using the principle of capillary attraction without any absorbent material. At the end of a hard rubber body, a silver nib with an iridium point is mounted on a feed. That feed, which is an essential part of the Bibax, is a hard rubber cylinder with four parallel grooves through which the ink flows when the nib is placed in an ink well. There is no reservoir, but a reserve that provides a flow of ink adequate to write six to seven pages, which is more than enough for most people.

used as an external ornament, it has little effect. However, a fountain pen with a body made of solid gold or silver would be not only very expensive, but very messy as well. The same can be said of pens with large reservoirs. Even half empty, such a reservoir can hold a very impressive amount of air. One should not confuse well-proportioned pens equipped with well-designed reservoirs and big pens merely having large reservoirs. There is a difference. Cartridges, as we will see later, soon replaced the massive, heavy pens on the market.

Feeds

All feeds operate on the same basic principle as the one invented by Waterman. In most cases, the feed is located under the nib, but some pens were equipped with feeds placed above the nib (first Parkers), and others, which

are quite rare (such as a few early **Swans**), were equipped with dual feeds, one on either side of the nib (over-under feeds).

For a long time, feeds were cut and bored from cylindrical black rubber rods. When synthetic resins became available, feeds were made by injection molding. Their convex shape is adapted precisely to the concavity of the nib (for upper feeds, the reverse is true). The external side is beveled under the tip of the nib, in order to avoid any friction with the paper. The other end of the feed is inserted into the section at the base of the nib. Thus wedged, the nib is maintained in close contact with the convex surface of the feed.

In the usual feed, the side beneath the nib has a grooved channel shaped like a trench, one end of which is inserted into the ink reservoir with the other extending to within 1 mm of the tip of the feed. When the feed is in place, its end lies under the nib, half-way between the eye and the tip.

Feed

ink

section

capillary groove

feed

canal

nib

hole

split

Cross-section of the Feed

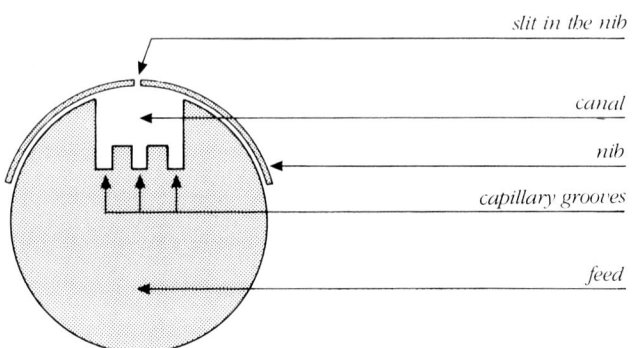

slit in the nib

canal

nib

capillary grooves

feed

During the process of writing, the flow of ink results in a decrease in the air pressure within the reservoir. To permit pressure equalization, there must be an intake of air, which acts as an air valve. The upper level canal is usually filled with ink, but it is through this channel that air bubbles travel up through the reservoir to equalize the pressure. Meanwhile, the lower grooves remain filled with ink, ensuring flow between the reservoir and the tip of the nib, even while air is passing in the opposite direction. The capillary attraction thus can remain constant.

Designed to collect the surplus ink resulting from variation in air pressure (altitude, body heat) are small pockets on either side of the central grooves, often represented by depressions or a series of fissures. There were none in Waterman's original patent. They first appeared in 1899 (Spoon Feed). The ink thus passes from the barrel reservoir to the tip of the nib, thanks to a series of capillary spaces, which include grooves, contact areas between the nib and the feed where the ink accumulates, lateral pockets, and a slit in the nib. When writing, the pressure applied by the hand causes these areas to fill and the tips of the nib to spread while the nib moves away from the feed and the ink flow increases. To obtain maximum capillary attraction at the tip, the width of the slit decreases from the eye to the point of contact with the paper.

Self-filling Swan (1913). Slightly more practical than the eyedropper. After the blue cap is removed, the pen is placed inside the opening. The bottle is turned upside down and the rubber half-sphere is squeezed to fill the pen.

Bottom: Travel ink wells. Some are equipped with an eyedropper (circa 1915).

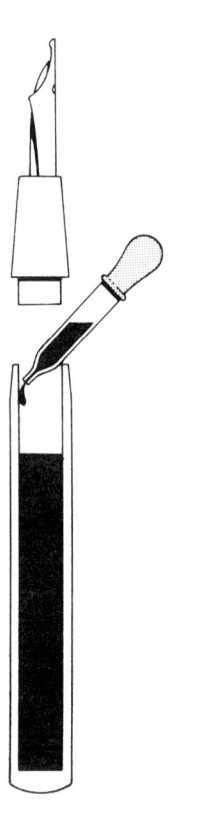

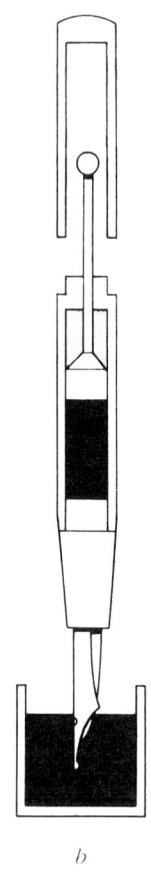

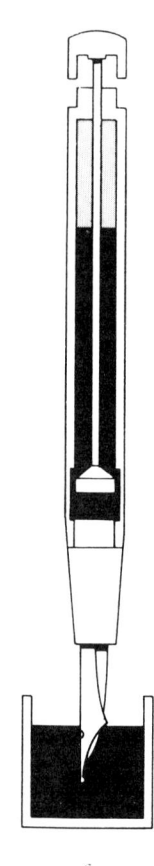

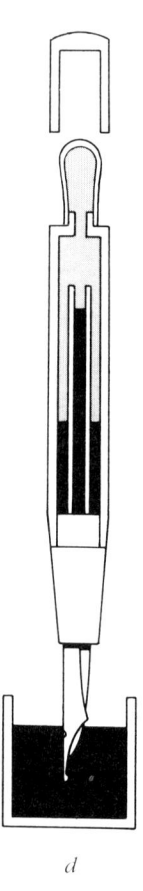

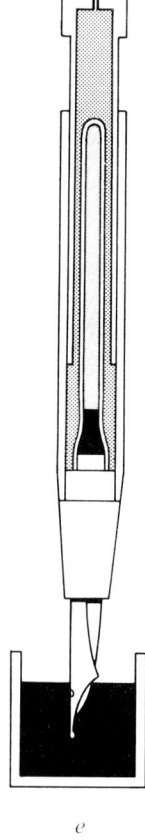

a   *b*   *c*   *d*   *e*

Filling Systems

To ensure the flow of ink to the nib, virtually all manufacturers developed feeds that operated on the principle of capillary attraction. Technical differences focused largely on the filling systems. From the end of the 19th century to the present, there have been two basic types of filling systems: the ink is either contained directly in the body of the fountain pen or in a separate reservoir.

The even flow of the ink is a critical element in the operation of a pen. Once that problem is satisfactorily solved, the filling system affects only the ease of operation. Manufacturers attempted to offer systems that ensured ease of operation, while at the same time they strove to be different from their competitors. Hence, there existed a multiplicity of systems, the major purpose of which was to be different and distinctive.

The filling systems in which the body is the receptacle can be divided into four major categories:

— Direct filling with an eyedropper or similar instrument (Fig. a). Used with the first standard fountain pens and later with the "**safeties**" with retractable nibs, it is the oldest method, the crudest, and the least convenient. It requires considerable dexterity on the part of the user.

— Filling using a simple piston (Fig. b). The piston may be mounted on a smooth shaft, as in a syringe, or on a threaded rod activated by the rotation of a knob. In both cases, air is ejected during the downward movement of the piston; the ink is then sucked up and always remains on the same side of the piston. A smooth shaft has the advantage of simplicity, but it reduces the capacity of the reservoir.

— Filling by plunger (Fig. c). Although there is a piston in this system, this process is very different from the preceding one. In its downward course, the piston expels the air in the cylinder and a decrease in pressure is created behind it. Near the end of its course, it reaches a portion of the body with a wider inner diameter, resulting in an upward ink flow that compensates for the pressure drop, and the reservoir fills without any additional movement of the piston. The reserve ink is behind the piston.

— Filling utilizing a vacuum tube (Fig. d). The process may be initiated using a button or compressible bulb acting on the membrane of a simple rubber tube (Parker **Vacumatic**) or by any other system resulting in the expulsion of a small amount of air to be replaced with a similar volume of ink. The tube is long enough so that its opening remains clear until fully filled. Such tubes are also used in fountain pens fitted with flexible reservoirs (Stylomine).

Systems with reservoirs independent from the body of the pen have an obvious advantage. They permit the use of materials that are not necessarily compatible with ink. These systems can be divided into two major categories:

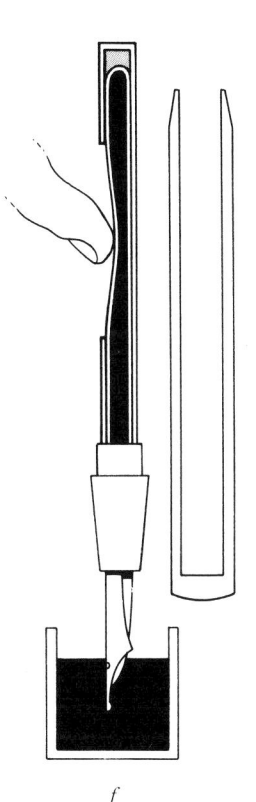

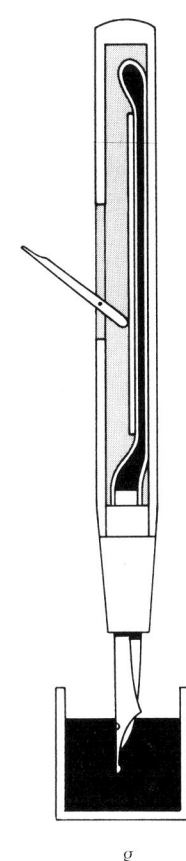

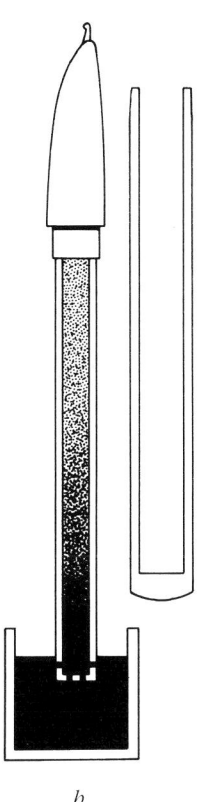

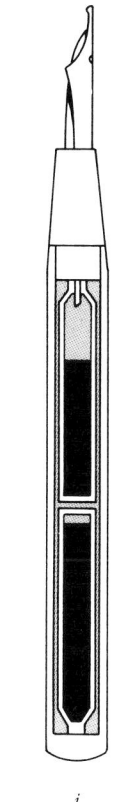

f   *g*   *h*   *i*

built-in reservoirs or removable reservoirs. When it is built-in, the reservoir is filled as a result of the expulsion of the air it holds or by capillary attraction. The built-in reservoirs are generally made of flexible material. Replaced by plastic materials today, the rubber sac was formerly the unchallenged master in that category. Since filling occurs following air expulsion, the difference between the systems rests only in the way the rubber sac is compressed. Four examples illustrate the systems that operate through the compression of a flexible reservoir:

— By torsion of the reservoir. A crude, little used method. (1903, A.A. Waterman's adaptation of Moseley's 1859 patent and Kollisch's 1841 patent).

— By the pressure of an air column compressing the reservoir (Fig. e). At the end of the downward course, when the air is released, the reservoir expands and fills (Chilton, Sheaffer, Pneu).

Safety First:

The Waterman safety pen, "the pen that can be carried in any position," held an important place on the French market for 30 years, from 1908 to 1939. It was produced in the United States until the 1940s, although it was largely replaced in the 1920s by lever filling models with which it had been competing since 1915. It is reputed that the safety pen patent recorded by Waterman was inspired by the mechanism of the mechanical pencil, registered in 1903. The safety appeared on the market in 1907, and interestingly enough, the mechanism of the first models was not the same as that described in the patent. This situation prevailed for 5 years, and it was not until 1912 that its manufacture reverted to the mechanism initially designed and recorded.

In the first design, helical grooves were cut inside the body to propel the nib outside the pen; in the second design, the grooves were replaced by a helical movable piece. In the first design, the nib revolved as it extended, and in the second, it did not revolve. In the first design, models were fitted with a threaded propulsion extension onto which the cap was screwed; in the second design, the propulsion extension was smooth.

After World War II, the success of the retractable nib encouraged many French manufacturers to increase production of these models, further enhancing its success. That success was perhaps due to the fact that the nib was continually immersed in ink and thus always ready to write. The attraction of the hidden mechanism and the elegance of the manipulation required to extend the nib may also have contributed greatly to its lasting success. In 1930, Stylomine, in order to eliminate the inconvenience of eye-dropper fillers, introduced a retractable nib model called the Self-Filler.

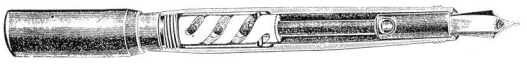

JiF fountain pens manufactured during World War II. These models were equipped with a glass cartridge and lever. Since the use of gold was prohibited, the nibs were made of steel.

– By direct pressure of the fingers (Fig. f), either on the sac or on an extension (Stylomine).

– Through a compression bar (Fig. g). There are numerous systems utilizing this principle: a pin, long or short levers, jointed, off-centered, push-buttons, rotating buttons, etc. Some models vary the systems just for the fun of it, but the composition of the fountain pen is very different from that of human beings. It is useless and precludes a good understanding of the subject when one creates variations without good reason.

Capillary attraction, essential to the filling system, was not very successful when variations of the basic system were employed. Major manufacturers, such as Parker and Waterman, tried them. When filled with stacked disks, a mesh fabric or other absorbent material to increase the surface area, the resulting reservoir had a very small capacity. In Fig. h, the filling is

provided by a spongy wick. Whether it is the nib that is immersed in the ink (Waterman **X Pen**) or the other end of the reservoir (Parker **61**), filling is a slow operation and takes an average of 20 seconds. Conversely, if the cap is not replaced, the ink dries very quickly. However, because these systems were unaffected by variations in pressure, they were relatively popular among aircraft crews and airline passengers.

Cartridges

The cartridge is the simplest and most practical filling system. It is also the most recently developed system and the one most innovative in design (Fig. i). Due to its simplicity and sturdiness, the cartridge succeeded in place of systems that were cumbersome, fragile, and sometimes incredibly complex. Not re-

Boxes of glass nibs

In 1936, when JiF introduced its cartridge models, which had been adopted from American pens, their shape did not conform to that of a cartridge and required modification so that the body could be opened to allow the insertion of the cartridge. The lever and its opening were eliminated, the feed was adapted so that it served as a plunger, and a rubber ring was added to make the cartridge leakproof. The assembly was all accomplished in France. World War II put an end to production. Models shown are deluxe examples having gold and silver trim (1936-1939).

quiring any mechanism, the cartridge frees the body of the pen and increases its capacity.

The average cartridge contains more ink than an equivalent rubber sac that can never be completely filled. It permits better control of ink flow and eliminates the need for ink wells and bottles (which are missed by some, who have obviously forgotten the rags and blotters required to wipe out stains, spills, and various other mishaps). With the cartridge, ink regains its positive characteristics and flows in the right direction, downward towards the tip, with sufficient consistency to permit writing, but never in sudden bursts as is the case with other systems. (It might be claimed that the forced passage of air and the strong flow of the ink theoretically "cleans" the channel. In fact, since the ink becomes more viscous because of the inevitable evaporation, the opposite might be more true.) Additionally, the cartridge prevents the writer from running out of fuel. Carried in a pocket or

in a travel case, one or two spare cartridges are much less cumbersome and messy than a bottle of ink. Pens with large ink reservoirs are now obsolete. The first cartridges, made of glass, were rather fragile, but with the advent of plastic this particular weakness has been completely eliminated. The history of the cartridge really began in 1936. Cartridges existed before then, but they were fleeting fads, without any longstanding influence on the future of the fountain pen.

The oldest attempt at a cartridge filler was that of the Eagle Pencil Company. It first offered glass ink vials in 1890. Unfortunately, they were very fragile; the tip of the vial had to be sectioned off carefully and mishaps were frequent, even more so when people insisted on using eyedroppers to fill them. Ten years later, Eagle abandoned the concept and adopted the rubber sac like everyone else.

The pen that Blair patented in 1898 and

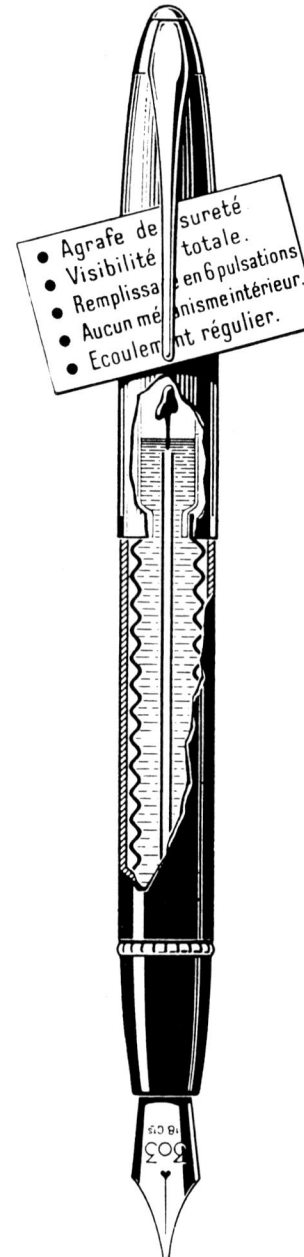

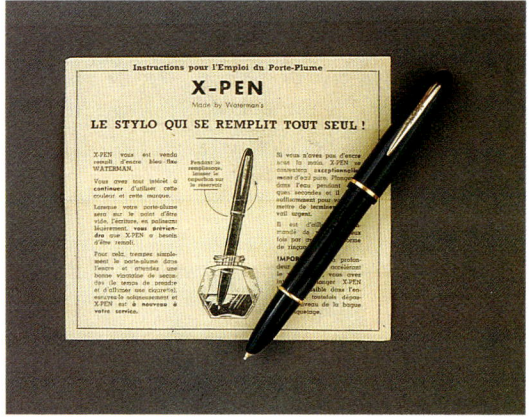

Waterman X Pen, *capillary filling (stack of absorbent disks), 1951 patent issued in 1953. Manufactured in France.*

Stylomine 303 *with retractable nib and automatic filling. The mechanism, which extends the nib, can be unscrewed to release a small rubber bulb (1930).*

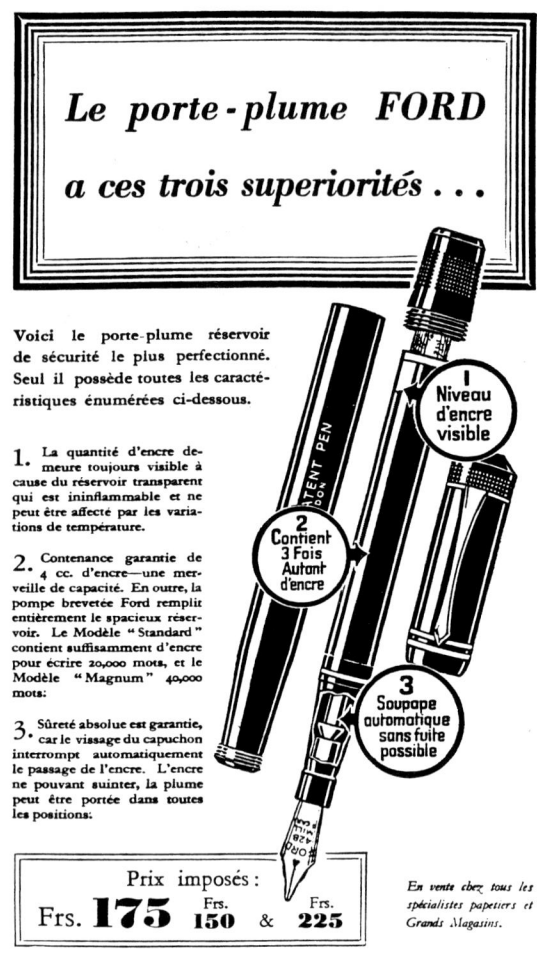

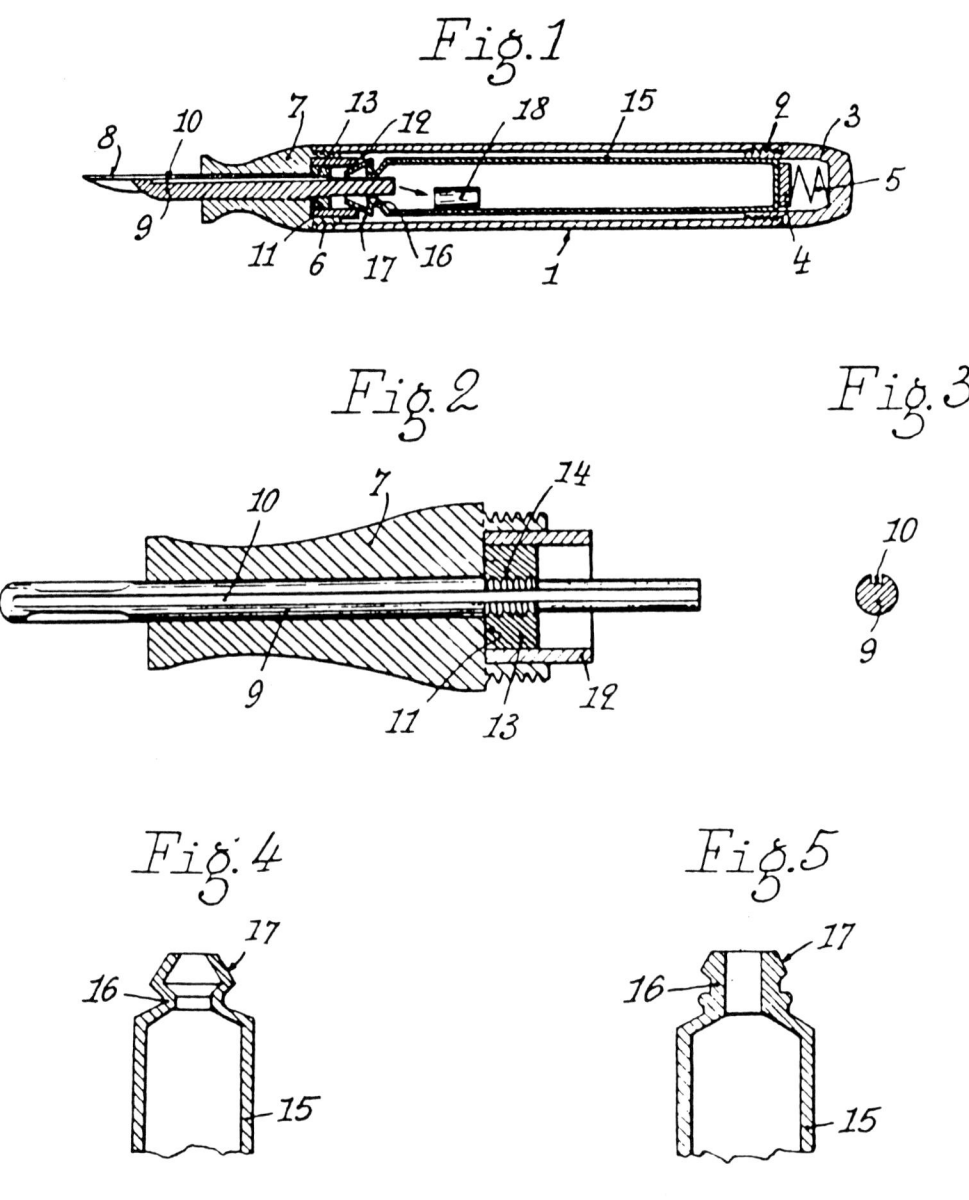

*JiF-Waterman patent for the glass cartridge with truncated neck,
the rubber ring holding the cartridge in the section,
and the feed extension (located at the end of the capillary passage),
which was designed to dislodge the cap.*

Mac Niven & Cameron (c. 1918).

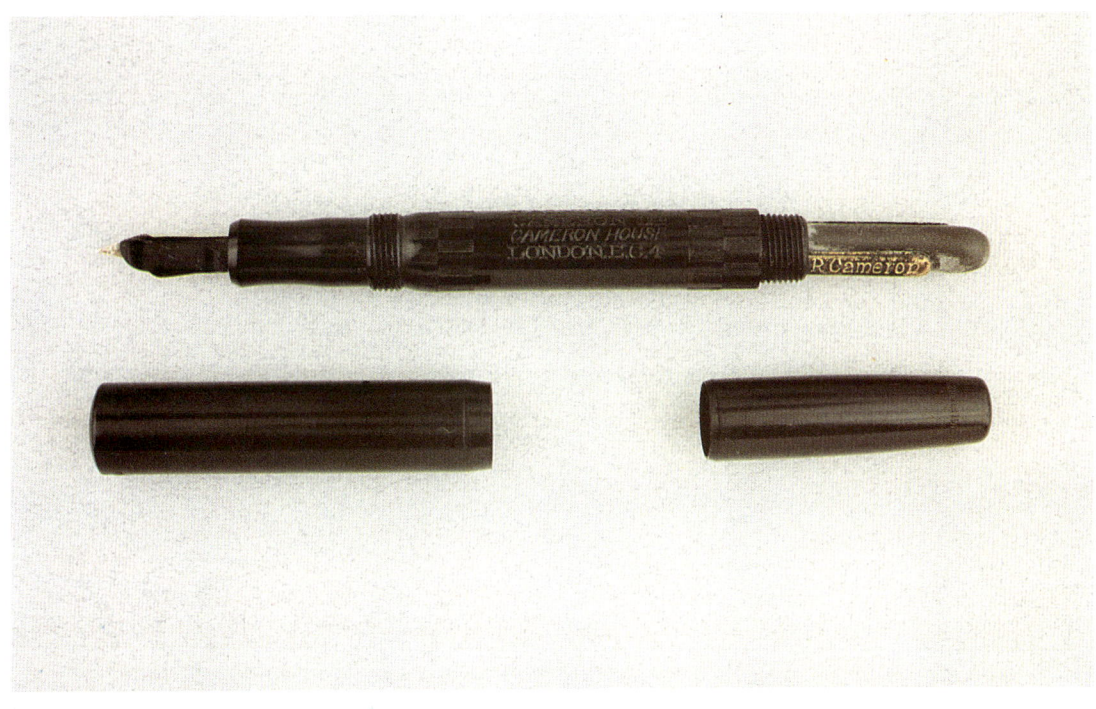

*Aurora fountain pen (circa 1932); the filling is done
(possibly with one hand) through a small lever located
at the end of the body (shown partially extended in this
photograph). First distributed in France in 1931 by
Edacoto. The Aurora fountain pen and the Edacoto
mechanical pencil were called the "duo moderne".*

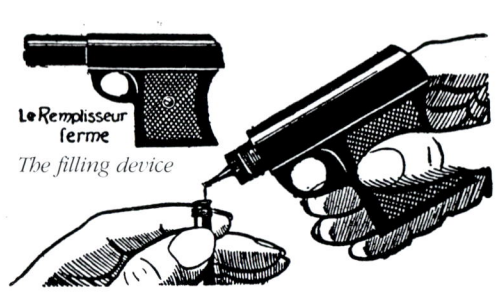

Le Remplisseur ferme

The filling device

Flacon d'encre incassable en ébonite,
pour remplir les Porte-Plume Réservoir

*Small unbreakable bottle of ink in black hard rubber
with which the reservoir of the pen holder could be
refilled.*

*Monograph pen holder, patented on May 17, 1889. The
revolutionary capillary filling system obviously had not
yet become popular.*

Waterman standard model with lever and cartridge (1953-1955). The Super Cartouche (with a gold dot on the cap) is equipped with a large capacity cartridge and visible ink level.

Flash Fill *by Waterman, with cartridge. Manufactured in France (1950).*

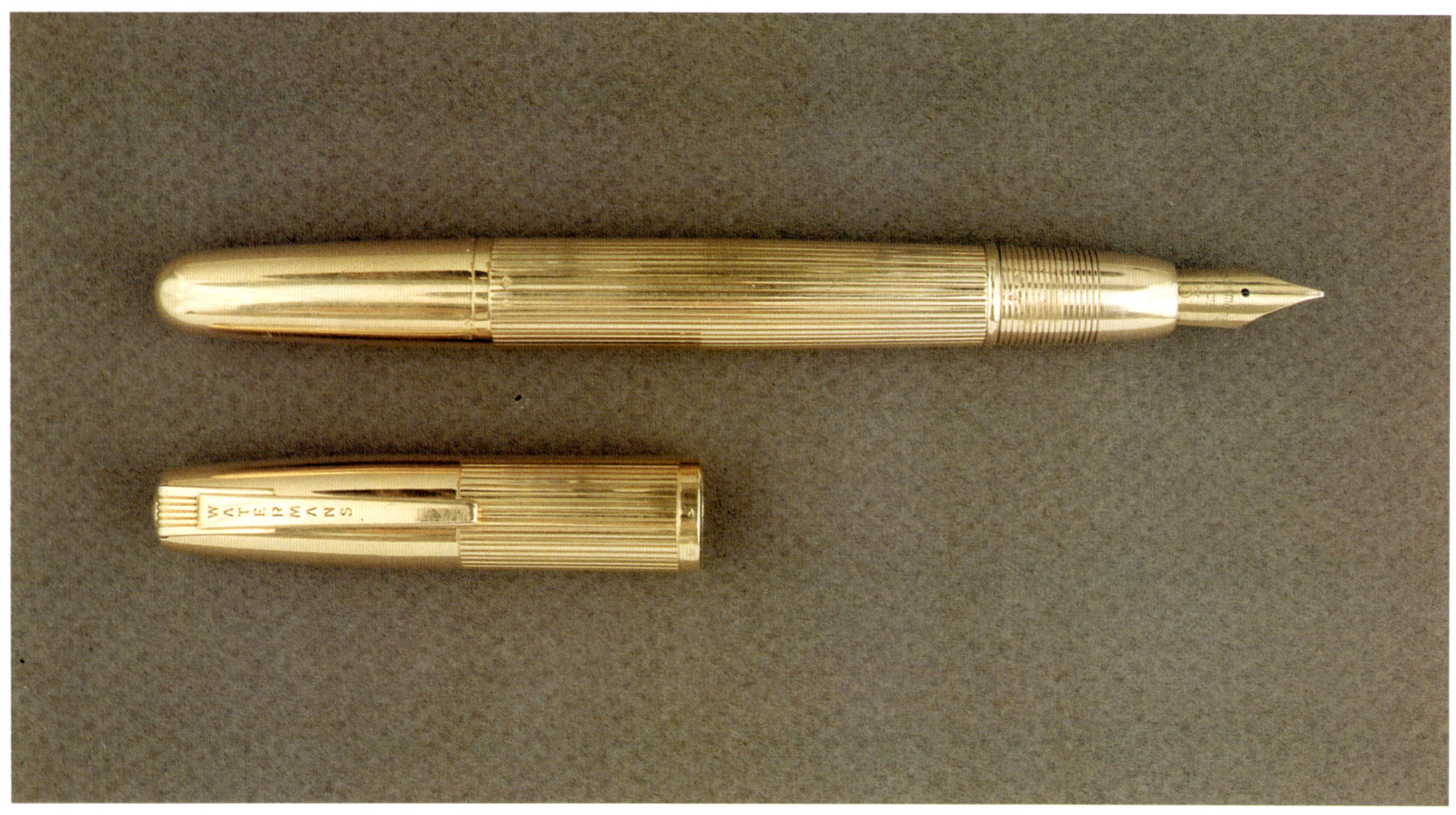

manufactured for many years is often cited as the first fountain pen to use a cartridge. Indeed, there was a cartridge used with this pen, but it was a container with solid ink. After it was inserted into the pen, it had to be filled with water. Thus, in reality, the filling system was not all that different. That model, as well as all others using water, was especially popular with people constantly on the move, such as explorers and the military. Even in the middle of

nowhere, running out of ink was no longer a risk. A single solid ink cartridge was enough to refill the pen several times. Other than that, the Blair pen did not offer any of the advantages of the modern ink cartridge.

In 1921, the Frenchman Jean-Baptiste Salmon invented a pen with an independent and rechargeable ink reservoir, which he called the *Stylo Tube*. The name was registered in 1923. The reservoir consisted of a glass tube with the

open end threaded and capped. The empty cartridge was unscrewed and discarded, and a full one was inserted in its place. In 1927, Salmon improved his tube. He replaced the glass with black rubber, a good idea but, unfortunately, a sales failure.

In 1936, Jif patented a fountain pen with a capsule, designed 7 years earlier by a Mr. Perraud, then technical manager of the company. The patent describes three compo-

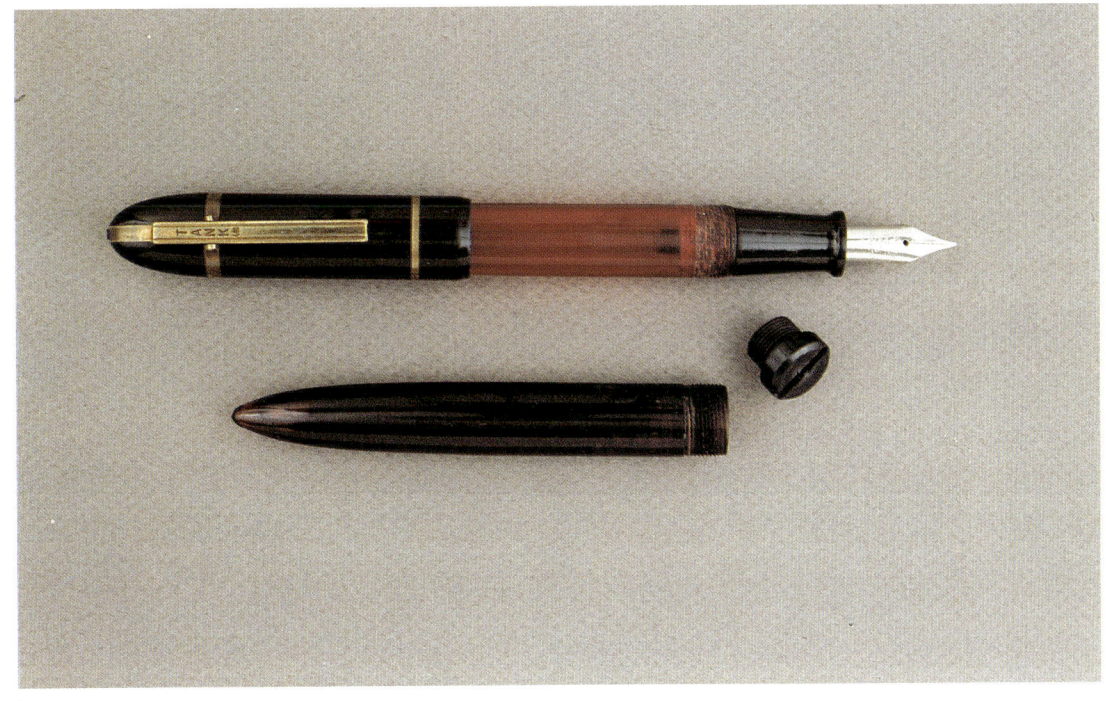

Tank 400 *by Pierre Bagnol, with a spare ink reservoir (1947).*

nents: a glass capsule with a narrowed neck, a body with an O ring that keeps the capsule in place, and a perforator that pierces the cap. Success was instantaneous. It proved to be the birth of the first practical cartridge, and thanks to this patent Waterman had exclusive production rights for the ink cartridge.

In 1947, the Pierre Bagnol Company launched the **Tank 400**, which was very aptly named. The whole body of the pen was a cartridge. Once empty, it was discarded. Its capacity was enormous; in a publicity release, Bagnol described his model as being the equivalent of 10 fountain pens. The **Tank 400** was a moderate success.

Nibs

Together with the feed, the nib is the most essential part of a fountain pen. Obvious? Not necessarily so! Many a fountain pen is purchased today on the strength of its good looks. The appearence of the written word is of lesser importance. When it comes down to making a choice, a few customers will try the feel of the nib, but more often than not the compatibility of the nib with the individual's handwriting will be secondary to the attractiveness of a lacquered finish.

The fountain pen nib must have several qualities. First and foremost, it must glide on

Glass nibs were used mostly for mulitiple copy writing because of their hardness. Despite their attractive shapes and colors, they were never widely used because of the unpredictability of the ink flow.

Colors
Lever filling Waterman #5 and #7 pens in marbled red hard rubber (1926-1930). Originally, the #7 was sold for $7.00 and the #5 for $5.00. The type of nib was identified by the color of the band on the cap. The color was engraved on the nib and the eye was in the shape of a keyhole.

the paper surface with ease and flexibility. Since it cannot be sharpened, nor is it practical to discard it after a few pages, it must also resist the acidity of the ink and the friction of the paper. Glass is impervious to acid, but it lacks flexibility. Laminated and shaped metals are flexible enough, but steel corrodes easily and gold wears out quickly.

Glass Nibs

Although glass is inflexible and breaks easily, this did not prevent it from being used as a writing instrument. In 1837, a man named Boulard registered a patent for a glass nib, a real nib with a split end and two points. According to him, its fragility was largely compensated for by its stainless and acid resistant

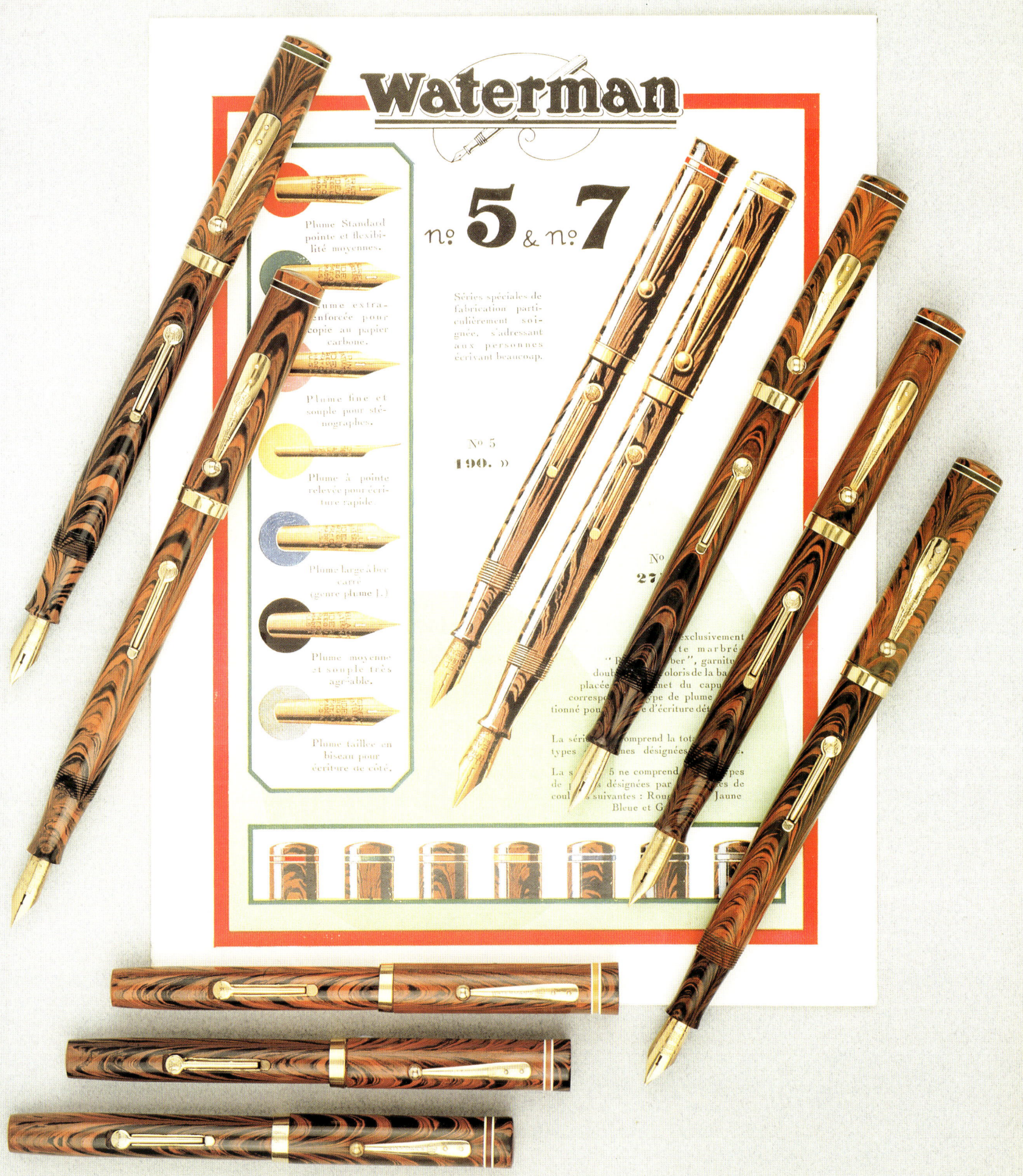

The thickness of the nib decreases from the tip to the back-end.

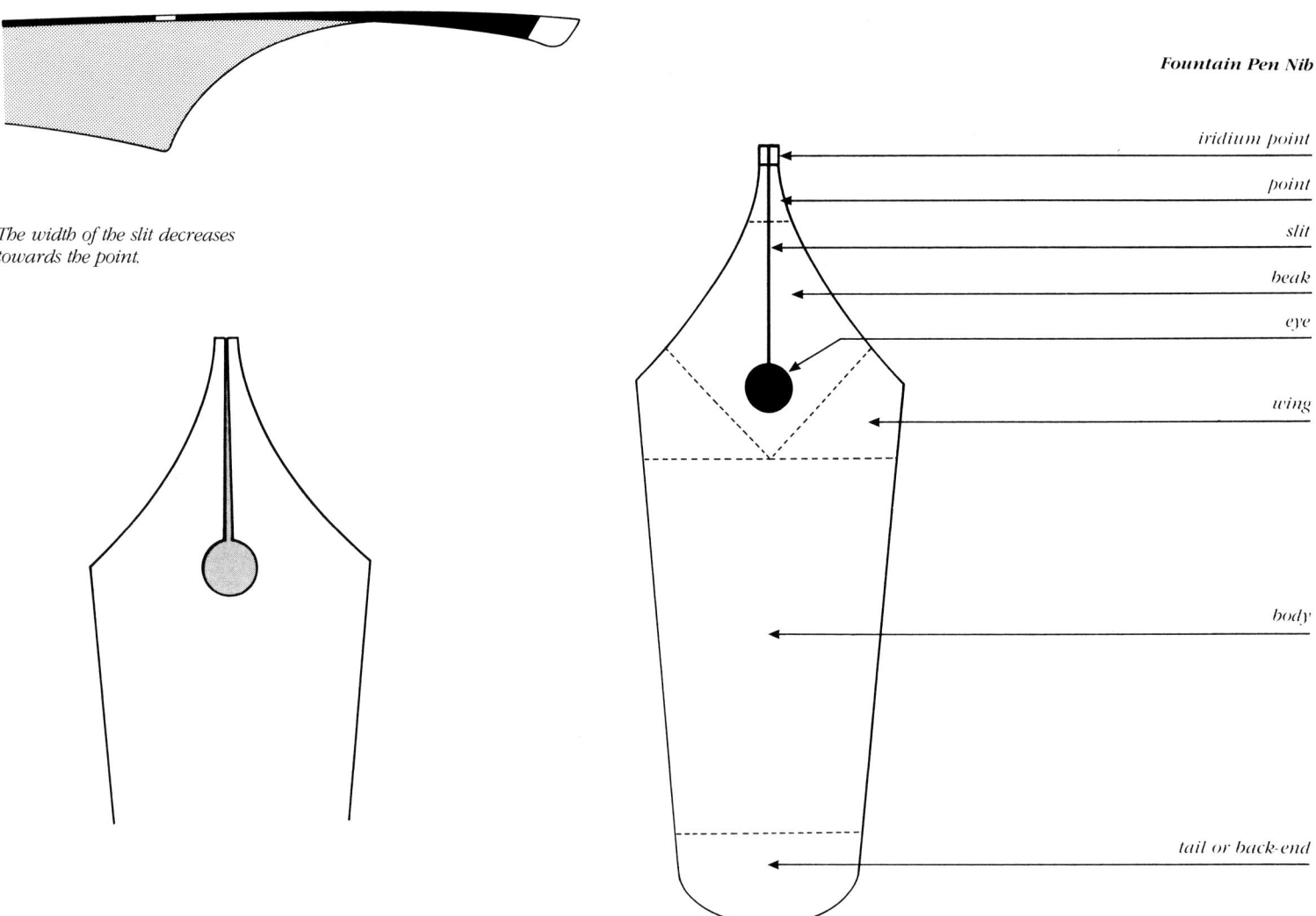

The width of the slit decreases towards the point.

Fountain Pen Nib

iridium point

point

slit

beak

eye

wing

body

tail or back-end

qualities; it was also durable and economical.

Although the patent was granted to Gay-Lussac, production remained dormant. Successful glass nibs were not actually nibs, they lacked sharp points and had no split end; they were simply pieces of twisted or corrugated pointed glass mounted on some type of holder. Other glass nibs, more beautiful, were mounted onto a glass handle or were drawn until they were a one-piece nib and holder, at the end of which a glass bird was formed.

The period following the end of the Victorian era was the golden age of glass nibs. Traditional glass blowing techniques created charming colored and decorated objects that graced the desks and writing tables of many refined young ladies.

At the beginning of the 20th century, particularly in the 1920s, some fountain pens were equipped with glass nibs. The hardness of their points made them ideal instruments for multiple copy writing or for writing with carbon paper. They competed favorably with stylographic and manifold nib fountain pens. During World War II, when steel was requisitioned for more pressing needs, glass nibs found patrons among accountants and some businessmen, but there were few other users.

Glass nibs were used largely on inexpensive fountain pens and no major manufacturer except Montblanc ever used them, and then only to a very limited extent. Their resistance to acids and corrosion and even their low price were not enough to offset their significant shortcomings. The hardness that made them attractive to carbon paper users was not really a plus to the majority of writers, since, in addition to being hard, they were very fragile. Glass nibs that were fitted onto fountain pens were either fixed or retractable. In the case of the former, the ridges or fluting that fed the tip dried up very quickly and it was then difficult to re-establish the flow of ink. With retractable nibs, the point was better protected and did not dry as easily, but the slight disadvantage of all

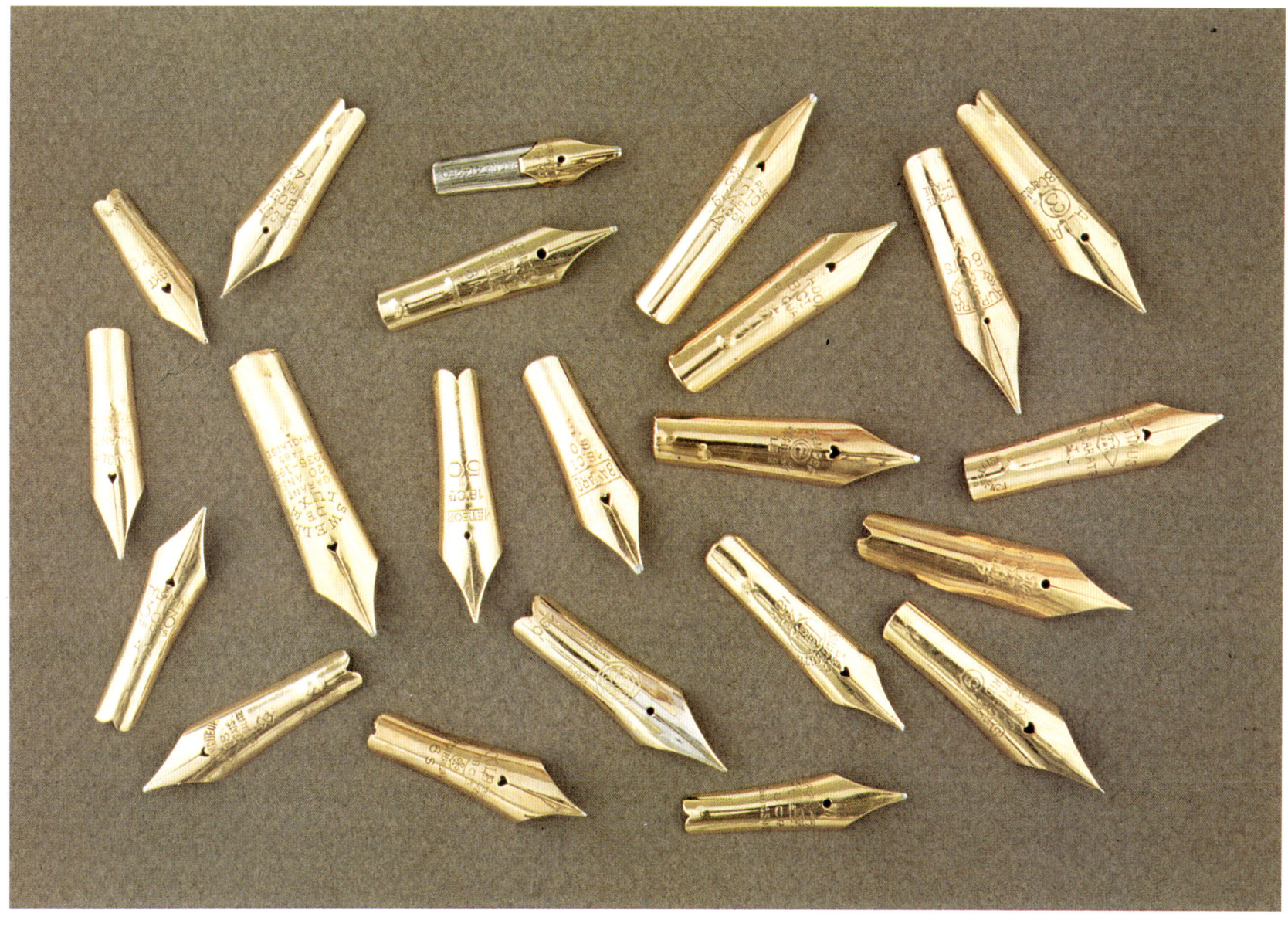

Nibs made by various manufacturers.

retractable nib pens became disastrous in this case. When the nib was extended, if the propulsion device were not fully extended, the ink would empty onto the paper as soon as the nib came into contact with the surface.

Manufacturing techniques being simple, glass nibs were made everywhere. One company that was able to make a name for itself in this domain was the German company, Haro. In France, most glass nibs were imported from Czechoslovakia.

Gold Nibs

Impervious to corrosion, gold is the ideal material for nibs once a way has been devised for dealing with the wear resulting from friction with the paper. The solution was to fix a hard element at the tip. Feather quill nibs were equipped with a similar component by the addition of bits of precious stones (diamonds or rubies). The hardness of these materials was unquestionable, but they also needed a round surface without which they inflicted irreparable damage to the paper. Around 1827, an Englishman named Doughty used ruby-tipped gold nibs. Although very expensive, his nibs were moderately successful.

Platinum has been known since 1735, but it was not until 1804 that two British chemists identified other metals in platinum ore.

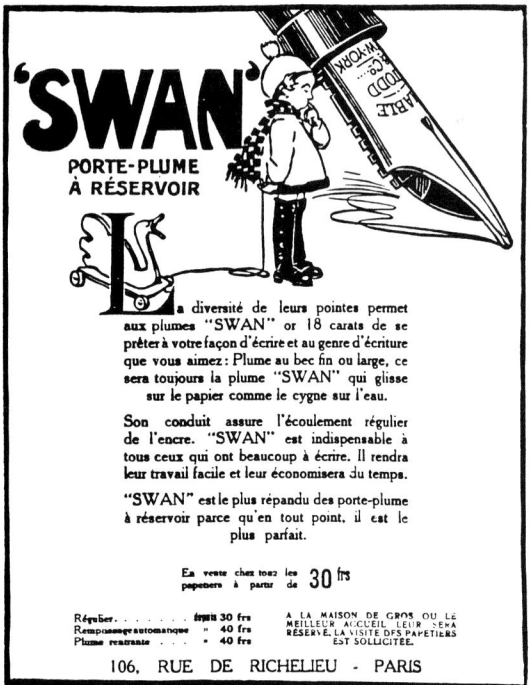

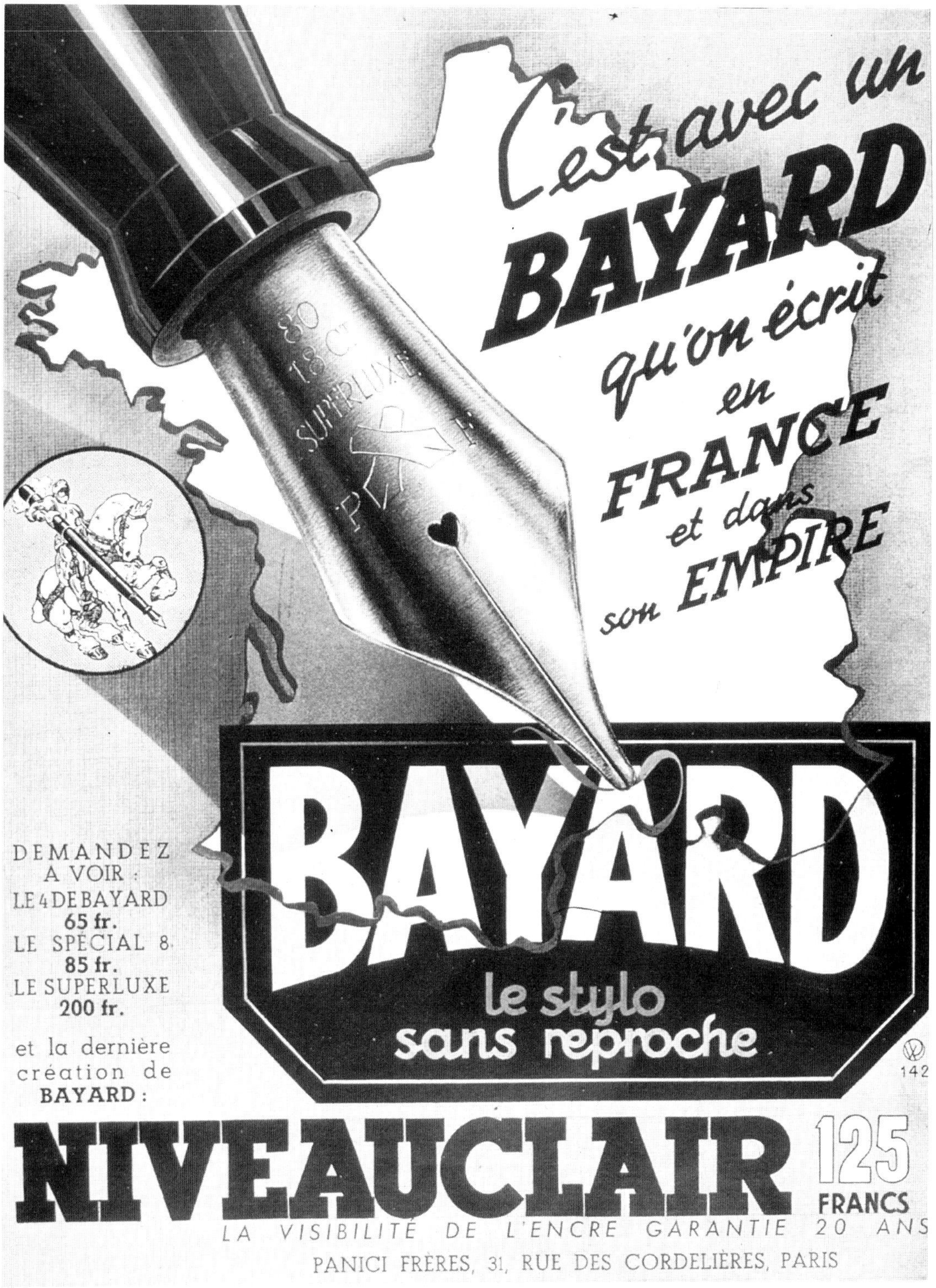

Smithson Tennant discovered osmium and iridium, and William Hyde Wollaston, palladium and rhodium.

It is generally acknowledged that the first individual to obtain satisfactory results with any of these metals was John Isaac Hawkins, who, in 1823, had started experiments with feather quills, using tortoise shell and horn nibs set with ruby tips. He understood that by capitalizing on the hardness of diamonds, rubies, and other precious stones, he could affix them to a grinding wheel and, thus, cut the iridium. At the same time, he was able to make improvements in gold nibs, rendering them more durable.

In 1843, after trying ruby tips, the Frenchman Jean-Benoît Mallat initiated the

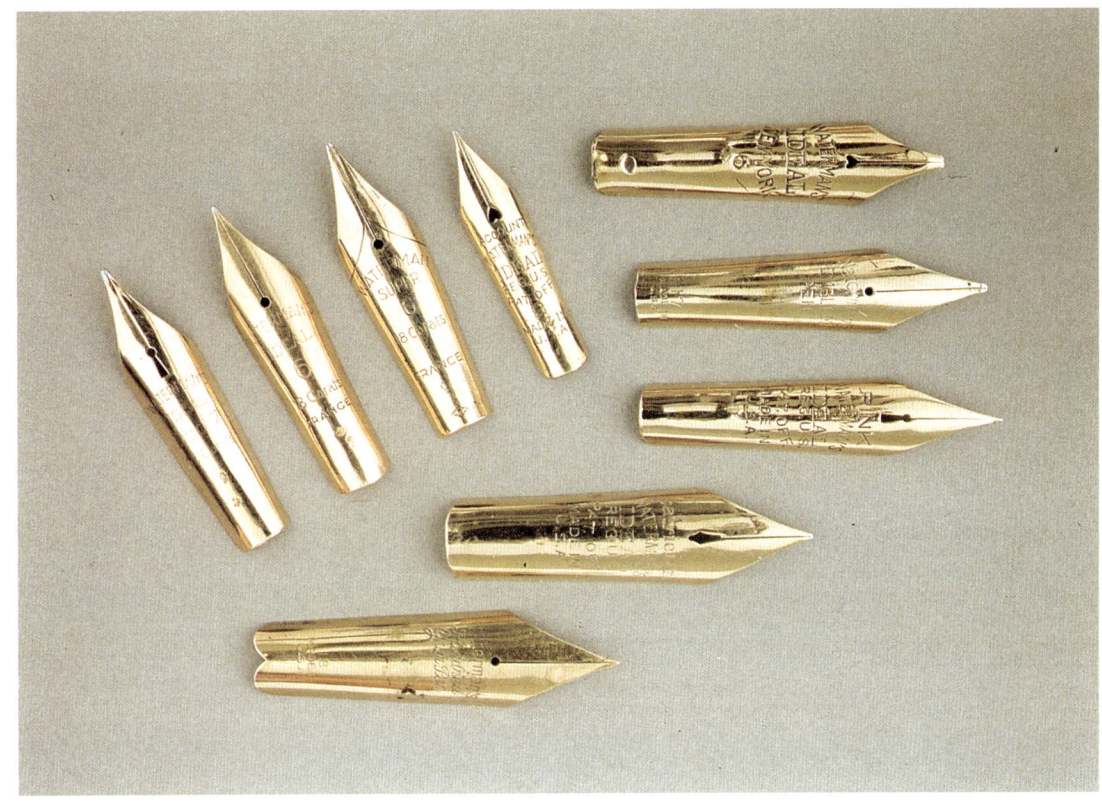

Assortment of Waterman nibs: Patrician, Hundred Year, Duo 7...

production of gold nibs with iridium points. However, it was not until the end of the 19th century in the United States that the industry was actually born. New York rapidly became the fountain pen capital of the world, and for several decades it supplied the world market. Sitting on innumerable steel nibs, manufacturers in Birmingham, England had missed the boat. Despite its expertise in the production of fountain pens, Great Britain played only a secondary role in the gold nib industry. It was the principal European producer, but lagged far behind the United States. As for France, it was only after World War I that an interest in gold nibs developed, and even then only the major companies began production (Bayard, Gold Starry, Paillard, Stylomine, Unic). A few specialized companies supplied nibs under their own name brands or under the trade names of small pen manufacturers.

The gold used in making nibs is so soft that it is necessary to reinforce it with a small cap of iridium or osmium. Even 14 or 18 karat alloys are too soft. A karat is defined as the quantity of pure gold contained in a gold alloy, expressed as a ratio of 1:24. Pure gold is 24 karat, 18 karat gold has a gold/gold alloy ratio of 750/1,000, and 14 karat gold has a ratio of 585/1,000 (the numbers 750 and 585 often appear on nibs).

Most fountain pen nibs are made of 14 karat gold, with the exception of those manufactured for export to a few markets that require 18 karat gold. In France, gold of less than 18 karats may not be sold. The other two elements in the alloy are copper and silver.

14 karat: 14 Au + 6 Cu + 4 Ag

18 karat: 18 Au + 3 Cu + 3 Ag

These alloys are subjected to very careful analysis. They must not contain any impurity that might alter their properties and make them more fragile.

The manufacture of gold nibs involves a large number of steps, the most important of which are as follows:

1. Rolling of an ingot, 10 to 20 mm in

Sabon workshop (Bordeaux) circa 1930.

thickness. Several passes and annealing (necessary to ensure flexibility) are required before obtaining a thickness of 0.3 to 0.6 mm. Annealing is performed after each rolling, except for the last one, when the gold is hardened. Further rolling and other operations on bench presses are performed on the cold gold; the hardness thus obtained is necessary to ensure the flexibility and resilience of the nib.

2. Cutting of the first dies.

3. Soldering of the iridium point with a blow torch.

4. Sanding the area around the iridium where the soldering has melted the gold.

5. Rolling of the form between two grooved cylinders. The sides of the nib are extended.

This rolling phase results in a thickness between 0.3 and 0.6 mm at the tips, but reduces the body of the nib to about 0.1 mm at the tail. For obvious reasons, the tip must be thicker. The thinning of the body improves flexibility. The reason behind the thinness of the tail is not to save gold, but to ensure a tight fit of the nib between the feed and the section.

6. Cutting of the other parts of the nib on a bench press equipped with a point and a die.

7. Marking and drilling of the eye on a press.

8. Impressing the curvature of the nib.

9. Splitting of the nib tip up to the eye with a cutting disk.

10. Repeat sanding of the iridium or osmium

point. At this stage, the nib is graded as either fine, medium or broad.

11. Polishing of the top of the nib and dulling of the underside (to regulate ink flow).

These processes are followed by various quality control tests (elasticity, point calibration, line drawing, etc.), which are automated today. Formerly, soldering with a blow torch had to be done before the last rolling. Now, electric soldering of the iridium is done after the curvature of the nib is produced.

The average standard nib weighs about 0.30 grams, the smallest weighs about 0.15 grams, and the largest rarely exceeds 0.50 grams. They may be partially rhodium-plated, creating a white surface that contrasts with the yellow of the gold.

The numbers that are sometimes stamped on the body indicate the size of a particular model. Nib size, point type, and nib quality should not be confused. Size refers to the nib dimensions (small, medium, large, etc.), type describes the point characteristics (extra-fine, fine, medium, large, square or broad, oblique, etc.), and quality refers to its behavior (soft, semi-soft, hard, etc.). All these characteristics can be combined; for example, a nib may be large or small, fine or broad, and hard or soft. This is one of the reasons why there was such an incredible number of models offered by the

Displays of French nibs in gilded steel (gold-plate is usually not used for nibs because of the difference in flexibility between gold and steel). These nibs were generally used on inexpensive fountain pens.

Before the Parker 51, other pens also had hidden nibs.

major manufacturers throughout the 1920s and 1930s.

After World War II, the decline in the popularity of the fountain pen resulted in a sharp decrease in the variety of nibs available. The number of models offered by major manufacturers, who had offered scores only a couple of decades before, could be counted on the fingers of one hand. Today, the resurgence in the popularity of the fountain pen has somewhat improved the situation.

Steel Nibs

Before World War II, a good nib had to be made of gold. Steel is harder than gold, but it is not resistant to wear. Iridium and osmium are very expensive, even more so than gold. It would have been absurd to use them as points on steel nibs since the latter were so corrosive. Steel was used for inexpensive models, low-end pens for students with limited incomes or would-be writers. When iridium was not used, the nib tips were doubled or thickened in order to ensure a smooth flow onto paper and resistance to wear, thus adapting techniques that had been used on nibs for dip pens for decades.

Today, things have changed a lot. Gold is still used for higher priced models and it retains its prestige, but the majority of contemporary fountain pens are fitted with steel nibs. Many factors contributed to this trend. During and immediately after World War II, there was a gold shortage in Europe, which, although insignificant when compared with other tragedies at the time, had serious repercussions. In France, it was forbidden to manufacture gold nibs until 1949. Beginning in 1971, gold prices, which

Lady's fountain pen, gold trim by an anonymous jeweler. The cap is embellished with an amethyst cabochon and a circle of rose-cut diamonds.

previously were stable, started to climb sharply. Finally, and most importantly, advances in stainless steel technology enabled the manufacture of steel nibs of a quality almost equal to that of gold nibs.

The resistance to corrosion and the mechanical properties of stainless steel nibs are close to those of 14 karat gold nibs. In these alloys, chromium plays an essential role in resisting corrosion, while nickel and molybdenum ensure thermal stability, and the carbon content is kept as low as possible. The processing of this type of steel requires a technology much more advanced than that required to produce 14 or 18 karat gold.

Steel nibs are sold in either their natural color or gold-filled. They even look like gold, but obviously are not. Contemporary stainless steel nibs are of excellent quality, which could not be said of steel nibs made in the past.

Nibs have been made of other alloys too, such as palladium and silver. Although these materials are slightly more subject to corrosion, their performance and price are close to that of gold nibs. The problem with them is their color; the market is not inclined to pay the price of gold for something that looks like steel.

Shapes

Whether gold or steel, the nib does not offer many options for its shape. This is unfortunate since there was an incredible variety of pens. They numbered in the thousands and were decorated with engraved figures or imaginative filigrees.

The ancestor of the fountain pen nib was nothing more than a simple tip mounted onto a hollow pen-holder, generally fed by a short tube. At the beginning of the 19th century, they were generally made of goose feather quills. The first real fountain pen nibs combined the curved line of the reed pen with the softness of the feather quill, which, together, ensured the strength and flexibility of the tip.

With its proven track record, the curved shape remained constant throughout the centuries and did not change, even with the advent of the fountain pen. For ink to feed properly, three parts of the pen must be fitted as closely as possible: the nib, the feed, and the section that keeps the parts together. For nearly 40 years, feeds and sections were bored from black rubber tubes or rods. The era of plastics and injection molding did not alter the roundness of the body. It did, however, permit some innovations; for example, a built-in nib in an interchangeable section.

117

Adjustable Wahl Eversharp nibs, which allowed a reduction or increase in tip flexibility for thin or broad writing (1932-1939).

Some of the "innovations" do not quite deserve the title. One example was the adjustable nib on some Wahl-Eversharp pens. Billed as revolutionary at the beginning of the 1930s, it was actually a copy of a gimmick introduced 75 years earlier. Tubular nibs, however tailored or aerodynamic, are basically of the same shape as the reeds, feather quills, and first metal nibs made by the Romans.

With its covered nib, the Parker **51** was a very good pen, a best seller in its day, and one that was copied by many; moreover, it radically (and some assert negatively) changed the world's perception of the fountain pen. The covered nib may have its defenders, who argue that it permitted the use of a faster drying ink, that the nib was protected, and that it had a design worthy of the Bauhaus architectural style. Nevertheless, it was the first fountain pen to conceal its nib. By hiding the nib, you could forget that it existed, and the fountain pen had a hard time recovering from such an assault on its image. Fortunately, the covered nib was just a fad. The current renaissance of the fountain pen is eloquent testimony; nibs have once again emerged into the light of day.

Materials

A nib must be flexible. Metal provides that property. As for the rest of the fountain pen (feed, body, cap, reservoir), its history is intimately linked to that of plastics. This poorly defined term in current usage equates plastics with synthetic resins. Following mechanical stress, an elastic distortion is temporary; however, any distortion of a plastic material is permanent. Therefore, any material that consists of macromolecules exhibiting this property is a "plastic" substance. Hence, there are natural plastics (amber, horn, tortoise shell, etc.) and artificial plastics made by man from natural substances (cellulose acetate, celluloid, black hard rubber, etc.) as well as synthetic resins that are completely man-made, especially from petroleum and coal by-products (bakelite, plexiglas, rilsan, etc.).

In 1839, after 8 years of unsuccessful attempts, Charles Goodyear inadvertently placed a mixture of rubber and sulfur on a stove. He could never have imagined that this incident would have such a huge impact on the evolution of writing instruments. Although it

Black hard rubber and red marbled rubber rods ready to be cut and drilled.

took 5 more years and bore the name of Thomas Hancock, vulcanized rubber had been invented, and sulfur had created the bond between its macro-molecular chains.

As long as ink was stored within its body, the fountain pen had to be composed of non-porous, acid-resistant, non-heat conducting materials that would also be inexpensive. Vulcanized rubber has all of these properties and, therefore, hard rubber was a critical factor in the birth and early expansion of the fountain pen industry. For more than half a century, it was the most widely used material. It was delivered to factories in the form of rods,

generally 1 meter long, and of varying diameter corresponding to the parts to be shaped on the lathes: bodies, caps, sections, and feeds. Excellent pens were created from this material and the body was seamless. Hard rubber is easy to identify; if you have any doubts, just rub the pen with a woolen cloth. If it is composed of hard rubber, the static electricity created will attract small pieces of paper.

After rubber came cotton or wood cellulose. Celluloid was developed in 1869 by John Wesley Hyatt in response to a competition designed to identify a material to replace ivory for use in billiard balls. Celluloid is obtained by

"Cardinal" red hard rubber Waterman pen (1910-1929).

Engraved Gold and Silver
From left to right, three standard and one safety fountain pens: a British Swan, silver, circa 1910; a French CM, silver, circa 1922; an American A.A. Waterman, gold-filled, circa 1914; and a French pen, circa 1916.

heating nitrocellulose with camphor, which gives it its characteristic smell. The manufacturing process was perfected in Germany during the last two decades of the l9th century and, as a result, it was used in the fountain pen industry in Germany much more so than in any other country. It was supplied in rods or tubes and, like hard rubber, was shaped by a lathe. Its plastic qualities were remarkable, but it had one major flaw that prevented it from outperforming hard rubber: it was highly flammable. Many a collector, trying to disassemble the section of a pen by heating it, has found himself with a small

heap of ashes on his hands. Any fountain pen that emits a faint odor of camphor after being rubbed a few times should be kept away from an open flame. Unfortunately, in the case of very old models, the smell is almost undetectable.

After 1920, celluloid was competing with cellulose acetate and, later on, with acetobutyrate of cellulose, both of which were much less flammable. Materials developed by DuPont de Nemours in the 1920s were derived from nitrocellulose, regardless of their name (i.e., radite [Sheaffer] and permanite [Parker]).

Two nameless models among the many manufactured by Fernand Laureau (circa 1930).

Ivory fountain pen with Japanese design (circa 1930).

Patricians

Faithful for a long time to hard rubber, Waterman moved into plastics in 1929, 6 years after Sheaffer. Although slow in joining the bandwagon, Waterman produced some of the most beautiful pens of that era - especially the Patrician. *It was offered in six colors: black, emerald, onyx (red and cream), turquoise (blue and gold), nacre (black and pearl), and moss agate (green, brown, and black). Its clip was no longer mounted with rivets but inset in the cap. The globe in the logo also disappeared from the lever. One year later, the ladies' model, the* Lady Patricia, *appeared (1930-1938).*

However designated, all these materials had a quality that black hard rubber lacked: they could be produced in bright colors. Lighter and less fragile, they also allowed greater freedom in the shape of the material and thus played a pivotal role in the evolution of the fountain pen. In 1923, Sheaffer was the first major manufacturer to use plastics, followed by Parker in 1926, and Wahl in 1927. Slower to react, Waterman did not follow suit until 1929, and this delay was one of the reasons for Waterman's decline in the 1930s. That same year, Sheaffer introduced designs with more fluid lines that could be injection-molded. Although Hyatt patented injection molding in 1878, it was not widely used in the fountain pen industry until the 1940s.

After cotton came cows...In 1899, the Austrians Kritsche and Spitteler developed a remarkable plastic from milk. Clotted, purified, and dried, casein treated with formaldehyde would become galalith (gala: milk; lithe: stone [Greek]). Parker first used it as early as 1904 (ivorine), but it was not produced in large numbers until much later. Its weakness was that in time it would invariably become discolored by ink. Fortunately, the introduction of the rubber sac helped correct that problem.

After the era of plant- and animal-derived products came the age of synthetic resins. The first of these was bakelite (1907). It owes its

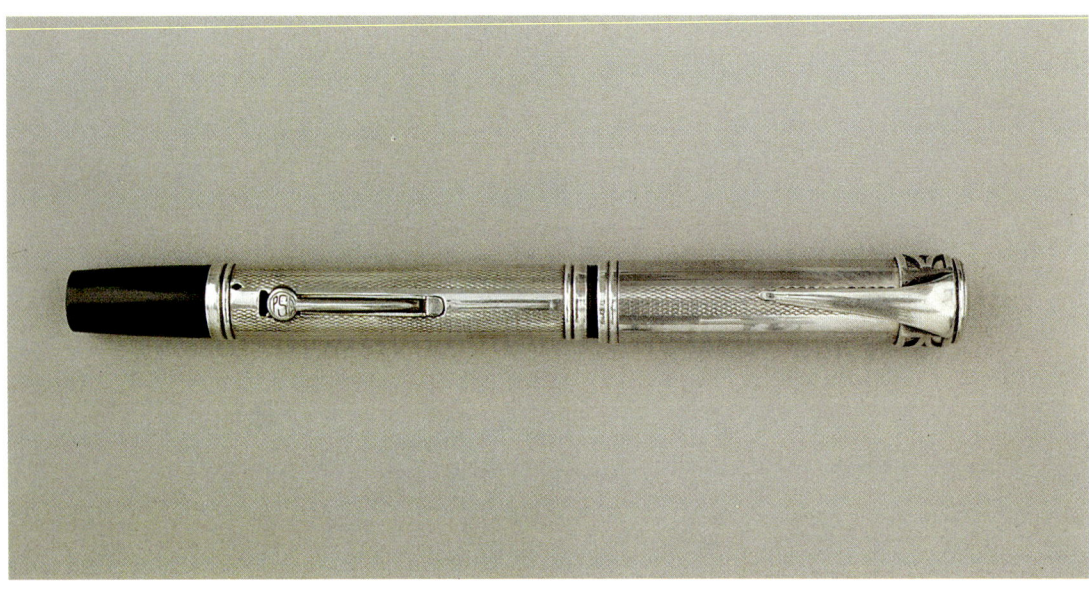

Grand Aigle Mercier *with lever, black hard rubber, silver trim (circa 1934).*

Retractable nib pens. Toledo style trim, possibly manufactured by Charcellay (circa 1925).

Waterman standard pens, gold and silver trim (France) on black hard rubber (circa 1910).

Lever filling Waterman pens in "two-tone" hard rubber (1928-1930).

"Continental" Dress
Retractable nib Waterman pens, black hard rubber, so-called "continental" trim in gold-plate (1920-1925). These gold-filled overlays and filigrees cover the entire body; the original clip matches the motif.

name to the Belgian chemist, Leo Hendrik Baekeland, who created it by condensing phenol and formaldehyde. This was followed by the development of a long list of synthetic materials that were known to the public by their trademarks, such as plexiglas (which is, in fact, methyl polymethacrylate). Since the 1940s, synthetic resins have been widely used in the fountain pen industry.

We have seen that in the first part of the l9th century, most early fountain pens were designed or manufactured in metal, for lack of better materials. Highly valued as trim and indispensable for the nibs, levers, and other filling mechanisms, metals are not suitable for the body of the fountain pen. Most metals oxidize, are corroded by ink, and, in most cases, are good heat conductors. In addition, shaping them is more difficult than is the case with plastics; in short, they are full of flaws. Yet, a few manufacturers offered inexpensive fountain pens in molded metal (brass, nickel, silver, etc.) The aluminum pen was moderately successful

during World War II because it made use of whatever scraps of metal the war machine did not use. In the 1940s, there were a few good examples made completely of metal.

The points of these nibs were made of rare metals, especially iridium and osmium. Pure iridium was obtained for the first time in 1885. The first nibs were equipped with points made of iridium-osmium, a natural alloy obtained from platinum ore during the first phase of processing. Later on, synthetic alloys of iridium and osmium, and sometimes ruthenium, were used. Eventually, various alloys, such as tungsten, cobalt, rhenium, titanium, and, in low-end products, nickel were used.

Methods of Transportation

A fountain pen is essentially an ink well in a pen and not a pen in an ink well. The fountain pen owed its early success to the fact that, in theory, it offered considerable advantages over

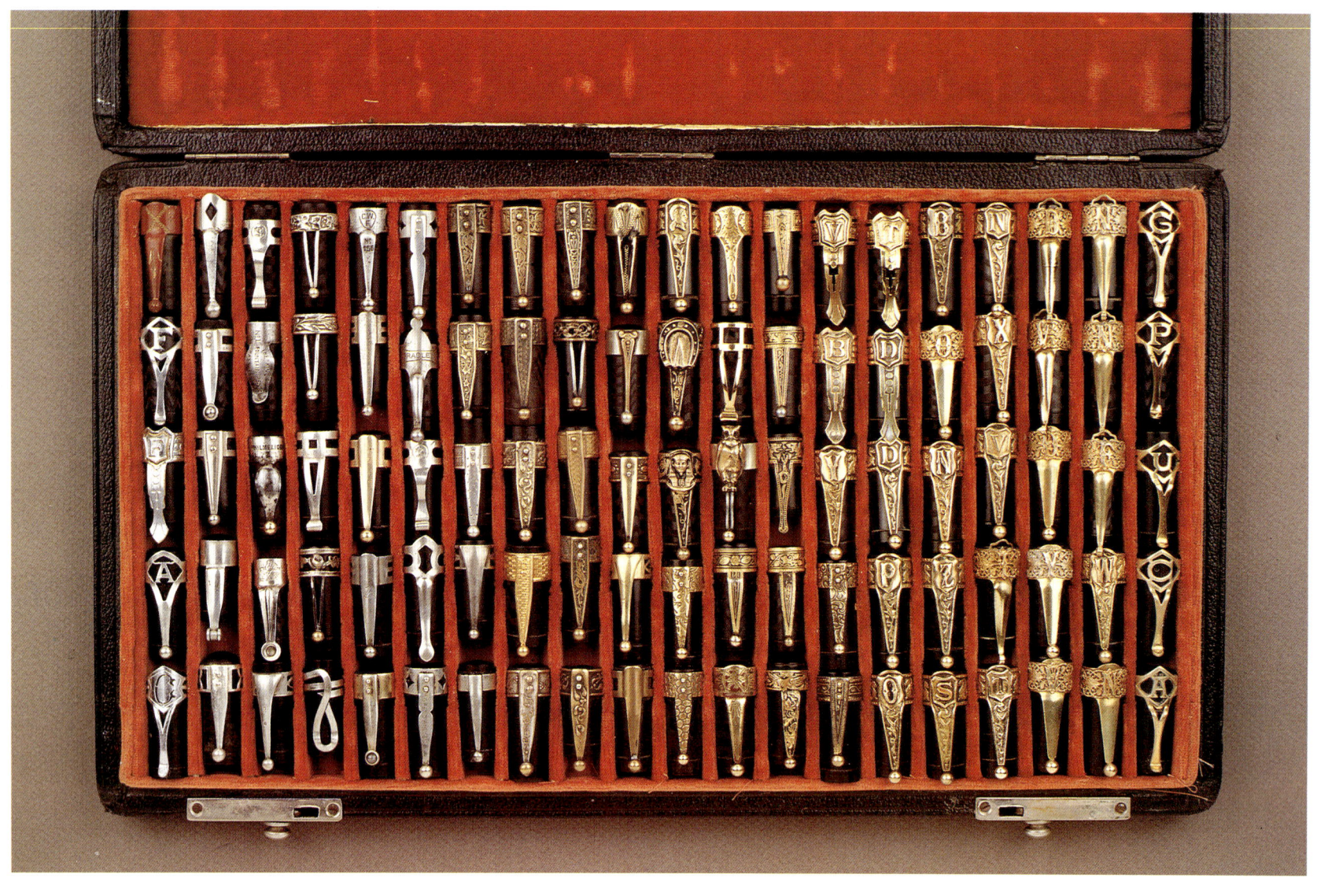

Case with French clips (1918-1935).

The "Transportable" Pen

Top, left to right: Knapsack *by* Waterman (1903) *with two compartments (one for the pen and one for the eyedropper); French leather case for* Mont d'Or; *metal cases (*Swan, 1908*) that fit in the pocket to hold a fountain pen; leather case by* Waterman *to be attached to a belt; leather case with two compartments. Bottom: English clip for three instruments; Parker case for the* Vacumatic *and its matching mechanical pencil designed for the Royal Canadian Air Force aviators (World War II); two English pen keychains, one in silver-plated brass and the other in sterling; small leather case for the* Viala Lilliput; *two Telescope Cap* Waterman *pens with an additional tasseled cap mounted over the regular cap (1914-1927).*

the pen AND the ink well: it was easily transportable and always ready and available. In practice, a few wrinkles had to be ironed out.

The cap of the first fountain pens was simply placed over the nib. Thus, leaks were unavoidable. It was recommended that a fountain pen be carried straight up with the nib in a vertical position. To achieve this, a number of devices were invented. A few were truly simplistic, such as vertical seams in pockets that would hold pens (or cigars) straight up - a little silly. Systems with clips or bands were preferable. Since it first entered the fountain pen market, Waterman has offered the **Ideal Pocket**, a sort of metal case that fitted into the pocket and could hold several writing instruments. Soon, however, manufacturers realized that it would be

smarter to place an accessory on the pen itself rather than in the pocket. This led to the development of the band around the cap that holds a clip. Such a system offered even more advantages. It prevented the pen from falling out of the pocket or rolling off a flat surface. The clip could also be adjusted to fit the depth of the pocket. For ladies, a ring affixed to the top of the cap permitted the pen to be hung by a chain or ribbon and worn as a pendant.

The screw cap and the retractable nib of the safeties improved the fit and reduced leakage. Keeping a pen in a vertical position was no longer a necessity. The manner in which pens were carried by men did not change much, since they were still positioned vertically in suit pockets. However, women now became less

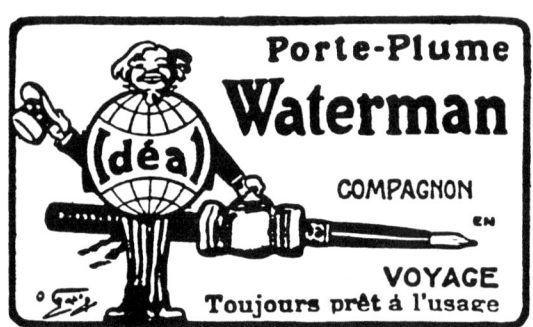

Une nouveauté pour votre sac
Madame,

Porte-Plume
Waterman
(déa)

COMPAGNON EN

VOYAGE
Toujours prêt à l'usage

Display case of clips in sterling, silver plate, and copper (1918-1935). It was an easy and inexpensive way to personalize a pen. They were very popular in France.

hesitant to carry pens in their purses and men could use their vest pockets. A leather case was sometimes used to separate fountain pens from handkerchiefs, notebooks, and other accessories. Many ladies' pens were trimmed with a ring and a ribbon or tassel attached for no other purpose than to assist their owners in retrieving them from the bottom of a purse.

Major manufacturers soon adopted the fixed clip. It was first offered as an option; later, its use became widespread. Waterman's **Clip-Cap** was introduced in 1905. Other than its obvious usefulness, the clip offered another advantage. Even when the pen is placed inside a pocket, the clip remains visible, allowing the model to be identified. Manufacturers engraved their names on the clip, which, in most cases, proved to be small and difficult to read. For ease of recognition, they gave their clips readily

identifiable shapes. Parker's arrow is perhaps one of the best known and most successful signatures. Created in 1932 for the **Vacumatic**, it survived many changes.

Clips were used more in France than in any other country. For years, Waterman exported fountain pens without clips to France, and until World War II, many French manufacturers distributed clipless fountain pens, allowing the retailer to sell clips selected by the buyer, who was then afforded an opportunity to personalize his or her writing instrument.

Demand was strong and a large number of models were produced. Some were strictly utilitarian, including a few with imaginative anti-theft devices. Others offered a more elaborate design, so that all tastes could be satisfied. The clips were sometimes made of gold, often of silver. In the less expensive models, the

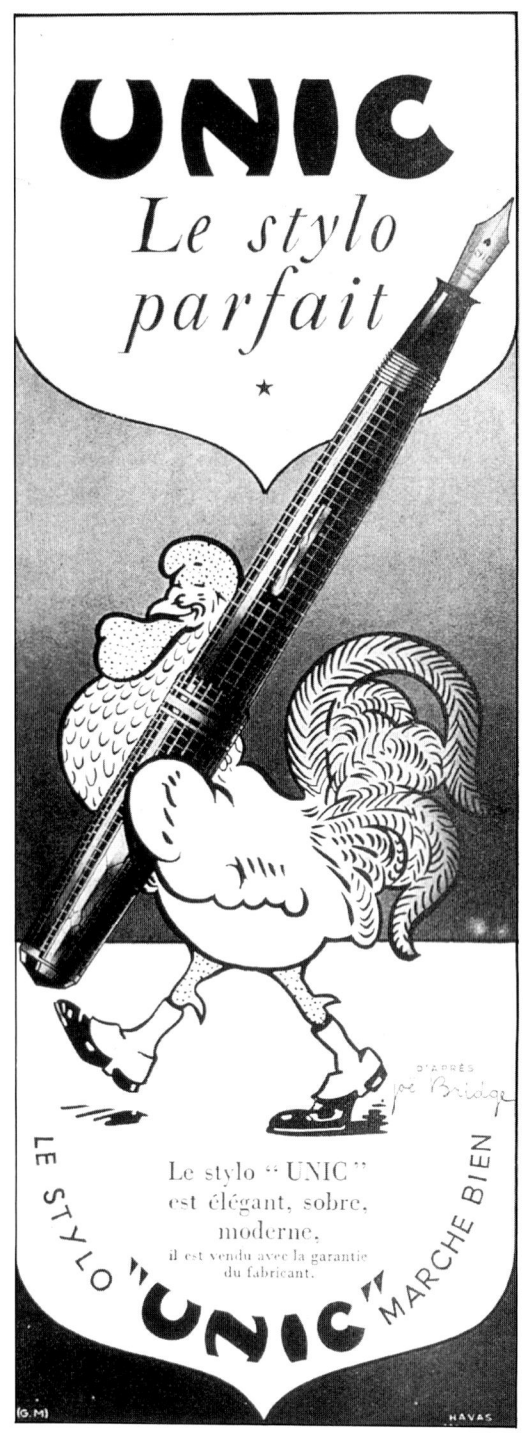

Gold-plated French clips shown flat to fully illustrate the design. Augis (1922).

clips were gold- or silver-plated, chromed or enameled. They were very fashionable during the 1920s and 1930s. Their demise is perhaps regrettable, as this was one of the rare instances in which the individuality and fancy of the user could be expressed at little cost.

State of Affairs

From 1880 until the end of World War II, there were hundreds of pen manufacturers. The Great Depression of 1929 caused the demise of quite a few in the United States. An abrupt drop

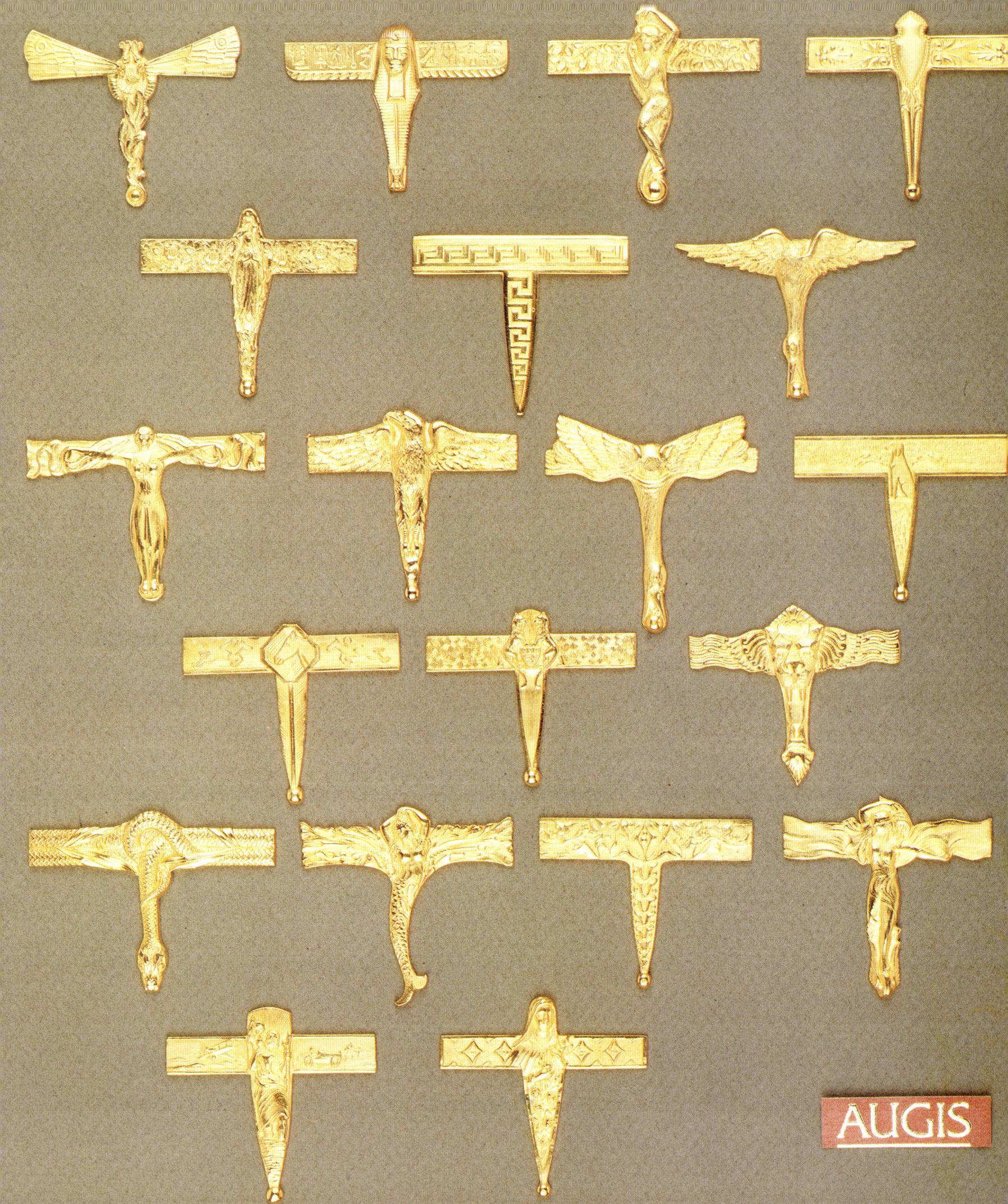

AUGIS

at least equal to that of the pens produced by large manufacturers. In the 1940s, injection molding upset the apple cart. Within a short period of time, only large manufacturers were able to afford the investment required for larger and more complex machinery. Increasing numbers of small craftsmen failed to remain competitive. After World War II, only the major manufacturers could survive and even then, only with difficulty.

The shortage of gold was a concern, but that situation was relatively short-lived. The real problems appeared with the introduction of a new instrument, the ball-point pen. Since it played such an important role in the chronology of writing, we should devote a few lines to its history.

Ball Versus Nib

The idea of using a ball as a tracing point was not really new. In 1888, the American J.J. Loud obtained a patent for a ball-point pen to be used on rough surfaces, such as packing crates. The primary ball turned freely against two small auxiliary balls maintained by a piston. In 1891, E. Lambert offered a model even more ingenious since it had only one ball. In 1899, Varley registered a comparable patent, and in 1910, the German Michael Baums obtained another patent for the ball-point pen. Why did it take half a century for this type of writing instrument to secure a foothold in the industry? The explanation lies in the fact that it could operate with neither the fluid ink of the fountain pen (which flowed without forming a film around the ball) nor the viscous inks of the time, which were too thick, clogged the mechanism, and were too slow to dry.

From 1935 to 1939, Frank Klimes and Paul Eisner manufactured and sold a few thousand **Rolpens**. However, they were not well designed. To force the ink down to the ball, a piston had to be twisted while a button was pushed at the same time.

The true father of the ball-point pen was the Hungarian Laszlo Jozsef (Ladislao José) Biro. He was born in Budapest in 1899 and died in Buenos Aires in 1985. At the age of 17, he

in production occurred in the 1950s. Until then, mass production and individual craftsmanship had co-existed peacefully; this explains the literally hundreds of trade names on the market at that time. The machinery required for a small-scale fountain pen factory was inexpensive and readily available. As a result, the level of quality of pens produced in small shops was

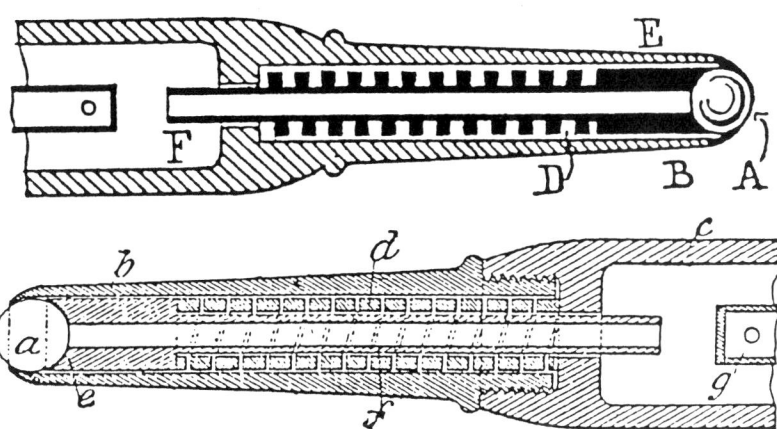

invented a washing machine and later designed an automatic gear box. In 1938, he obtained a patent for his ball-point pen in Hungary. It was a good design, but the environment for further development was not conducive. He took refuge in France and when war broke out, he fled to Argentina where he manufactured a few models and went into partnership with a British financier named Henry George Martin, with whom he founded the Eterpen S.A. Company. A contract with the Allied Armed Forces led to a series of licensing agreements in the United States. The first was with the Eberhard Faber Pencil Co., which, in turn, sold the license to Eversharp. These new instruments appealed to the Air Force because they were less sensitive than fountain pens to variation in atmospheric pressure. At the time, a reliable ink had not yet been developed and the rapid wear of the ball resulted in leaks.

In 1945, Milton Reynolds appeared on the scene. An entrepreneur and opportunist, he realized very quickly that the new instrument could be very successful. Without too much concern for Biro's patents, he commissioned his engineers to design a ball-point pen. His factories churned them out, with his models wholesaling for 70 cents and retailing for $12.50 at that time. On October 29, 1945, the first pens were placed on the market. In the first week, Reynolds sold 25,000 pens. In February 1946, production reached 30,000 pens per day. However, these instruments were disaster prone; they leaked and their thick ink resisted all attempts at cleaning.

All the major producers jumped on the band wagon, including those companies, like Eberhard Faber and Eversharp, who purchased the distribution rights, as well as dozens of smaller manufacturers. Prices fell precipitously to under a dollar. In 1948, having amassed a fortune, Reynolds retired. Faber withdrew from the market in 1947. Although Eversharp had sold millions of ball-point pens, it lost $10 million and would never recover from this setback.

In the early 1950s, there was an upswing in the economy. The major manufacturers took the time to test their models before releasing them. Seech, also a Hungarian, developed an ink better adapted to the ball-point pen. Improved technology and a better selection of materials finally led to the production of reliable instruments that wrote as well as a small metal ball would allow.

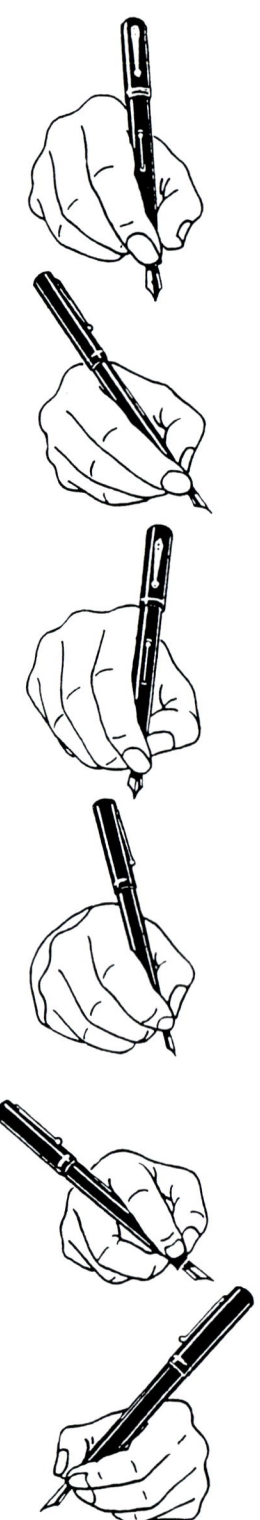

Waterman Hundred Year Pen *(1940)*.

Today I

From top to bottom: Gentleman in silver *by Waterman, men's* Opera *by Waterman, men's* Centenaire de la Révolution Française *by Waterman,* Lady Patricia *by Waterman,* Premier Athens *(lacquer and gold-plate) by Parker,* Parker 75 *in sterling,* green Duofold *by Parker (limited edition), Parker 180* in sterling, latticed *Sheaffer* Slim, *Sheaffer* Nostalgia *in gold-filled sterling,* Connaisseur Prestige *by Sheaffer,* gold-filled Targa *by Sheaffer, (P.K.).*

Writing

One has only to compare personal diaries from the 1920s with more recent examples to realize that the art of writing has been lost. Of course, children today are not less intelligent than their grandparents, but their terrible penmanship is appalling! Some may blame the fountain pen for having rendered its predecessor, the metal dip pen, obsolete. But this is not entirely true; during the first half of this century, they co-existed in perfect harmony. Of course, little by little, the fountain pen replaced the dip pen in business and personal use. This evolution was appreciated by everyone, except drycleaners. Nevertheless, it was not the fountain pen, but rather the ball-point pen that usurped the traditional metal nib in the school-room. A traditional gift for important milestones, birthdays, and graduations, the fountain pen was ineptly wielded by young hands that had become used to ball-point pens.

Today, some elementary school students are once again using fountain pens, one reason being that manufacturers have begun to produce inexpensive models for these young users. However, these fountain pens come equipped with large spherical nibs that react very slightly or not at all to variations in handwriting. The ball eliminates the need for careful positioning of the hand. Hence, the difference between these fountain pens and the ball-point pen is minimal. Additionally, the ink used in the fountain pen is less greasy and dries more quickly than that used in the ball-point pen.

In the first section of this book, we stressed

Silver Cartier (1938).

Today, the fountain pen has largely regained its place, although the new market has a slight disadvantage. The trend is toward nostalgia; the shapes of the 1920s are back with a vengeance, which is understandable since the shapes and designs of that era have never been equaled. All the major manufacturers are offering fountain pens of unparalled quality, only with new and improved technology and filling mechanisms. Although the market is demanding fountain pens "like before", we will never again see the variety and range of models offered in bygone eras. A good example is the 34 different nibs offered by Waterman in 1909. When all the different permutations of the various sizes and variations of the three base models are taken into account, there were 12,444 possible combinations. In 1933, Waterman alone offered 302 nibs and 375 models.

Fountain pen nostalgia does have its limits, which can only be satisfied through the collection of period pens. If this desire to imitate the past is kept under control, it will be a positive influence, but if it is carried to an extreme, then it will freeze the fountain pen as an image of the past and will entice manufacturers to copy from old catalogs rather than develop new models and technologies. The latter will certainly be more expensive. We can only hope that once the clientele has been regained, thanks to the nostalgia for the old pens, innovations will continue.

Today II

From top to bottom: Pelikan M 800, Pelikan Toledo, gold-filled Cross, Lamy 2000, Montparnasse by Dupont, retractable Pilot, lacquered Vendome by Cartier, Parapen by Omas, a briar-colored Omas, gold-filled Montblanc 146, sterling Montblanc 146, black Montblanc 146, (P.K.).

the indispensible character of the fountain pen as the writing instrument of our time. Will it remain so into the next century? We can only hope so. Of course, all sorts of innovations in materials, inks, and shapes will appear. But if the writing instrument of the future is a nib with a reservoir, whatever its facade, it will still be a fountain pen, or at least the descendant of the fountain pen. Some say that tomorrow's pen will utilize a laser beam. So be it. We will then have a remarkable instrument, reliable and with considerable autonomy. But we will have to give it another name, because it will no longer be a fountain pen. It will replace the ball-point pen, but not the nib. The nib is timeless; the feather quill nib was used for more than a thousand years and the steel nib for more than a century and a half. The fountain pen has already celebrated its centennial. Those who predict its demise are the same individuals who predicted the death of the theater with the birth of the movies. Although it is true that the ball-point pen posed a serious challenge to the fountain pen, it did not replace it. What it did was eliminate a few manufacturers who were unable to compete on the open market.

Lever filling Waterman,

black hard rubber,

American made

silver trim

(1915-1929).

SECTION III

A Pen and More...

To own two or three hundred beautiful fountain pens

and to write with a ball-point pen; doubtless, is collecting.

To own ten times more or one hundred times fewer,

but to occasionally dip the nibs in fresh ink

and let them glide across paper,

this is certainly the way to become a "collector".

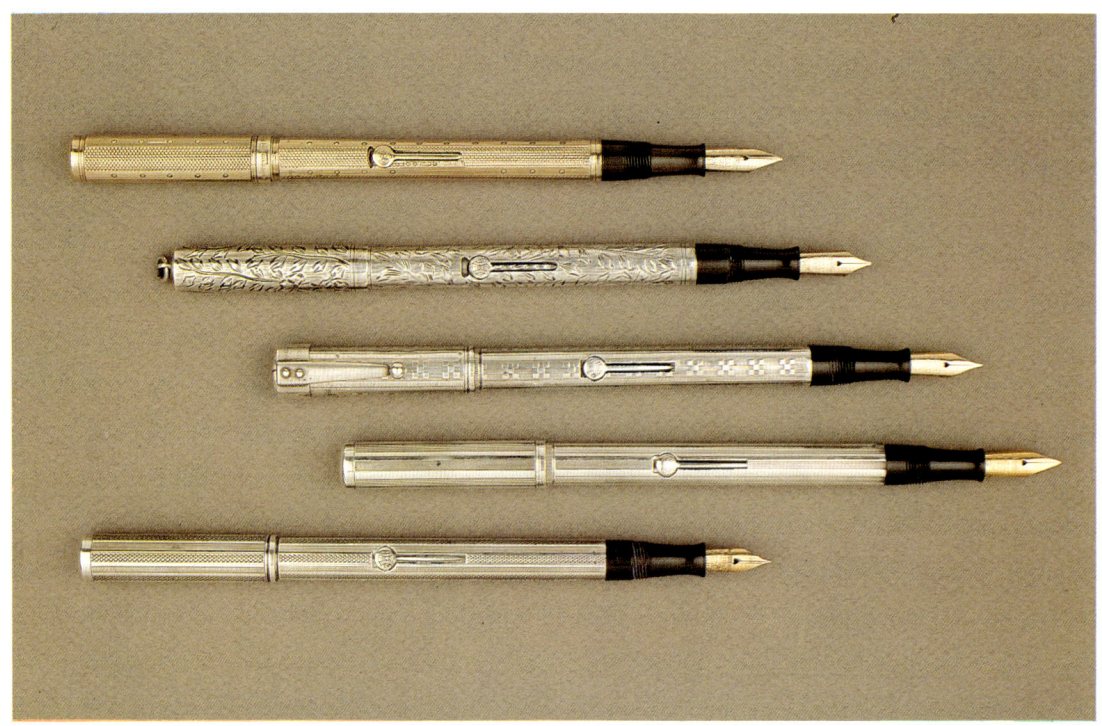

Elegant trim: barley grain, floral, and checkered. Waterman E.C. (end covered) slim models (52 1/2). From bottom to top: Three French models and two English models.

Waterman "Filigree"
These 12 pens are good examples of the "filigree" motif prevalent between 1905 and 1930. From bottom to top: Three standard models, four safeties, five P.S.F.s (pocket self-fillers). These pens, with American style trim, did not sell well in France.

Collecting Pens

It is not surprising that more and more people are becoming fountain pen collectors. Many different things are collected, whether or not they are generally considered to be valuable, all the way from Frank Sinatra autographs to cigar bands. Some collections are slightly bizarre, others are enviable, and almost all are useful, at least to the collector, who finds in them pleasure or a distraction from an increasingly demanding world. Whether they represent a source of profit or of nonprofitable knowledge, what motivates individuals is as diverse as the collections themselves, and is irrelevant; what matters is that we all benefit from the impulse. The contribution of major collectors, and especially of pioneers, is that at some point in time they are able to salvage a number of objects and knowledge that might otherwise have been, if not lost, then at least threatened with obscurity. Collectors often remedy the shortcomings of cultural institutions. When a given object or category of work does not meet the market demand or the priorities for preservation, the bold amateur remains its only chance for survival and restoration. Antique shops and museums would be empty were they not supplied by collectors estates, since personal collections frequently end up in one or the other of these after the demise of the collector.

The fountain pen is no exception to the rule. It is again in vogue, and the dark years are only a bad memory. You will hear no complaints, in spite of the corollary accompanying this resurgence in popularity: the prices of the older model fountain pens have increased exponentially. This is one more reason why the amateur collector should be careful and observe a few basic rules.

During World War II and the post-war years, the scarcity of gold had serious repercussions. Not only were gold nibs no longer manufactured, but existing gold pens and nibs were melted down. In the 1950s, the decline in popularity of the fountain pen and its very small number of collectors exacerbated the problem. Since its value had dropped to almost nothing, a few shrewd individuals started hunting for old fountain pens just to obtain their gold nibs.

Top of the line pens had beautiful cases, but the rest had to make do with modest cardboard boxes, which nevertheless have their own charm.

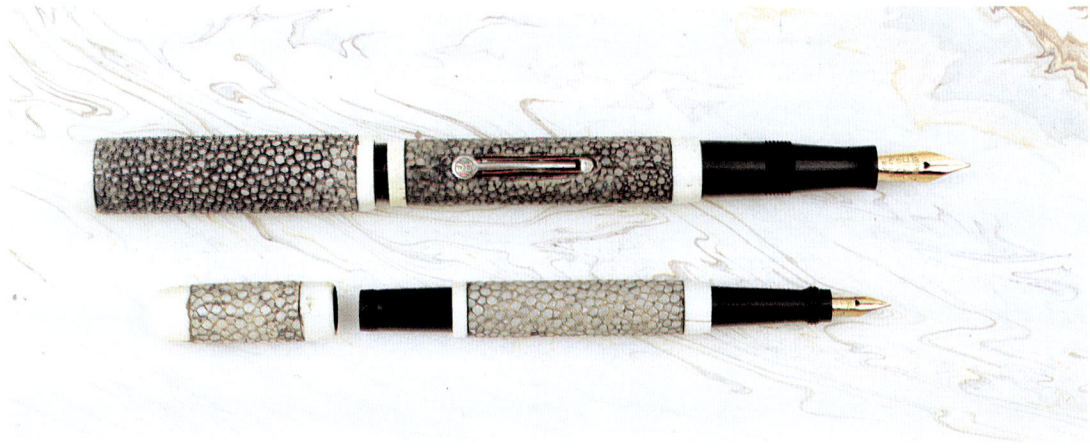

In the 1920s, the fountain pen did not escape the sharkskin fad. Two French models in ivory and sharkskin on black hard rubber.

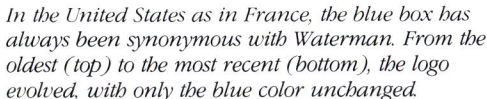

In the United States as in France, the blue box has always been synonymous with Waterman. From the oldest (top) to the most recent (bottom), the logo evolved, with only the blue color unchanged.

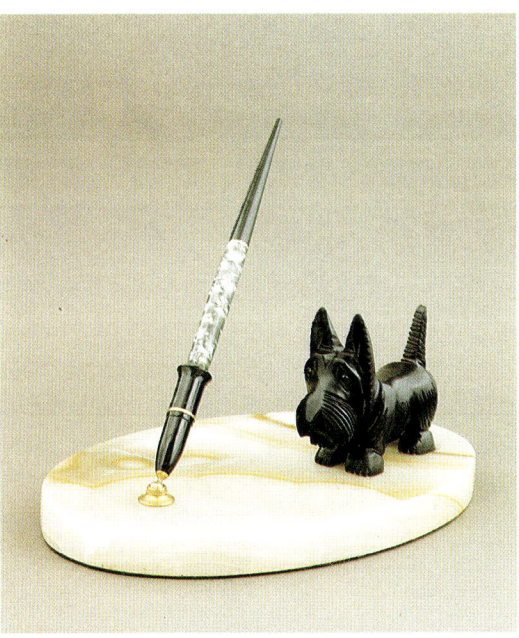

Waterman desk fountain pen with cartridge (1936-1939).

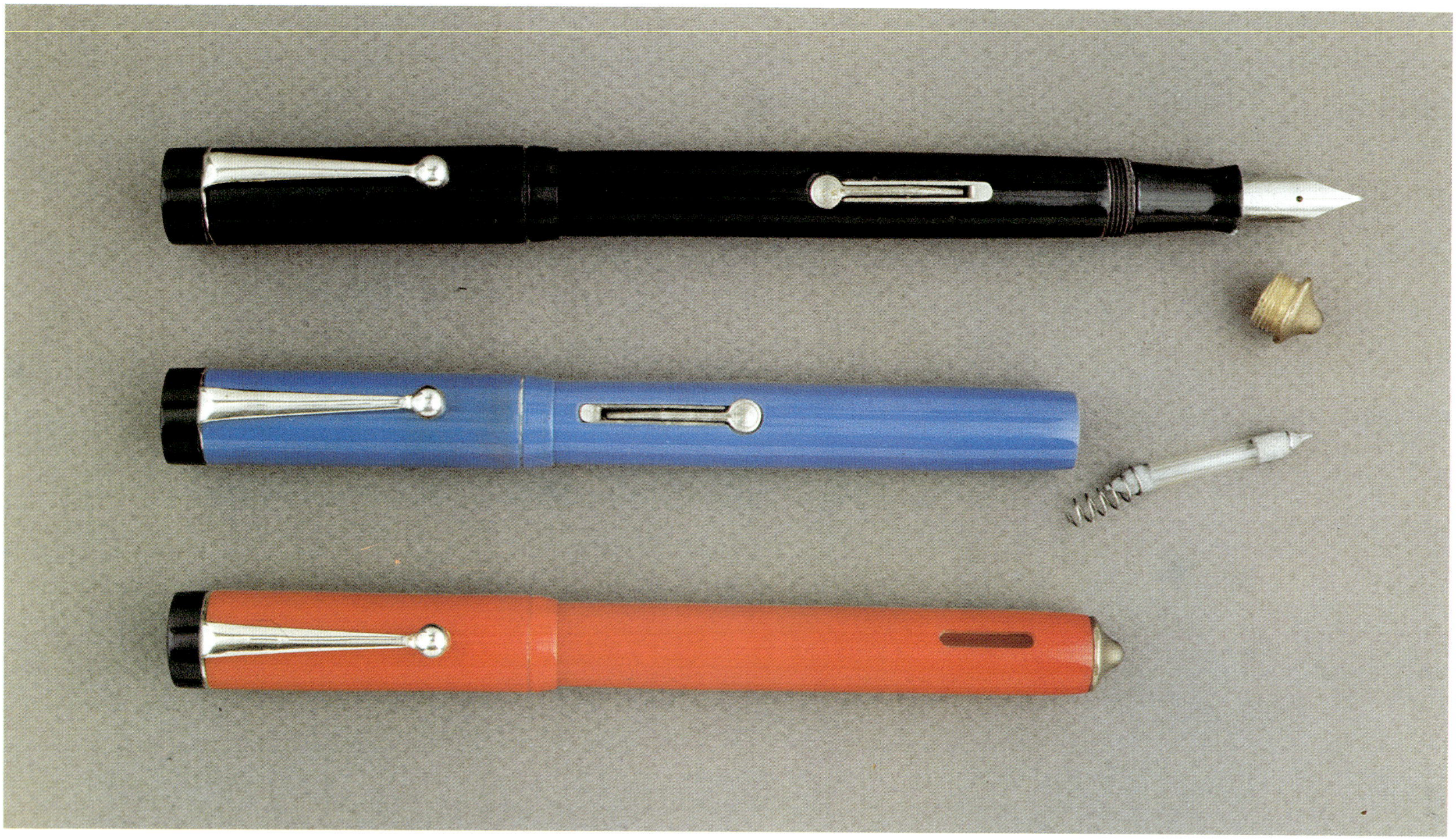

For the driver.

These instruments were made by Bayle and Griffon after the patent was obtained (1928). A neon vial linked to a brass terminal is used to check spark plugs; a small red indicator lights up when the spark plugs are operational.

The Collector

It is a well-known phenomenon: the fountain pen collector browsing in flea markets or antique shops falls in love with a model new to him or her. When the cap is removed, a razor, magnifying glass, thermometer, or even a weapon may be revealed. The link with a writing instrument is rather tenuous...even if it is not a pen, it looks very much like one...it has to be taken home to be added to the collection.

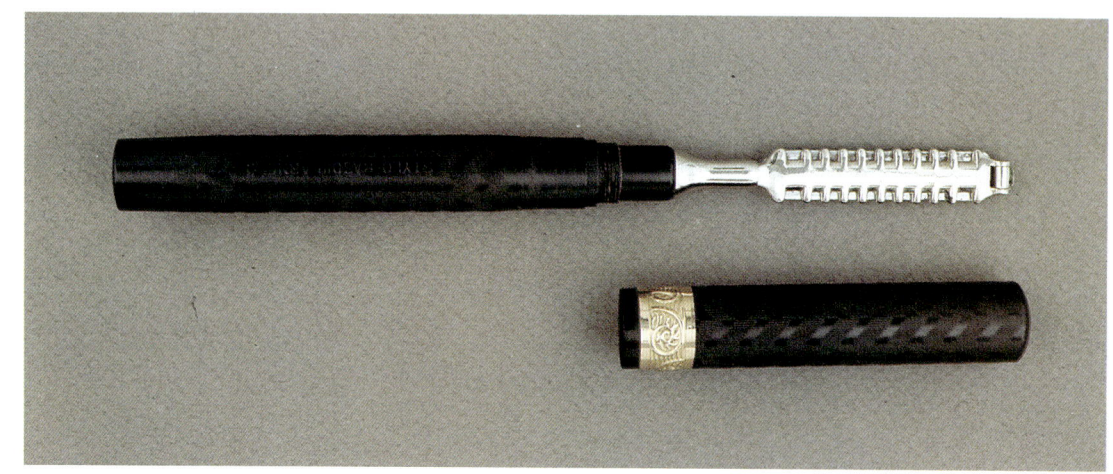

Arnold razor (1913). Of course, it does not write, but it does not shave too badly.

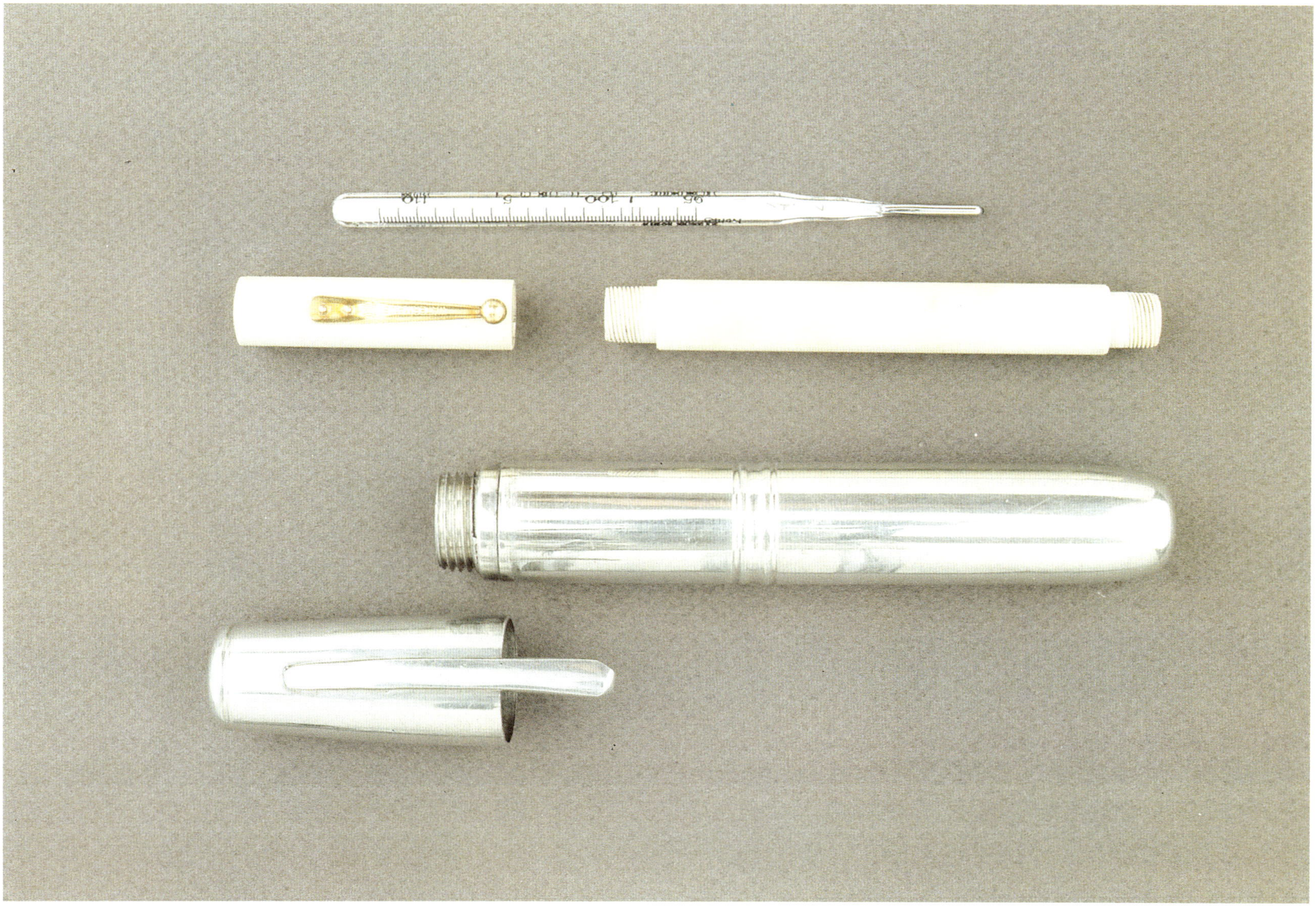

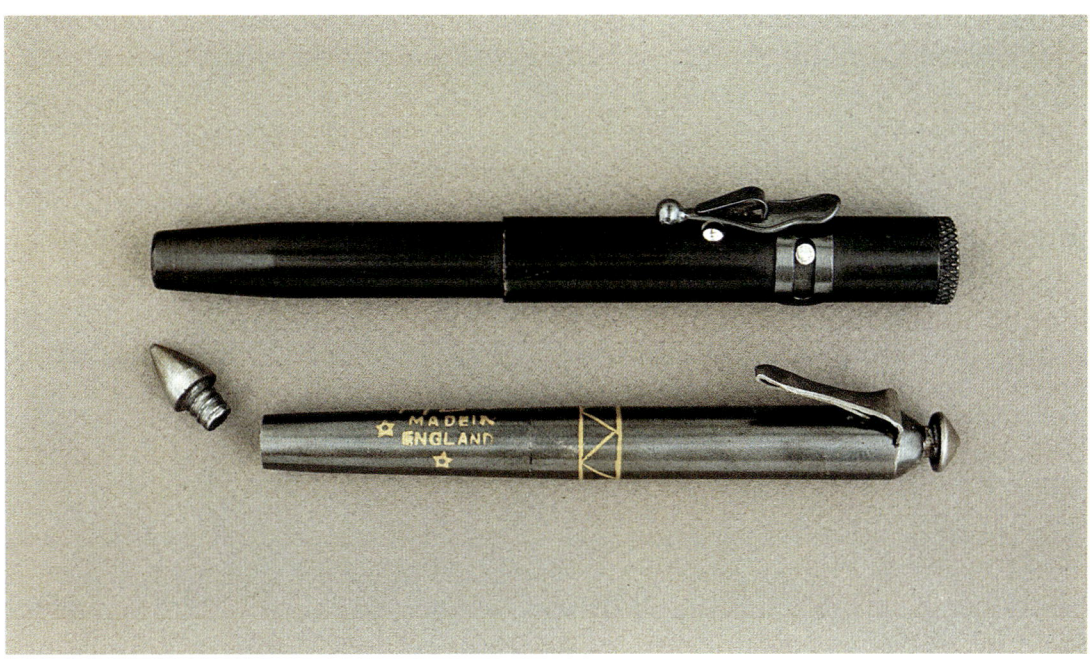

Two pens and two ways to take care of one's health. One contains a thermometer (Waterman, 1927). The other, once the cap is removed, emits a powerful odor of gin (P.H.-L.V.).

Contrary to their harmless appearance, these two "pens" are dangerous weapons. The English model is a pistol with real bullets. The other is an American "pen" that fires tear-gas cartridges.

Gold Starry case in which the history of the company's production is traced. From left to right: Standard 8 Bis (1912), 1 (1920), safety 86 (1929), safety (1933), 35 (1935), Staroid (1935), 27 (1933), silver (1935), (1938), Luxe (1938), 13 (1938), Luxe (1945).

A Stack of Safeties
Waterman pens with retractable nibs, black hard rubber and red marbled rubber, in various sizes (from 42 1/2 to 46) that were offered in the early 1920s. French bodies, clips, and bands.

The less luxurious models fitted with steel nibs were thrown away without much thought. The resumption of production and renewed interest in collecting has put an end to this wanton decimation.

Today, collectors of old fountain pens are numerous and ecclectic. Some are guided by a spontaneous love at first sight. A Parker, a Bayard, an Aurora, a Sailor, no matter what: "I like it, I want to buy it." Others are more selective. There are some Japanese aficionados who only collect Japanese pens, Italians who only have eyes for Eversharps, and Belgians for whom only a Sheaffer will do. They all have valid reasons for collecting specific models. All collectors are confronted with the pitfalls of buying and trading. Old fountain pens were once new pens and, thus, utilitarian objects that, for most part, have been both used and abused. Their

owners carried them everywhere...and who could blame them? As a result, a number of surviving pens show their scars.

To the inevitable wear and tear, there are additional problems. Since a fountain pen was frequently an object to which its owner was emotionally attached, each mishap led to repair. During World War II, repairs may not have been made with the proper spare parts, and not all repairmen were equally dexterous. Today, many models cannot be restored because the original spare parts are not to be found.

With luck, a thorough knowledge of the subject, and careful searching, you can find marvelous "old timers" for less money than you would expect to spend on mediocre newcomers. The opposite can also be true. Every day somewhere in the world, and especially during weekend excursions to flea markets,

— Oh ! un porte-plume réservoir pour dix francs ! Je cours l'acheter.

..Et, il le fit, le malheureux !

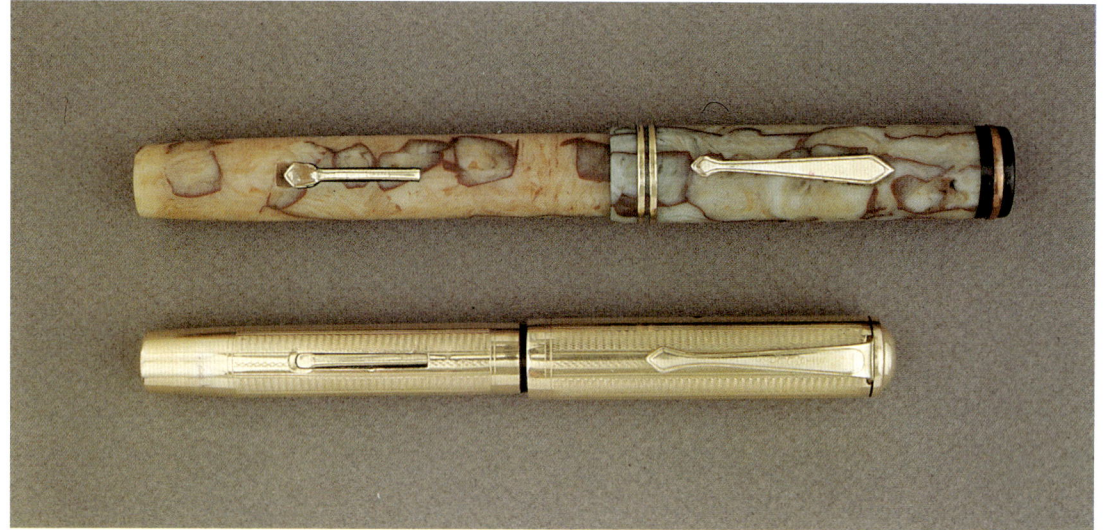

Lever filling Stellor in plastic (1932). Gold-filled (1938).

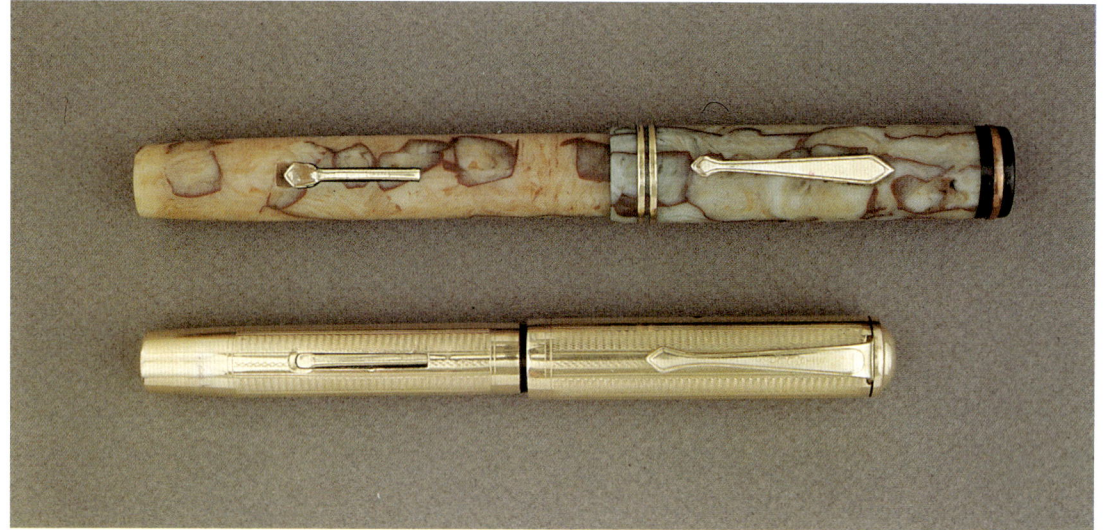

Pens Galore
French ladies fountain pens, from inexpensive celluloid to solid gold (Cartier). All date from the 1930s.

irreparable old fountain pens are bought for much more money than excellent new models.

Careful Acquisition

Except when received through inheritance or as a gift, a collection is built up through buying or trading, and in both cases a certain number of precautions should be taken.

Scratches, slight discoloration of the black hard rubber, a worn inscription, and a dried up rubber sac are all marks of wear that are totally acceptable. Conversely, some defects greatly depreciate the value of a fountain pen, especially if they are not reparable. Before making

any purchase, a thorough examination should be undertaken.

The Cap

You should insert the tip of your thumb into the inside of the cap to feel around for cracks or dents not visible from the outside. A bright light inserted into the cap will often illuminate a hairline crack not otherwise visible.

Note that the band around the rim of the cap may not always be the original, and may have been placed there to hide a dent or a crack. It is advisable to familiarize yourself with the characteristics of any particular pen. This is

Two Conklin Endura pens, with lever, in red and blue sapphire plastic (1927-1932).

![pen icon]

To Twist or Not to Twist
Gold-plated Waterman pens with retractable nibs, sizes 42 and 42 1/2, with French trim, produced from 1907 to the 1930s. The grooved models are the oldest (1907 and 1912). The propulsion mechanism is threaded with a spiral groove; the nib extends in a rotating movement. In the other models, the nib extends without revolving.

especially true of fountain pens in marbled black hard rubber or with engraved metal trim: the cap may have been replaced and no longer exactly matches the body of the pen. You should evaluate the condition of the cap threads by fully unscrewing the cap (in the case of retractable nibs, you should also check the retraction mechanism). If the threads are worn or the cap is not the original one belonging to that particular pen, it will not fit snugly. You should also check to see that the cap fits snugly

onto the other end of the pen. If it does not fit well, this might indicate that it has been replaced, or that the body of the pen has been vigorously polished to hide, for example, tooth marks made by a nervous writer. Some manufacturers used to mount the pen clip on the cap with small rivets, which were not very resistant to abuse. If there is no fixed clip, the mounting holes may have been hidden under a mobile clip or may have been filled with wax or another material.

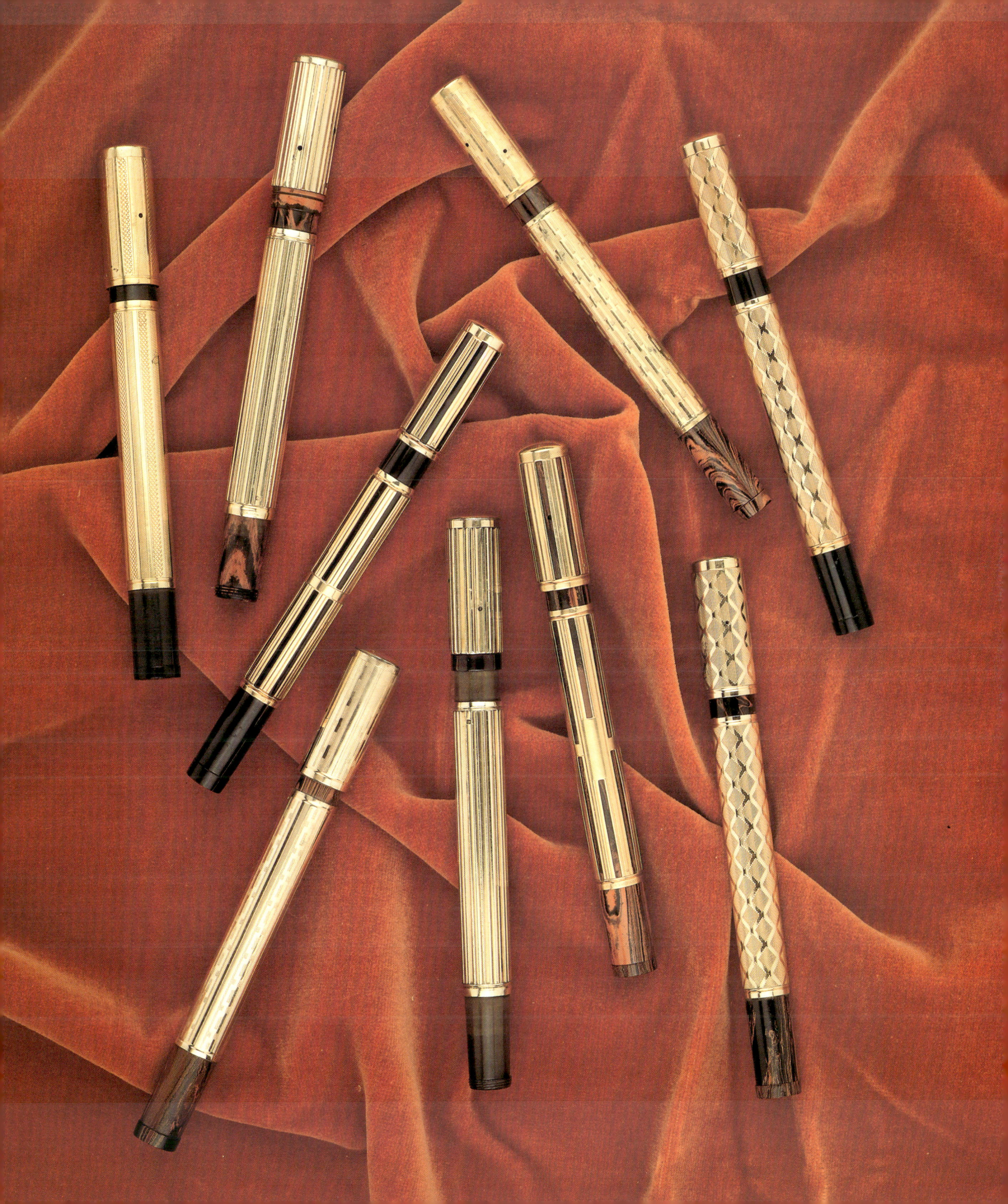

Waterman pen with European trim. Model with ring for hanging (circa 1920) and model with clip (circa 1930).

Dunhill-Namiki
Lacquered pens by Namiki (Pilot) for the Paris Dunhill store. From left to right: 1930, 1927, 1938, 1932, 1932. (K.T.).

The Body

With the cap screwed on, you should rotate the body between your thumb and forefinger in order to spot warping or other distortions. You should check to see that there are no cracks, especially between the joints and other parts, such as the section, lever, or propulsion mechanism.

The Nib

It goes without saying that a fountain pen without a nib is not worthy of its name, unless an identical replacement part is available. The nib is a very important factor in the potential depreciation of the pen. You should check to see that it is not cracked and does not show any superfluous "slits".

Ink-Vue by Waterman with visible ink level. Filling is accomplished using a jointed lever (1935-1940).

L.E.C.s for Ladies
French and American trim on E.C. or L.E.C. (lower end covered) Waterman ladies' pens (52 1/2). Black hard rubber, lever filling. American made trim is recognizable by examining the cover of the cap, which (unlike the French cap) is made of two pieces with visible joints. (United States, 1917-1929; France, 1924-1939).

The condition of the iridium tips should also be examined. Reasonable wear and tear is not harmful, but the complete erosion of one of the two tips renders the nib unusable and significantly reduces the value of less expensive pens. New iridium can be applied.

The Mechanism

With retractable nib models, you should try to retract the nib several times. If it retracts too easily, this may mean that the cork seal is loose. If the propulsion mechanism rotates without the nib appearing, this may mean that the nib is missing or, more seriously, that an internal part is missing or broken. If you acquire a retractable nib fountain pen and the propulsion mechanism does not rotate, you should not apply force because the mechanism could be damaged. Rather, you should fill the pen with cold water to soften up any dried ink, the probable cause of the malfunction. Do not be impatient, this process can be lengthy. When you are dealing with levered fountain pens, gently lift the lever while at the same time pressing a finger on the area where the axis pin is located. You will avoid breaking the lever if the compression bar encounters a dried, rigid rubber sac.

Personalized Pens
A stamping machine allowing the inscription of two to three lines of text on the body of the fountain pen. This text could be the name of the client or the name of the retailer. The process permitted the creation of countless inexpensive brand names. Large department stores or mail order companies often offered articles under their own names rather than under the name of a little known manufacturer. With a few exceptions, such as Kirby Bird for Waterman, the name of the retailer does not appear on the major brands, but the name of the owner often does.

Tools
There was a time when all reputable stores selling fountain pens had a workshop with several employees. Small repairs and modifications were performed. A few manufacturers, such as Atlet, offered complete tool kits, such as the ones pictured here.

If the pen has a push button, activate it. If it does not respond, this may indicate that the rubber sac has dried up. If it remains retracted, this may mean that the sac is missing, or even worse, that the compression bar is missing or damaged.

Piston models must be handled with great care because they are very difficult to repair. Try to manipulate the piston, but be aware that it is often adhered to the wall by dried ink. For more sophisticated models, such as Parker's **Vacumatic** or certain Stylomines, it is very difficult to judge their state of repair when you buy them at a flea market.

The Wise Buyer

Whether it is acquired through a purchase or a trade, an antique fountain pen without any major flaw will still need cleaning. This operation is not without potential pitfalls. It is always advisable to read the user's guide, when one is available.

You should also know what comprises the material of the fountain pen. Most materials are sensitive to heat, especially hard rubber. Celluloid is extremely flammable, and other nitrocellulose plastics are only a little less so.

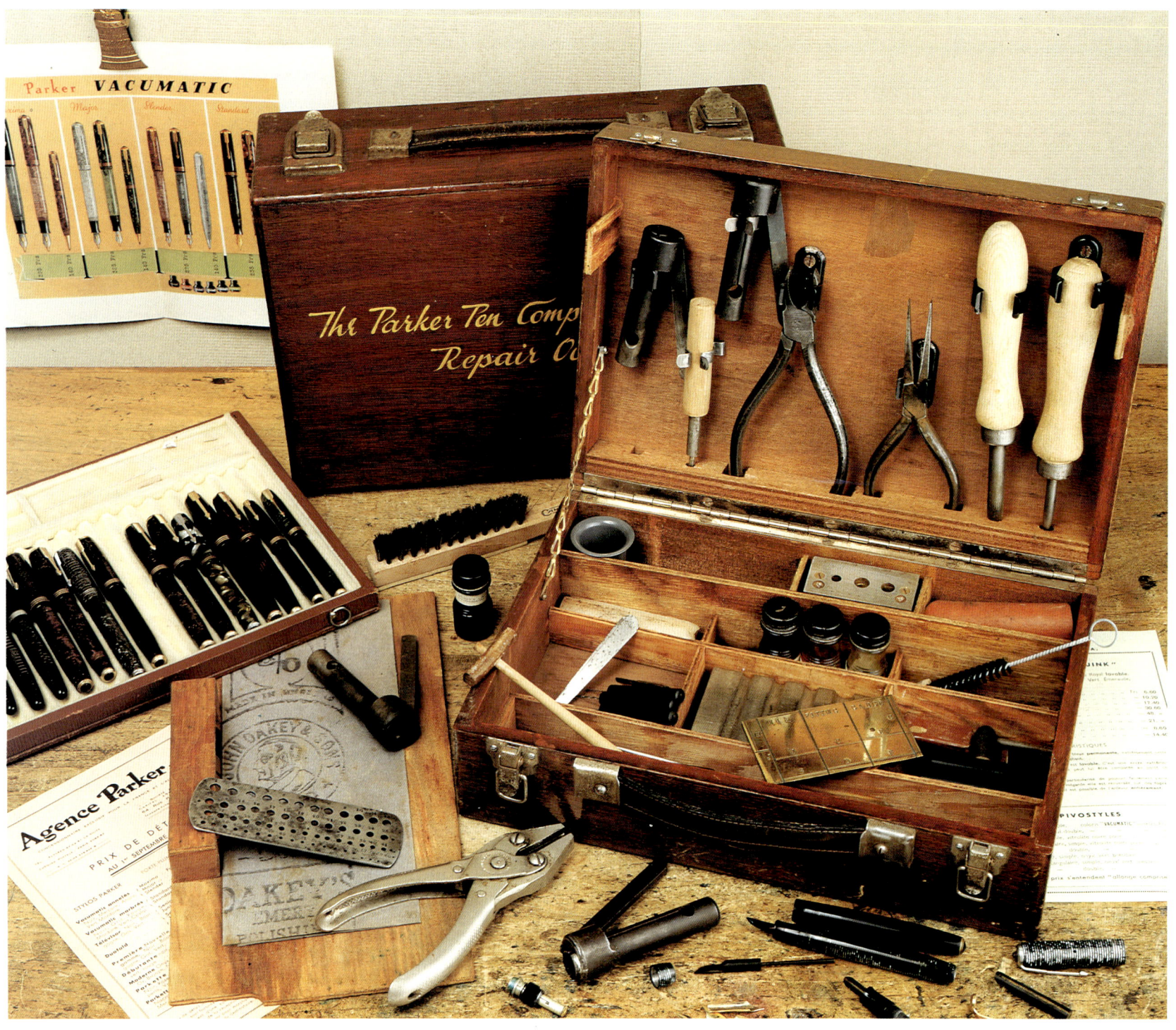

Repair Kit

The major fountain pen brands gave their distributors tool kits especially designed for their models. The one pictured above is for Parker. This kit allowed a full range of repairs for the Vacumatic. *After World War II, the temporary decline of the fountain pen and the tendency to throw away the pen rather than repair it rendered these kits obsolete.*

Therefore, considerable care should be used when applying heat. The part should be moved through the heat source.

To dissolve dried ink, you should use only cold water. This should be done with care because certain materials become discolored or distorted when they remain immersed in water for any length of time. You should be extremely wary of bleach; it is very useful in removing ink stains but, even when heavily diluted, it can damage gold nibs. Do not use rubbing alcohol because it damages plastics. Therefore, use cold water and only cold water. In most cases, a simple bath is not going to be enough to restore the appearance of old fountain pens. You will need to tinker with them...but only on

Illustration for the cover of a 1912 Kaweco catalog. Two years later, the call to arms was in significant contrast.

the condition that you feel the pen is worth the effort involved.

A word of caution...if the repair required exceeds your competence or if you do not have the proper tools, it is far better to go to a professional; there are still a few very competent individuals left.

Those who have the knowledge, tools, and skill necessary also will need the spare parts. Today, one of the best ways of obtaining these is to buy fountain pens in poor condition. From these rejects, there is always at least one part you can salvage that can be used to restore a perfect body. A good repair job should not only produce a fountain pen with its former appearance, but also should ensure its proper operation, namely, its ability to write well.

If the nib and the section have been removed, they must be replaced very carefully. Frequently, the nib slightly distorts the inside of the section by creating its own imprint. The position of the nib relative to the feed is easy to determine. The tip of the feed is generally located approximately half-way between the point and the eye. If the two ends of the nib are spread apart, they should be bent slightly towards the point. If they are overlapping, they should be bent slightly away from the point. If the point is rough and does not glide easily across the paper, a few figure eights scribed onto super fine sanding paper should restore its smoothness.

In principle, all parts should be original spare parts, with the exception of rubber sacs. Whether dried up, cracked or missing, they have to be replaced. The source of the new rubber sac is of little importance.

Once the fountain pen has been cleaned and repaired, it can be filled with ink if you wish to write with it. It is important to use the correct

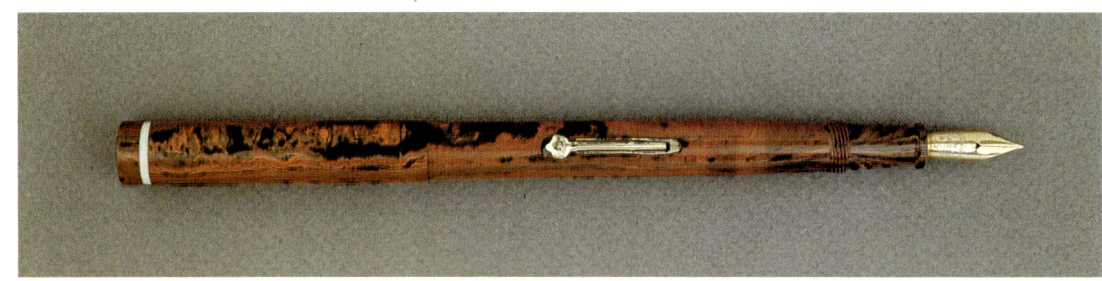

Lever filling Meteore, *marbled red hard rubber (1926).*

Lever filling Semper *by Paillard, black hard rubber (circa 1935).*

ink (e.g., blue or blue-black) for any given fountain pen. Once your prized pen is ready to join its fellows in your collection, do not forget to empty it and rinse it out several times in cold water. Never leave ink in an unused pen. It will not only clog the capillary grooves (which is not serious for a pen not used for writing), but the acidity of the ink will also increase with evaporation. In that case, there can be considerable damage, since plastics may be discolored and the metal parts may corrode.

Black rubber is sensitive to heat and also to light, which discolors it over a period of time. This means that a collection of black hard rubber fountain pens should not be left in a case exposed to direct sunlight. However, this does not mean that, like vampires, black hard rubber fountain pens cannot withstand a moderate amount of light.

If you wish to use an antique fountain pen, a few precautions are in order. Use only fresh ink. Any bottle of ink that has been open for more than 1 year should be discarded. In case of an interruption in use, even for a few weeks, you should empty and rinse your fountain pen. Do not expect that a nib shaped by another hand will adjust easily to yours. On the contrary, compatibility will take some time, but will eventually occur. So, without being rude about it, try not to lend your fountain pen to another person for any extended period of time; however, a few words written by another hand will not alter the shape of the point.

French Dressings in the 1920s
Lever filling Waterman pens, sizes 52 1/2 and 52, in black hard rubber or red marbled, French bodies (1917-1933). Four in solid gold and four gold-filled.

Ch. Leummel

Depuis le haut Moyen-Age jusqu'au XIX° siècle, la plume d'oie fut le seul procédé employé pour écrire...

De nos jours, le Stylo est universellement utilisé.

Pratique, élégant et propre, il est vraiment le compagnon indispensable et fidèle de l'homme moderne.

LE STYLO **Rally**

RALLIE TOUS LES SUFFRAGES !

EN VENTE : CHEZ TOUS LES SPECIALISTES ET PAPETERIES
USINES : 35, RUE DU RETRAIT, PARIS (XX°)

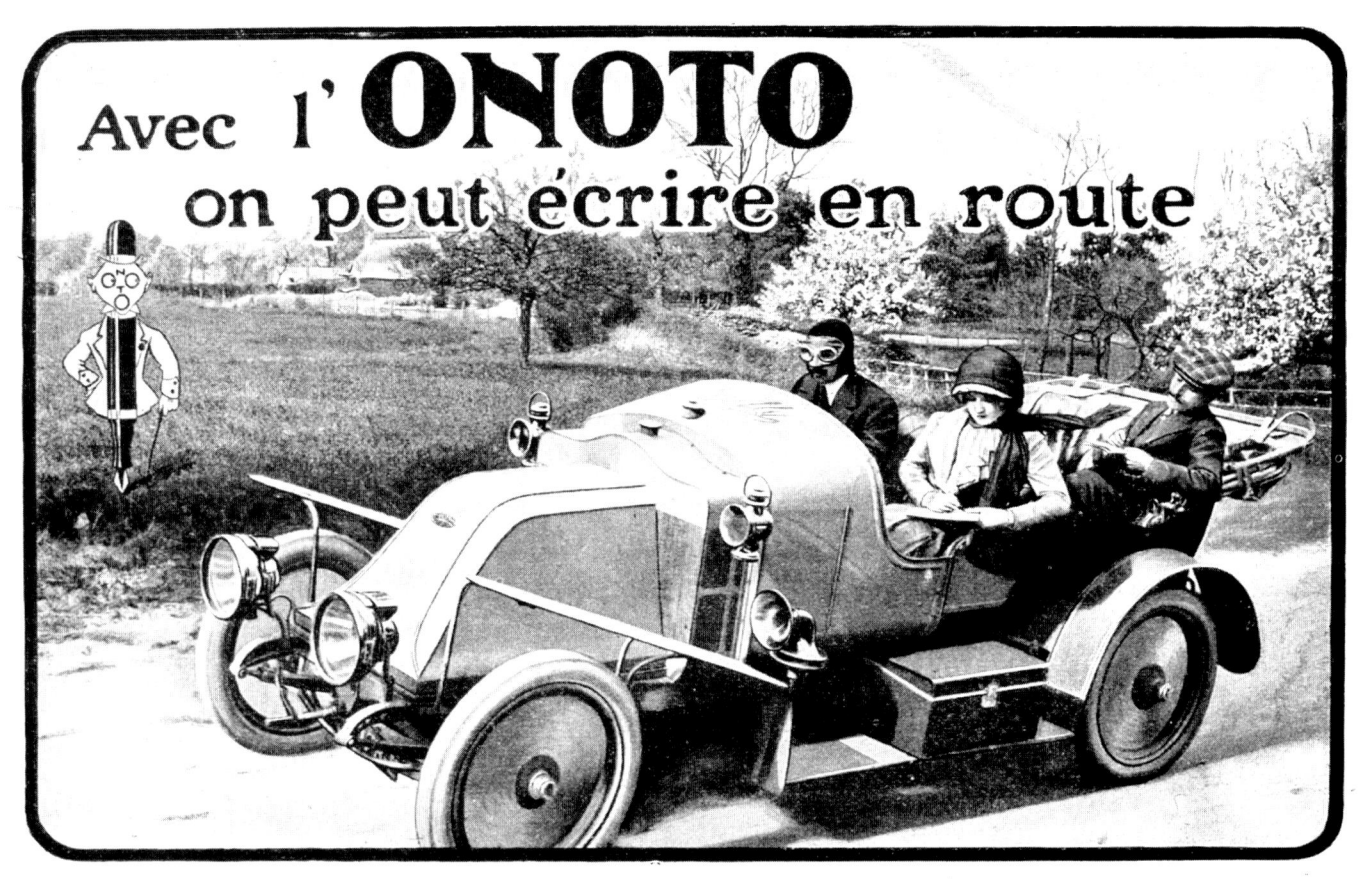

Avec l'ONOTO
on peut écrire en route

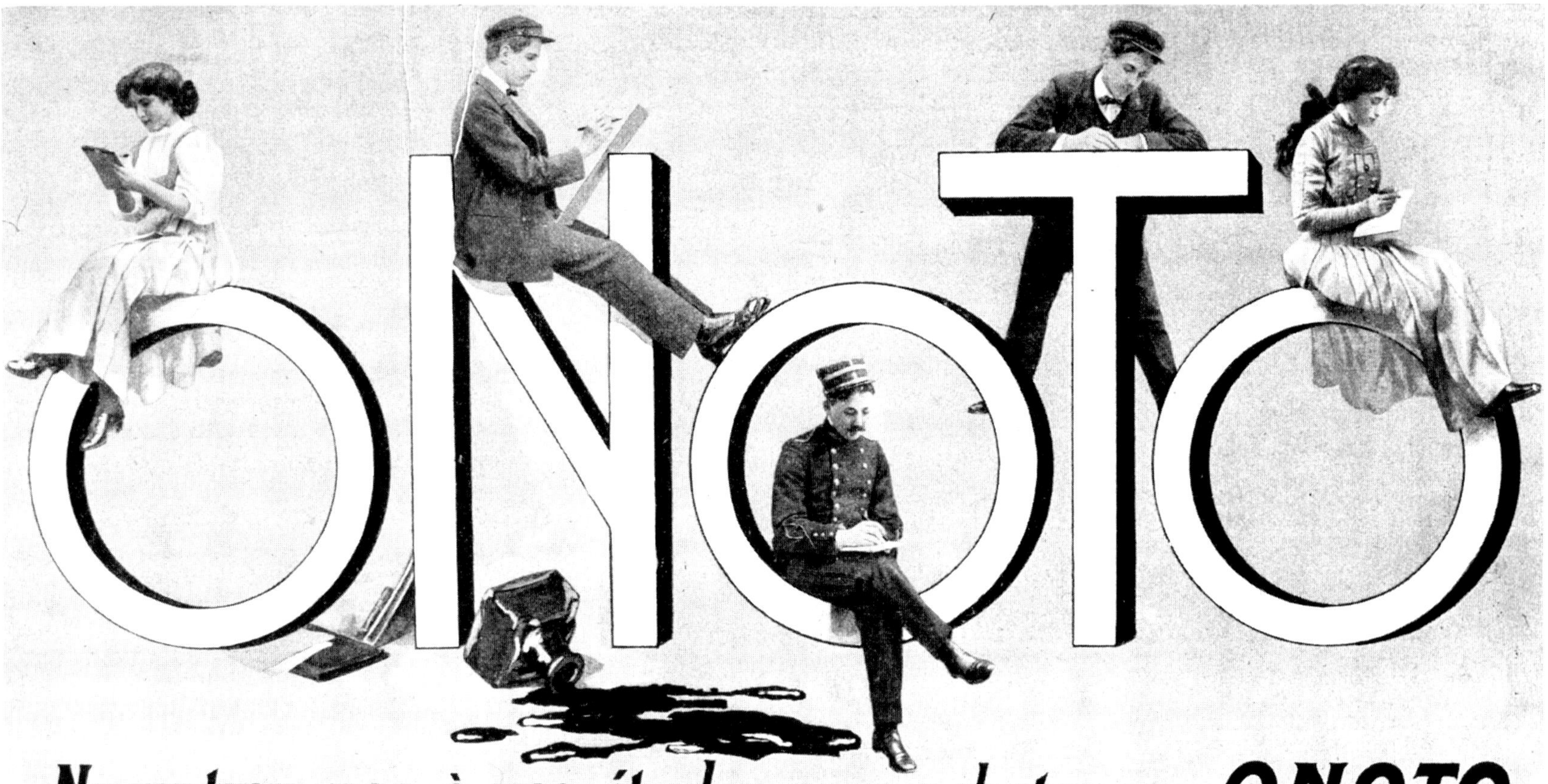
ONOTO
Ne rentrez pas à vos études sans acheter un ONOTO

En qualité... toujours plus haut !

ROYAL
Stephens'

COMPAGNIE DES ENCRES
SOCIÉTÉ ANONYME AU CAPITAL DE 2.625.000 FRANCS
57 RUE DEGUINGAND
LEVALLOIS-PERRET (SEINE)

Waterman ladies fountain pens, L.E.C. casings, silver, gold, gold-filled (1924-1930).

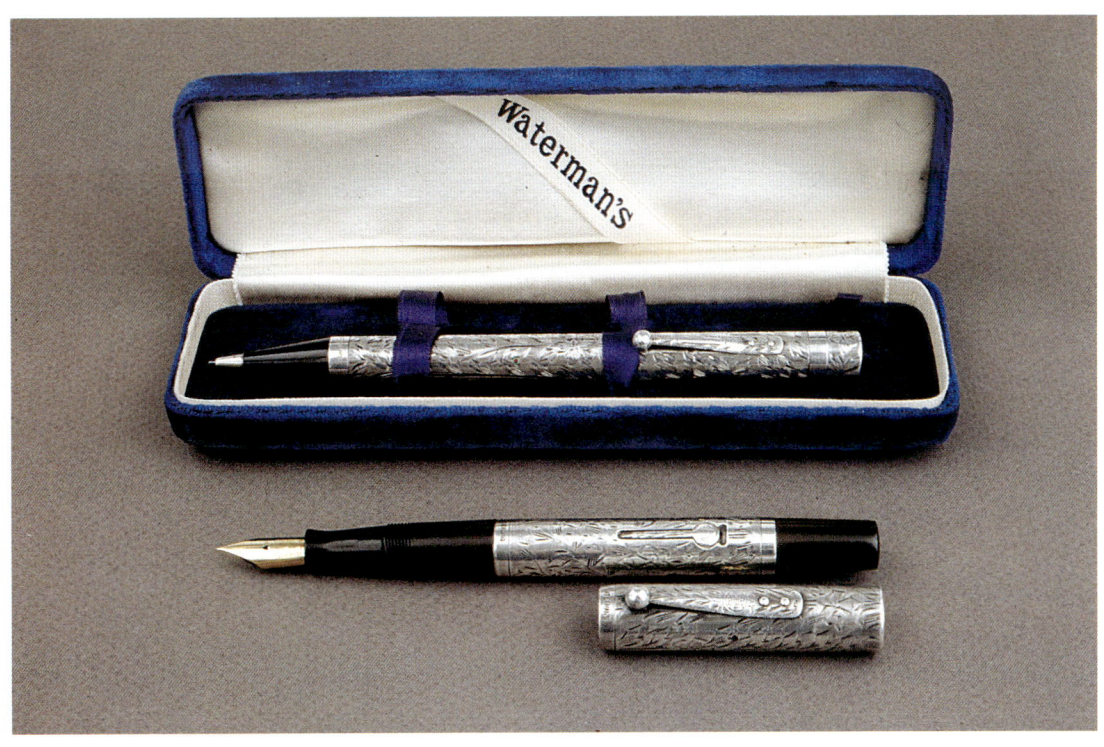

Waterman fountain pen and mechanical pencil set, silver body, floral trim (1915-1929).

Lever filling Waterman pens (52 v.), French I.E.C. casings over black or red marbled hard rubber (1924-1939).

Que de progrès en écriture
avec cette plume
"Waterman„
Johannès -

LE DERNIER
LA DERNIÈRE
Les 2 Etapes de la vie !
Le premier poil et.....
la première plume.....
Waterman

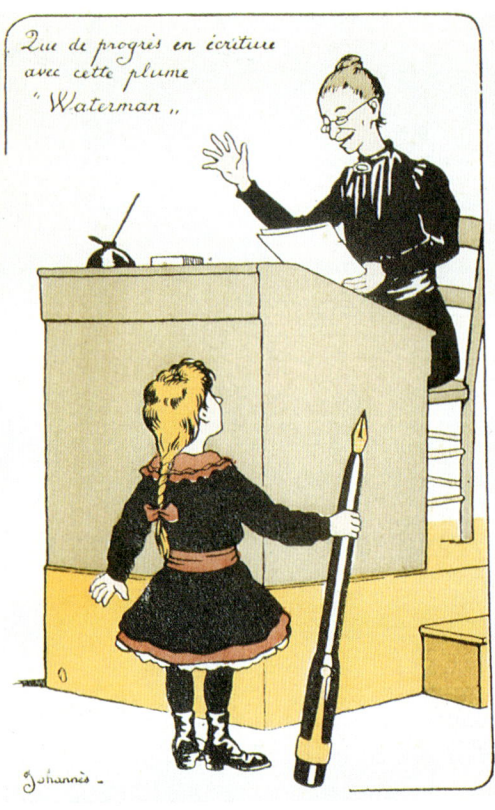

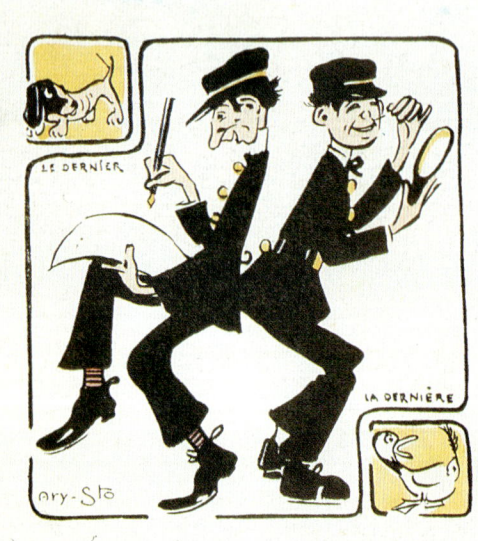

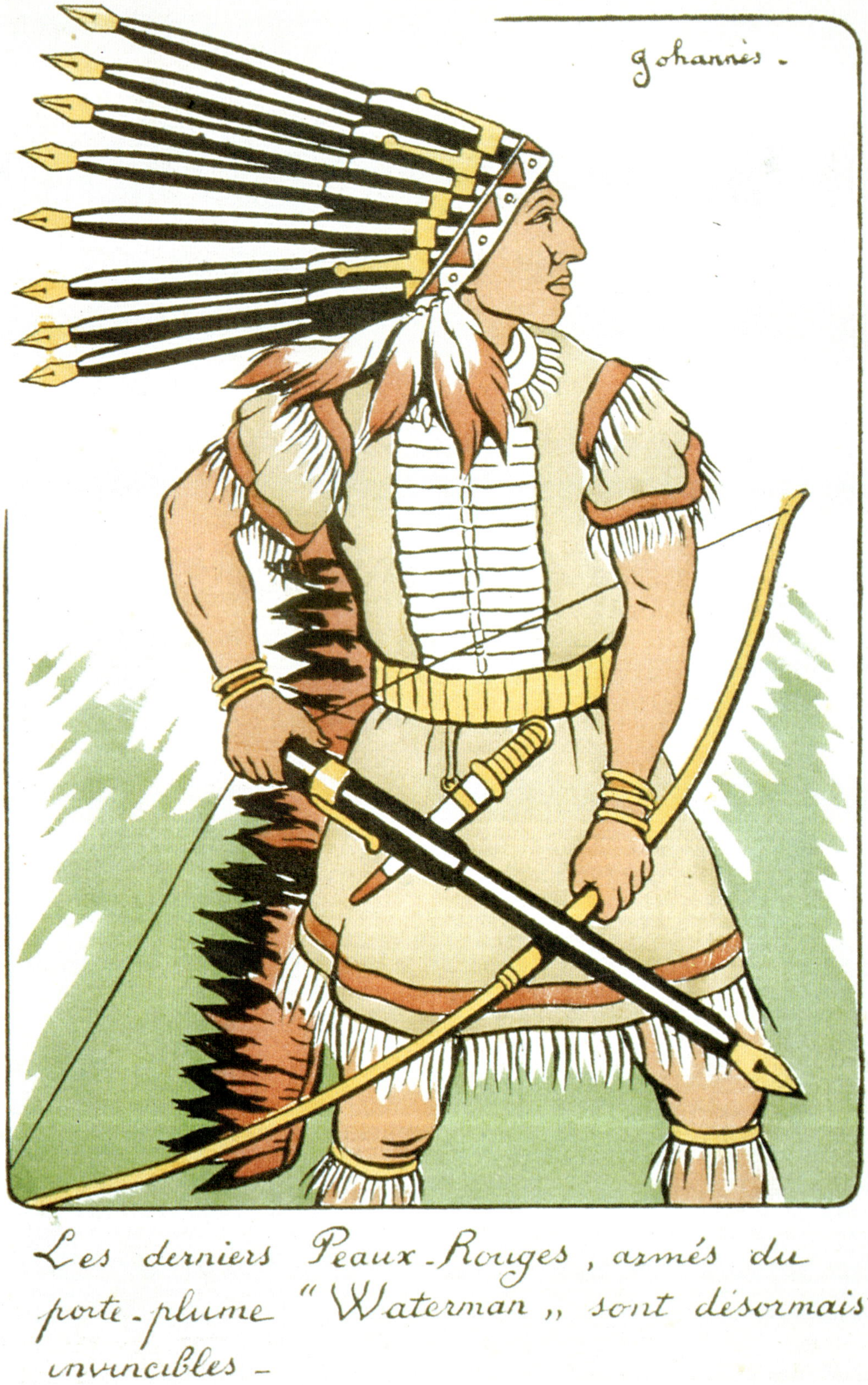
Johannès -
Les derniers Peaux-Rouges, armés du
porte-plume "Waterman„ sont désormais
invincibles -

At the beginning of this century, Hardtmuth represented Waterman in France. Soon after the opening of the Paris office (1904), the company published these promotional postcards that were given away to customers.

For Holiday Gifts Buy

Waterman's "Ideal"

Fountain Pen,

Office, 136 Fulton Street, N. Y.

over.

SEM

Avec une plume Onoto
On écrit bien, même en Auto!
Edmond Rostand

Waterman promotional cards (1884).

Glastnost

The ability to see the ink level while writing contributes greatly to the user's sense of security. Despite a few short-lived attempts (Waterman in 1903 and Swan 10 years later), that luxury remained unavailable for a long time. Hard rubber is not transparent and neither is the rubber of the ink sac. With the introduction of plastics, a see-through ink level was a very important sales pitch. In the 1930s, all the manufacturers joined the band wagon. The Nozac model by Conklin had an exclusive "word gauge"; its transparent body was graduated according to a unique measuring unit: 1,000 words. Determining the ink level was possible since all or part of the body was transparent. In most models, it was necessary to unscrew the body to view the reservoir or the cartridge, or to view the transparent plunger located in the barrel.

AU SOMMET DE LA QUALITÉ

LE Superstyl DE

BAYARD
le stylo sans reproche

PUBL. M. GAUBERT

BIEN VISIBLE, *le niveau d'encre*

Un coup d'œil à contre-jour sur votre Eversharp *transparent*, à niveau d'encre bien visible, et vous êtes fixé.

★ Pas besoin d'encre ? Rien d'étonnant, si votre Eversharp *transparent* est du modèle "à piston" : il contient au moins *deux fois plus d'encre* qu'un stylo classique.

★ Besoin d'encre ? Alors, pour le remplir : *trois coups* de piston. L'encre monte, attirée par le vide : le remplissage est instantané.

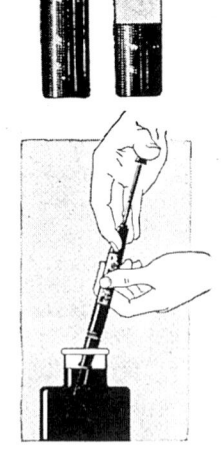

Modèles transparents et à piston, modèles classiques : Tous bons papetiers, libraires, spécialistes, grands magasins. Gros : Frazar-France, 33, Rue de Miromesnil, Paris.

EVERSHARP

PIPO

aucun obstacle n'est insurmontable...

TANK-400

*Le stylo à grande contenance
garanti pour l'existence.*

*C'est un bon stylo
qu'IL désire..!*

— ALORS, c'est le TANK-400
qui LUI fera le plus plaisir...

car c'est la grande nouveauté. Ignorant
la panne, supprimant l'encrier, c'est le
stylo de l'homme de lettres, du journaliste,
de l'homme d'affaires, du comptable, de l'étudiant.
Un instrument de travail moderne et chic,
dont le corps formant cartouche interchangeable
à niveau visible, permet d'écrire *à la plume
et à l'encre* sans arrêt.

Le TANK 400 en écrin de
luxe avec ses quatre
cartouches de rechange
remplies d'encre
BLEU RADIO ou BLEU NOIR
Stephens'
extra fluide

GARANTIE A VIE — *Où que vous
soyez si le TANK 400 ne vous donne
pas satisfaction entière, présentez
votre bon de garantie au papetier
de la ville; il vous sera échangé
immédiatement et sans frais*

DESCRIPTION

1 le **CAPUCHON** avec son
clip de sûreté, véritable pièce de mécanique de précision.

2 la **CARTOUCHE** interchangeable formant
le corps du stylo à niveau d'encre visible.

3 la **SECTION PLUME**, qui
avec ses perfectionnements, constitue l'âme
du stylo le plus moderne.

Autres avantages
Entièrement en PLEXIGLAS, donc INCASSABLE, Clip, joncs et plume en métal
doré à l'or fin INALTÉRABLES

Ets Pierre BAIGNOL & Co

USINES & BUREAUX : 19, rue de SARTORIS
LA GARENNE - COLOMBES (SEINE)

APPENDIX

Significant Names in the Fountain Pen Industry

Charles Abel (Paris, France). *Clebs*, *Million* (1934), *Oldchap* (1921) fountain pens.

Eugene Abel (Paris, France). *Atlet* (1924, tools for repair), *Babel* and *The Traveller* fountain pens.

Agap (Paris, France). *Analpen* and *Club* fountain pens.

Aikin Lambert (New York). Company founded in 1864. Manufacturer of gold nibs. Began manufacturing its own fountain pens circa 1890. Victim of the Great Depression of 1929, it was acquired by L.E. Waterman in 1932.

Akira Seishindo Seisakusho (Tokyo, Japan).

Alkovitszky (Paris, France). Nibs and trim.

Amalgamated Gold Pen Makers (London/Liverpool, Great Britain). Nib manufacturers.

The American Fountain Pen Co. (Boston, Massachusetts). Founded in 1899. One of the first to manufacture retractable nib fountain pens, the *Moore Non-Leakable*, without a rotary mechanism, but with a slide (patented by Morris W. Moore). Became the Moore Pen Co. in 1917. Adapted the innovations of major manufacturers in later years. Went out of business in 1956.

Ancora (Arona, Italy). Founded in 1909 by Giuseppe Zanini. After his death in 1929, his son Alfredo took over the business. The trademark is symbolized by an anchor (ancora). Went out of business in 1975.

Anglo American Co. (Paris, France). 28, boulevard Poissonnière. Importer since 1887. First exclusive distributor for L.E. Waterman.

Artus (Heidelberg, Germany). Artus Fullhaltergesellschaft Kaufman & Co. See Lamy.

Ateliers Francais (Issy-les-Moulineaux, France). Jacques Bonhomme (1920).

Augis (Champagne-au-Mont-Dore, France). Jeweler and medal manufacturer. Established in 1830. Produced a large range of high quality clips.

Aurora (Turin, Italy). Fabbrica Italiana di Penne a Serbatoio. Founded in 1919 by Isaia Levi. Products sold in France by Edacoto (1931). Still in operation.

Badois (Paris, France). Trademark registered in 1921 by Louis Badois, one of the partners of La Plume d'Or.

Pierre Baignol (Paris, France). *Tank 400* fountain pen (circa 1947).

Baruzzi-Ostal (Nice, Alpes-Maritimes, France). 1910. *Champion*, *Mignon*, and *Scribo* fountain pens.

Baudinière (Paris, France). *Luxor* fountain pens (circa 1930).

Bayard (Paris, France). In 1903, Étienne Forbin was a distributor for Nauheim & Co. (New York). In 1912, he registered many trademarks of the fountain pens that he distributed (*Bayard*, *Excelsior*, *Alpin*, etc.). Some were manufactured at his factory in Arbois (Jura). In 1922, his nephews took over the business and the trade name was changed to Panici Frères et Cie. The initials P.F. are inscribed on the nibs. The workshops on the rue des Cordelières in Paris gave the company a new distinction. It was one of the most prominent fountain pen companies until it went bankrupt, like many others, in the 1960s.

Bayle (Lyon, Rhône, France). *Mon Plaisir* fountain pens (circa 1929).

Beaufils (Paris, France). See Stellor.

A. Bendoni (Paris, France). Nib manufacturer.

B & D (Brussels, Belgium). Beirlaen and Delen. See Bermond.

Bermond (Brussels, Belgium). Trademark registered in 1919 by Beirlaen and Delen (B & D). Bermond is the contraction of BEirlaen and RayMOND. Another trademark: *The Scout Pen*. Manufactured in Germany by Mertz and Krell. After World War II, Bermond imported Biro ballpoint pens. The company still operates under the management of Penn & Co.

Blair (New York). Solid ink pens with a water reservoir.

Blanzy-Poure (Boulogne-sur-Mer, Pas-de-Calais, France). Founded in 1846 by Pierre Blanzy and Eugene Poure. One of the largest steel nib manufacturers. Produced nibs for the *Chromix* fountain pens.

The Boston Pen Co. (Boston, Massachusetts). Founded in 1894. Acquired by the Wahl Adding Machine Company in 1917.

Bourbon (Saint-Lupicin, Jura, France). Manufacturer of pen bodies.

Brause & Co. (Iserlohn, Germany). Founded in 1850 (steel nibs).

Camel Pen Co. (Orange, New Jersey). Founded in 1935 by Joseph V. Wustman. Solid ink pens filled with water. Good quality but poor sales. The company went bankrupt after 3 years.

Carey Pen Co. (New York). Founded in 1890. Went out of business in 1915.

Carpentras et Donarier (Nantes, Loire-Atlantique, France). *Solveig* fountain pens (1945).

*****Carter** (Cambridge, Massachusetts). The Carter Ink Co. was founded in 1858 by John W. Carter. It quickly became one of the major ink manufacturers in the United States. From 1926 to 1931, it manufactured high quality fountain pens in unusual colors, but of classic design.

Cartier (Paris, France). Established in 1847. Jewelers. Began manufacturing gold dip pens in 1860. Early in the 20th century, Cartier began designing trim for fountain pens. In the 1930s, the company designed a numbered series of small fountain pens. Since 1968, it has been involved in the development of high technology production. The *Must* of Cartier. The Compagnie des Technologies de luxe was founded in 1988.

Castela (Toulouse, Hautes-Pyrénées, France). *Wildaup* fountain pens circa 1922.

Caw's Pen & Ink Co. (New York). Manufacturer of ink and fountain pens (1890-1915). Received a silver medal at the International Exposition of Decorative Arts in 1900.

Charcellay (Paris, France). In 1910, Charcellay established the Franco-British Manufacturing Pen Cie. After World War I, the company expanded rapidly and became one of the most important in the French market. In the 1930s, it took the name of the Compagnie française pour la fabrication de P.P.R. Despite the quality of its products, Charcellay is not very well known because, like Laureau and Sabon, its models were marketed under other trademarks.

Chemol (Budapest, Hungary).

Chilton (Boston, Massachusetts). Founded in 1923 by Seth Chilton Crocker. The company moved to Long Island City, New York in 1932, later to Summit, New Jersey, and went out of business in 1941. The fountain pen was filled through two tubes and pressure was applied by a column of air on the sac. See Crocker.

Christian (Paris, France). Christian Boursier. See Evergood.

Cisea (Turin, Italy). *Radius* fountain pens.

*Conklin (Toledo, Ohio). Founded in 1898 by Roy Conklin, it was the first manufacturer to offer a satisfactory filling system utilizing the compression of a rubber sac (1901). Roy Conklin sold his shares in the company in 1903. Conklin remained one of the top four United States manufacturers until the early 1920s when it was surpassed by Wahl. Entered the French market in 1920. Went out of business in 1947.

Conté (Paris, France). Pencil manufacturer. *Monte Cristo* fountain pens.

Conway Stewart (Enfield, Great Britain). Founded in 1905 by Thomas H. Garner and Frank Jarvis. Manufacturer of the first Gold Starry pens. Went out of business in 1975.

Crocker Pen Co. (Boston, Massachusetts). Founded in 1902 by Seth Crocker. His son, Seth Chilton Crocker, took over the business in 1907 and in 1923, founded the Chilton Pen Co. In 1931, he sold Crocker Pen to N. Zaino. See Chilton.

A.T. Cross (Boston, Massachusetts/Lincoln, Rhode Island). The date when the company was established is difficult to determine, because the frequently quoted year 1846 refers to the birth date of Alonzo Townsend Cross (1846-1922), who succeeded his father, Richard Cross, and his great uncle, Edward Bradbury, who had made writing instruments since 1843. The elder Crosses were English and had only recently settled in the United States. Alonzo was born in Birmingham. Until 1881, the company was called Richard Cross & Son. The initial products were largely mechanical pencils and pencil caps. Beginning in 1877, Alonzo Townsend Cross manufactured the needle pen and was the first to market an instrument called the *stylographic pen*. A few years later, he became the first manufacturer of that type of instrument, while his production of nib fountain pens remained insignificant. In 1916, the company was acquired by Walter Russell Boss. In 1935, the distinctive black half cone trademark appeared. Since 1946, the superb *Century* has been produced without major modifications. In 1953, the company launched the production of ballpoint pens. In 1963, the word "Pencil" was dropped from the company's name and it became A.T. Cross Co. Still in business, it is the dean of all United States writing instrument manufacturers.

Daussy (Paris, France). *Le Pneu* fountain pens.

De La Rue (London, Great Britain). Founded in Guernsey in 1813 by Thomas de la Rue, who moved to London in 1816 and made a fortune by printing playing cards. Throughout the 19th century the company developed and diversified. It produced stamps, bank notes, stationery, and writing instruments. After manufacturing a few unsuccessful models (*Swift*), real fountain pens were first produced in 1895 (*Pelican*) and appeared on the French market in 1898. The first *Onoto* appeared in 1905 and its success lasted for many years. It is said that the name was chosen because it is pronounced the same way in most languages. The *Onoto* was produced for more than half a century. In 1958, De La Rue gave up manufacturing fountain pens and the rights were acquired by its Australian distributor.

Delolme (Saint-Claude, Jura, France). *Jemco* fountain pens.

Demilly & Degan (Paris, France). See La Plume d'Or.

Devarson (London, Great Britain). See Lincoln.

Dhome (Paris, France). DOM nibs.

Dolfina (Doorn, The Netherlands).

Dunhill (London, Great Britain). Founded in 1907 by Alfred Dunhill, who was originally a purveyor of fine tobaccos. In 1930, Dunhill sent its fountain pens to be lacquered by Namiki (Pilot). These pens are manufactured today by Montblanc (which belongs to the Dunhill group).

Dunn (New York). Founded in 1921. Went out of business in 1924.

Dupont (Paris, France). Founded in 1872 by Simon Tissot-Dupont. Manufacturer of luxury leather goods and of lighters since 1939. Manufacturer of fountain pens since 1973. Production facilities in Faverges (Haute Savoie).

Eagle Pencil Co. (New York). In 1856, Henry Berolzheimer founded a company in Furth, Bavaria. He moved to New York in 1860 and shortened his name to Berol. He became one of the most important pencil and nib manufacturers in the United States. The company produced the first fountain pens with glass cartridges in 1890 and, in subsequent years, produced low-end, affordable fountain pens.

Edac (Paris, France). Originally, the company was a mechanical pencil company. However, it produced a few fountain pens, one of which was metal with an automatic filling system. In 1931, the company distributed Aurora pens in France and sold them as sets, together with automatic pencils, under the name, *Duo Moderne*. In 1959, it became one of the manufacturers of the *Visor Pen*.

Edacoto (Paris, France). See Edac.

E.J.S. (Paris, France). See Laureau.

Eskesen (Copenhagen, Denmark).

Elmo-Montegrappa (Bassano, Italy). Founded in 1921 by Alessandro Marzotto.

Evergood (Paris, France). Facilities in the Conflans-Sainte-Honorine. Manufacturer of mechanical pencils. Christian Boursier, its founder, began producing fountain pens during World War II.

Faber-Castell (Nuremberg, Germany). Faber's history dates back to 1761. Kaspar Faber founded a pencil factory, but the initials of his successor, Anton Wilhelm Faber (1758-1819), appear in the trade name. In the second half of the 19th century, three brothers headed the company. Eberhard moved to New York in 1849 and founded his pencil company. Johann remained in Nuremberg and in 1878 established a company bearing his name (on the French market: *Le Métro* |1904|, *Neptune*, *Cardinal*). The eldest brother, Lothar, managed A.W. Faber until his death in 1896. In 1898, Count Castell-Rudenhausen, who had married a Faber, became head of the company and added his own name to the trade name (on the French market: *Flamingo* |1904|, *Novellus* |1905|). A.W. Faber-Castell strengthened its position in the fountain pen market by buying the Johann Faber company in 1932 and buying into Osmia in 1935. Faber-Castell is today a very important company in the area of writing and drafting instruments, but it gave up manufacturing fountain pens in 1975.

Forbin (Paris, France). See Bayard.

Fortin & Cie (Paris, France). 59, rue des Petits-Champs. Stationery manufacturer since 1802, specialized in steel nibs. Began manufacturing fountain pens circa 1894.

The Franco-British Manufacturing Co. (Paris, France). See Charcellay.

I. Frank (Paris, France). 15, rue des Petits Carreaux. Stationers under Napoleon III and distributors of John Mitchell (metal nibs). I. Frank began selling fountain pens circa 1894. In 1934, the company changed its name to Penlex.

Frazer & Geyer (New York). See Lincoln and A.A. Waterman.

Fukunaka Mannenpitsu Seisakusho (Tokyo, Japan).

Geha (Hanover, Germany). Founded in 1818 by Heinrich and Conrad Hartmann.

Globe d'Or (Paris, France). Manufacturers of *Gold, Black* (1945), *Dominator* (1946).

Goldirca (Hanover, Germany). Derived its name from the words Gold-IRidium-CAoutchouc (rubber). Founded in 1919.

Gold Star (Paris, France). See Gold Starry.

Gold Starry (Paris/ Saint-Leu-la-Forêt, France). In 1909, Maurice Jandelle, at the time a salesman for Éditions Delagrave, concluded an agreement with the Conway Stewart Company for the distribution of its fountain pens in France under the trademark "Gold Star". Since the name was already registered, it was changed to "Gold Starry" (1912). In 1919, two men, a technician, Paul Janvrin, and a merchant, André Petit, began producing high quality fountain pens as a small business in Saint-Leu-la-Forêt, with direct distribution but inadequate financial backing. Jandelle wished to become independent and distribute French products. In order to establish these goals, in 1921, the Gold Starry company was created from a merger of the houses of Jandelle and Petit & Janvrin, with an initial capital outlay of 750,000 francs. Factories were built in Saint-Leu-La-Forêt. Gold Starry was the first French manufacturer to offer cellulose acetate pens in bright colors. The company remained very successful until 1933, but thereafter declined. Mr. Jandelle retired and management was passed to a Mr. Pérouse, who managed a small company that produced the "Viala

Lilliput". After World War II, the situation worsened with the advent of the ball-point pen. Gold Starry changed direction and became a producer of gold and silver trim for fountain pens. The company launched the production of high-end fountain pens. It remained successful for the next 20 years. In 1973, skyrocketing gold prices and a price freeze combined to push Gold Starry into bankruptcy. It went out of business in 1980.

Grafex (Brussels, Belgium). Trademark registered in 1926 by Louis Pauwels. Belgian manufacturing facilities. Other trademarks include *Perfex*, *Pratex*, and *Victory's Pen*. Went out of business in 1950s.

Grand Aigle (Toulon, Var/Toulouse, Hautes-Pyrénées, France). See Mercier.

Grand Perret (Saint-Claude, Jura, France). *Universal Fountain Pen*, 1930.

Gravade & Sachet (Paris, France). 29, boulevard Saint-Michel. Retailers circa 1894.

Grieshaber (Chicago, Illinois). Founded in 1842. Important fountain pen and nib manufacturer.

Guillement et Servet (Paris, France). *Omo* fountain pens (circa 1920).

Haro (Regensburg, Germany). Founded in 1926 in Fromsdorf (Silesia) by HAnns ROggenbuck. Specialized in glass nib fountain pens. Factories in Frankenstein and Weisswasser. In 1946, following the post-World War II partition, the Frankenstein factory found itself in Poland and the Weisswasser factory found itself in East Germany. Roggensbuck moved to Bad Mergentheim, then to Regensburg (West Germany). The company continued manufacturing glass nibs, then moved into the production of paper goods and stationery.

H. Hebborn (Heidelberg, Germany). Founded in 1925. Acquired by Parker in 1970.

Heintze & Blanckertz (Berlin/Frankfurt, Germany). Founded in Berlin in 1849 by Heinrich Siegmund Blanckertz and Rudolph Heintze. One of the largest German steel nib manufacturers and, before 1914, one of the fountain pen pioneers. Nationalized in East Germany after World War II and took the name of Schreibfedernfabrik-Berlin-Oranienburg.

Highley Pen Co. (Highley, Great Britain). Founded in 1946 by A.A.S. Charles (son of T.H. Charles, owner of T. Hessin & Co., manufacturer of steel nibs). Since 1949, it has had controlling interest in D. Leonardt & Co. and Hessin & Co. Took over the nib production department of Brandauer in 1960.

John Holland (Cincinnati, Ohio). Founded in 1841 (George Shepard). Originally a manufacturer of gold nibs, from the 1860s on John Holland was a true fountain pen pioneer. Some think that he was the first to market a more or less operative fountain pen in 1869. The company discontinued manufacturing fountain pens in 1950 but remained in business as stationers until 1980.

Hosonumma K.K. (Tokyo, Japan).

Houston Pen Co. (Sioux City, Iowa). Founded in 1911 by William A. Houston. Went out of business in 1924.

Inubushi & Co. (Tokyo, Japan).

Jewel Pen Co. (London, Great Britain).

JiF (Paris, France). Initials of Jules Fagard. See Waterman S.A.

Kaweco (Heidelberg, Germany). Heidelberger Federhalter Fabrik KOch, WEber & CO. Founded in 1892 by Otto Koch and Rudolph Weber, it was one of the first companies to offer *safeties*. Entered the French market in 1911. It was acquired by Friedrich Grube in 1929 and went out of business in 1970.

Kintz (Antwerp/Brussels, Belgium). See Le Tigre.

Kunz (Vienna, Austria).

Lamy (Heidelberg, Germany). The "Orthos Fullhalterfabrik C.J. Lamy" was founded in 1930 by Joseph Lamy, then director of the German subsidiary of Parker. Acquired Artus after World War II and is still in business.

Lancaster (Baltimore, Maryland). Founded in 1879 by Warren N. Lancaster. One of the true fountain pen pioneers.

Lang Pen Co. (Liverpool, Great Britain).

Laughlin (Detroit, Michigan). Founded in 1880. Went out of business in 1925.

*Laureau (Paris, France). In 1922, Fernand Laureau registered the trademark *Loro*. He manufactured fountain pens bearing the trade names of his customers, with or without nibs, and subcontracted to large manufacturers, such as Parker, for the production of beautiful pen trim. He received a silver medal in 1925 at the International Exposition of Decorative Arts in Paris. In 1929, he went into partnership with J. de Soultrait to establish E.J.S. Because he did not put his name on his products, Laureau's name is unjustly forgotten today.

*LeBoeuf (Springfield, Massachusetts). During the 1920s and 1930s, the company marketed exceptionally attractive fountain pens, utilizing many different plastics not employed by other manufacturers. The company survived until the late 1930s.

Lecocq (Paris, France). Manufacturer of clips.

LeFranc (Marseille, Bouches-du-Rhône, France).

Legorrec & Billaud Founded in 1923. Nib manufacturer, still in business.

Lieber (Lyon, Rhône, France). *Fontencre* trademark.

Lincoln (New York). Founded in 1894. Sold in 1900 to Frazer & Geyer Company. Two years later, after going into partnership with A.A. Waterman, Frazer and Geyer sold Lincoln to Perry, the largest nib manufacturer in the world. Nibs were manufactured in Great Britain under the trademark Devarson. Frazer and Geyer founded the New Lincoln Pen Co., which manufactured A.A. Waterman's low-end products.

C.W. Little (New York/Whitewater, Wisconsin). Manufactured *Century* fountain pens for approximately 30 years, beginning in 1900.

Lombard (Neuilly-sur-Seine, France). *Orego*, *Argeco*, and *Eco* fountain pens.

Lopy (Paris, France). Founded in 1934 by J. Lopy. *Jerzon* fountain pens.

Loro (Paris, France). See Laureau.

Luschi (Paris, France). Nib manufacturer. Significant contributor to the development of nib production in France through the creation of nib production divisions at the facilities of several fountain pen manufacturers.

Luxor (Heidelberg, Germany). See Hebborn.

Mabie Todd (New York, United States/London, Great Britain). In 1873, Mabie Todd & Bard was created from the association of John H. Mabie and Henry H. Todd, on the one hand, and of Jonathan Sprague Bard (Bard Bros. gold nib manufacturers since 1843), on the other. In 1884, a subsidiary was opened in London and the French market was entered in 1898. *Swan* fountain pens were distributed in most European countries. In 1909, fountain pens began to be manufactured in Great Britain. The *Swan* became *The Pen of the British Empire*. The parent company foundered, but the subsidiary flourished. In 1915, the British firm bought all rights for Europe and the British colonies. In 1921, the *Merle Blanc* was launched in France. The United States subsidiary went out of business in 1938. In 1952, Mabie Todd was absorbed by Biro and became Biro Swan, which was sold to BiC (France) in 1957.

MacKinnon (New York). Duncan MacKinnon is said to be the first to have offered a good needle point pen (1875). His stylographs were manufactured by John Holland.

MacNiven & Cameron (Edinburgh, Great Britain). Founded in 1770, the company was a leader for nearly two centuries in the area of stationery items. Its role was far more modest in the area of fountain pens. *Cameron* and *Waverley* fountain pens.

Maillocheau (Tours, Indre-et-Loire, France). *Magna*, *Speed-Point*, and *Walk-Over* fountain pens.

Mallat (Paris, France). Founded in 1842 by Jean-Benoît Mallat, an eclectic inventor who perfected the steel nib and manufactured the famous *Syphoïde* (1864). The company began manufacturing pens in 1916. *Integral* (1936), *Plexigraph* (1943). Still in business (writing and drafting instruments).

Manufacture Française de P.P.R. (Paris, France). See Richard.

Manufacture Lorraine de P.P.R. (Metz, Moselle, France). *The Kid*, *Griff*, and *Le Lorrain* fountain pens.

Manufacture Parisienne de P.P.R. (Paris/Nanterre, France). See La Plume d'Or.

Maroncini (Florence, Italy).

Le Matador (Paris, France). See Richard.

Matador (Wuppertal, Germany). See Siebert & Lowen.

Mauram (Saint-Claude, Jura, France.) M & A Benoit Frères.

Menard & Deluzy (Paris, France). 108, rue de Rennes. Distributors of Hicks fountain pens, circa 1894.

Mercier (Toulon, Var/Toulouse, Hautes-Pyrénées, France). Founded by Joseph Mercier in 1915 in Toulon. Moved to Toulouse in 1932. *Grand Aigle* trademark.

Mercury (Brussels, Belgium). Trademark of Dammaerts (circa 1947), an importer of Montblancs.

Météore (Paris/Nanterre, France). See La Plume d'Or.

Molinier (Marseille, Bouches-du-Rhône, France). *Roberry's* fountain pens.

Montblanc (Hamburg, Germany). Trademark registered in 1911 by Simplo-Fillerpen GmbH, which had been founded in 1908 by August Eberstein, Max Koch, Alfred Nehemias, and Klauss Voss (C.W. Lausen and W. Dziambor acquired shares in 1909). *Rouge et Noir, Simplo,* and *Diplomat* trademarks. In 1924, the high-end pens were given the generic name of *Meisterstuck.* In 1934, the trade name was changed to Montblanc Simplo GmbH. The white star is a symbol for Mont Blanc, and its altitude of 4,810 meters is inscribed on all nibs of the *Meisterstuck* pens. Still in business today, it is owned by the Dunhill group.

Mooney Pen (Chicago, Illinois). Founded in 1875 by Frank H. Mooney, gold nib manufacturer. Went out of business in 1917.

Moore (Boston, Massachusetts). See American Fountain Pen Co.

E. L. Moreau (Paris, France), 1898. Business office in Paris, 17, rue de Lancry, factories in Mouy, in Oise. In 1904, the company was acquired by and changed its name to J.M. Paillard. See Paillard.

Namiki (Tokyo, Japan). See Pilot and Dunhill.

Ohmi Yoko (Osaka, Japan).

Omas (Bologna, Italy). Officina Meccanicha Armando Simoni. Founded in 1919 by Armando Simoni (1891-1958). Still in business.

Onoto (London, Great Britain). See De La Rue.

Orthos Fullhalter-Fabrik (Heidelburg, Germany). See Lamy.

Osmia (Dossenheim, Germany). Founded in 1919 by Georg Bohler. Sold to Parker in 1928, which soon sold it back. Faber-Castell bought into the company in 1935.

Pagliero (Turin, Italy).

Paillard (Paris, France). Trade name used since 1904 by E.L. Moreau. Factory in Mouy (Oise). Specialized in colors and drafting instruments. Distributors in France of the *Simple* (Montblanc). In 1919, many of the partners of the J.M. Paillard Company founded the SAPR (Société anonyme pour la fabrication des P.P.R.). *Semper* and *Scriptor* fountain pens. Still in business as a manufacturer of drafting instruments.

Panici Frères (Paris, France). See Bayard.

*Parker (Janesville, Wisconsin). Founded in 1892 by George Stafford Parker. The success of the *Vacumatic* fountain pen, introduced in 1933, allowed Parker to exceed Sheaffer's sales. Today, it is the largest fountain pen manufacturer in the world. Recently acquired by the Gillette Company.

Pauwels (Lons-le-Saunier, Jura/Paris, France). Manufacturer of nibs, supplies, and pen trim.

Louis Pauwels (Brussels, Belgium). See Grafex.

Pedersen (Copenhagen, Denmark).

Pelican (London, Great Britain). See De La Rue.

Pelikan (Hanover, Germany). Founded in 1871 by Gunther Wagner following his purchase of the chemist Caro Horneman's business (created in 1832), where Wagner had worked since 1863. A manufacturer of stationery and drafting supplies (dyes and inks), Pelikan entered the fountain pen market in the 1920s. Known in France for its nibs and *Graphos* pen (industrial drafting). Still in business, but since 1984, it has belonged to Condorpart AG, Switzerland (today, the Pelikan Holding AG).

Pellet (Paris, France). *Plexipell, Stylopell, Montcalm,* and *Writter* fountain pens.

Pelletier (Brussels, Belgium). Ink and stationery manufacturer. *Pelletier* and *Imperial Pelletier* fountain pens.

Penlex (Paris, France). Formerly L. Frank Company. Manufacturer of fountain pen nibs.

Penola (Helsinki, Finland).

Pentel (Tokyo, Japan). Founded in 1946.

Perry & Co. (Birmingham/London, Great Britain). Founded in 1824 by James Perry. It was the largest manufacturer of steel nibs in the world and also produced fountain pens, but its success in that area was far less spectacular. See Devarson.

E.S. Perry, Ltd. (London/Gosport, Great Britain). Founded in 1921 by Edmund S. Perry, the director of Perry & Co., Ltd. in Birmingham, first manufacturer of steel nibs in the world. *Osmiroid* nibs and fountain pens.

Pilot (Tokyo, Japan). Trade name since 1938 of the Namiki Manufacturing Co., founded in 1918 by Ryosuke Namiki and Masao Wada.

Platinum (Tokyo, Japan). Trade name since 1942 of the Nakaya Manufacturing Co., founded in 1919 by Shyunichi Nakada.

La Plume d'Or (Paris/Nanterre, France). Name taken in 1921 by a company founded in 1916 as Manufacture Parisienne de P.P.R. Trademark of *La Météore*. Other trademarks are *Zodiac, Prompto* (1922), and *Pullman* (1932). It is also one of the most important European manufacturers of gold nibs. First in Paris, 63, rue des Archives, then 48, rue des Vinaigriers, the factories were finally located in Nanterre, 26-30, rue des Amandiers. Nibs are marked with the initials D&D (the founders' [Demilly and Degen] initials). During World War II, gold nibs were replaced by steel nibs stamped with the word *Vaedium*. Went out of business in 1956.

A. Poulain (Paris, France). 1892. Distributors of Caw's *Dashaway*, 7, avenue de l'Opéra. The former stationery company specialized in the distribution of English steel nibs, having been founded by Roux and agents of E.W. Cuthbert (Birmingham).

Pratex (Brussels, Belgium). See Grafex.

Regnault (La Ferté-Millon, Aisne/Valence, Drôme, France). Factories were established in 1927 in La Ferté-Millon. *Ludo* fountain pens. In 1945, the company moved to Valence. In 1948, it began manufacturing Reynolds ball-point pens (United States) under license. In 1954, it acquired the patent for that trademark. Still in business.

Reynolds (France). See Regnault.

Richard (Paris, France). Before World War I, F.J. Richard opened a factory in Paris for the manufacture of fountain pens bearing the trademark *Le Matador*. Other trademarks include *Imperial, Royal, Le Gracieux, Le Piou-Piou*, and *Le Parigot*. In 1920, the company changed its name to Manufacture Française de P.P.R.

J.G. Rider Pen Co. (Rockford, Illinois). Founded in 1905, went out of business in 1925.

Roggenbuck (Regensburg, Germany). See Haro.

Rotring (Hamburg, Germany). Founded in 1928. Manufacturer of tubular fountain pens.

Roubeaud (Paris, France). *Pousse-Pouce* (1897), *Star* (1899) fountain pens.

Ruyter (Chicago, Illinois).

Sabatier (Paris, France). Manufacturer of *Mors, Rip, Execo*, and *Wattman* fountain pens.

Sabon (Bordeaux, France). Manufacturer of heavy equipment until 1920. Began producing fountain pens during the 1920s, manufacturing its own supply of ebonite. In 1932, it switched to nitrocellulose plastics. With the exception of two fountain pens, *Sprell* and *Yale*, most of its products were sold under their clients' trade names. Went out of business in 1950.

Sakata Seisakusho (Japan). Founded in 1911 by Kyugorou Sakata. *Sailor* fountain pens.

Salz (New York). Founded in 1907.

Sertic (Paris, France). Manufacturer of *Inoxstyl* (1928).

Sheaffer (Fort Madison, Iowa). Founded in 1913 by Walter A. Sheaffer, a jeweler and inventor of the lever filling system. In 1923, Sheaffer was the first to use a material called pyroxylin and to manufacture colored pens. In 1929, he also was the first to capitalize upon the potential of pyroxylin, introducing a line called *Balance*, which would give him an advantage in the market of the 1930s. Sheaffer, who had refused to produce pens with 18K gold nibs, did not export his products to France until the 1950s.

A. Shipman's Sons (New York).

Siebert & Lowen (Wuppertal, Germany). Founded in 1895. Manufacturer of *Matador* fountain pens.

Simplo (Hanover, Germany). See Montblanc.

Soennecken (Bonn, Germany). Founded in 1875 by Friedrich Soennecken (1848-1919), who was a calligrapher and the author of penmanship manuals. The company is the oldest German manufacturer of steel nibs (1890) and remained one of the most influential during the next 50 years. Upon Friedrich's death, his son, Alfred, succeeded him. The factories were destroyed during World War II. The 1950s were a difficult period. Despite a partnership with the Bayard Company, the company went out of business in 1967.

Stabil (Brussels, Belgium). Trademark used by Chaim Jakubowicz, a distributor for Sheaffer. Sold fountain pens bearing the trademarks *Stabil-Drake*, *Majestic* (1946). Went out of business in 1974.

Staedler (Nuremburg, Germany). Pencil factory founded in 1662 by Friderich Staedler. While retaining pencils as its major product, the company launched the manufacture of fountain pens after World War I. It is today the largest manufacturer of drafting and writing instruments in the world.

Stellor (Paris/Pavillons-sous-Bois, France). Founded in 1918 by Joseph Beaufils. 39, rue Doudeauville in Paris, then 288, avenue Aristide-Briand in Pavillons-sous-Bois. Factories in Nurieux (Ain, France) and La Ferté-Millon (Aisne, France). Closed from 1942 to 1945, the company went out of business in 1956.

Stephens (Levallois-Perret, France). Founded in the 1930s by an influential English ink manufacturer. *Autograph* and *Royal* fountain pens.

Stortz (Graz, Austria).

Stroesser (Paris, France). *Matcher Pen*, *Matcher Colombes*, and *Jeep* fountain pens.

Stylomine (Paris, France). Originally the Y.E. Zuber Company, specialized in the cutting and stamping of metals. Produced, among other items, nibs, clips, and mechanical pencils. The latter were sold under the trademark *Stylomine* (1921). Fountain pen manufacturing began in 1925, and in 1930, the launching of the *303* was an enormous success. It was filled through a system using air compression of a rubber sac. This pen with a retractable nib is one of the rarest examples of automatic filling. In 1934, the company changed its name to S.A. des Établissements Stylomine. In later years, the company introduced the tube and accordion filling system, which was copied by most French manufacturers after the original patent expired.

StyloPneu (Neuilly-sur-Seine, France). Filling was accomplished through an external rubber bulb, which compressed the reservoir, or by blowing into the pen.

Swan (Great Britain). See Mabie Todd.

Tabo (Bologna, Italy). Founded by Tantini. (TAntini BOlogna).

Tardy (Paris, France). *Optimus* (1919) and *Le Parisien* fountain pens.

Tibaldi (Florence, Italy). Founded in 1916.

Le Tigre (Antwerp/Brussels, Belgium). Registered in 1918 by Rene Kintz, it is the best known trademark in Belgium. Other Kintz trademarks are: *Le Lion*, *Le Loup*, *Le Régional*, *Lyceum Pen*, *Régent*, *Jubilé*, and *Regency*. In the 1960s, Kintz sold low-end fountain pens, such as the student model called *Tintin-Kuifje*, which was made in Germany. The company went out of business in 1985.

Tonnelier (Cholet, Maine-et-Loire, France). *Eric Pen* (1924), *Gallia*, *Reservo*, and *Lido* fountain pens.

Tourneries du Rhône (Lyon, Rhône, France). *Stylox* is the trademark.

Tourteau (Paris, France). Clips; *L.T.* is the trademark.

Tropen (Ludenscheid, Germany). Founded by Gustav Schroeder. Injection molds for plastics. Began manufacturing fountain pens in 1925. Still in business today.

J. Ullrich & Co. (New York). Founded in 1884. *Independent* and *Elk* fountain pens.

Unic (Paris, France). Founded in 1919 by Kothe and Vannier. 51, rue Rochechouart.

Viala Lilliput (Paris, France). See Gold Starry.

Visconti (Florence, Italy). Founded in 1988 by Dante del Vecchio and Luigi Poli. Specializes in fountain pens and other writing instruments made from celluloid following the original process for making celluloid as developed by the Hyatt brothers in 1869.

Gunther Wagner (Hanover, Germany). See Pelikan.

Wahl-Eversharp (Chicago, Illinois). Founded in 1905, the Wahl Adding Machine Company took over the Japanese company Ever-Sharp Pencil in 1914 and the Boston Pen Company in 1917, becoming the Wahl Company. Entered the French market in 1922 (Frazar France). The best known pen trademarks are *Personal Point* (1929) and *Doric* (1931). Wahl and its affiliate Eversharp merged in 1940. The *Skyline* model was introduced in 1941. In 1957, Parker acquired the writing instrument division of Eversharp and liquidated it 5 years later.

A.A. Waterman (New York). Founded in 1897 by Arthur Waterman (no relation to Lewis Edson Waterman). In 1902, he launched the *Modern Middle Joint Fountain Pen*, one section of which extends all the way to the middle of the body to avoid leaks and stains on the fingers. Introduced the *Automatic Self-Filling Modern Fountain Pen*, which was filled by twisting the rubber sac. The company went into business with Frazer & Geyer in 1902, which proved to be a bad move. In 1905, Frazer & Geyer took over control of the company and the name. Lewis Edson's heirs objected to the use of the name and went to court in 1912. It was decided by the court that from then on, catalogs and advertising should mention that there was no connection between A.A. Waterman and L.E. Waterman. Four years later, A.A. Waterman stopped producing fountain pens.

L.E. Waterman Co. (New York). Founded in 1888 by Lewis Edson Waterman 4 years after he registered a patent on a feed design. Circa 1910, the company controlled three quarters of the U.S. market, and until 1925, it was the largest pen company in the U.S. A reluctance in accepting technological innovations, such as the replacement of black hard rubber by plastics with a nitrocellulose base, led to its decline in the 1930s. Production stopped in 1954. The U.S. trademark was sold to Baron Bich, who sold it back to Waterman S.A. (France) in 1971. In 1972, the English trademark was also acquired by Waterman S.A.

Waterman S.A. (Paris, France). In 1914, Jules Fagard was the distributor for L.E. Waterman Co. in France and Belgium. In 1926, he founded Jif-Waterman. His widow and daughter managed the company, which became Waterman S.A.. His granddaughter, Francine Gomez, made Waterman S.A. the premier European fountain pen manufacturer and the second worldwide. The company was sold to the U.S. company Gillette in 1986. From 1967 on, all Waterman fountain pens have been manufactured in France in the factory of Saint-Herblain located near Nantes.

Wearever (North Bergen, New Jersey). David Kahn Inc. Specialized in the low-end fountain pen with steel nibs. For years the company produced more pens than Waterman, Parker, Sheaffer, and Wahl-Eversharp combined.

Weidlich Simpson (Cincinnati, Ohio). Founded in 1895 (Wright Pen Co.). Went out of business in 1921.

Wirt (Bloomsburg, Pennsylvania). The most important manufacturer of the last century. In 1878, Paul E. Wirt registered a patent for a simple fountain pen. A few were manufactured by hand, and in 1885, he designed his own machinery and launched mass production. He was the first to mechanize the production of fountain pens and claimed that one million had been made in his factories over a 10-year period; a number four times that made by Waterman. In 15 years, he claimed to have manufactured more fountain pens than all of his competitors combined. Beginning in 1900, competition would inexorably drive Wirt out of business, which finally occurred in 1937.

Wyvern (Leicester, England). Founded in 1896 by David, Alec, and Alfred Finburgh. Stayed in business until 1955.

Y.E. Zuber (Paris, France). See Stylomine.

INDEX

Bibliography

Bowen Glen, *Collectible Fountain Pens*, Glenview, IL, 1982.

Castruccio Enrico, *La Penna*, IdeaLibri, Milan, 1985.

Columbain Marcel, *l'Aventure multiple des outils de l'écriture*, 1963.

Desechaliers, *Annuaires de la papeterie et de l'imprimerie.*

Edgar G., "The Story of the Fountain Pen", *London Magazine*, 1904.

Fischler George and **Schneider** Stuart, *Fountain Pens and Pencils*, Shiffer Publishing, West Chester, PA, 1990.

Fournier Lucien, "Le stylo, c'est la vie", *la Science et la Vie*, December 1925.

Fritz Paul, "La Plume: partie essentielle du stylo", *Papetier de France*, March 1962.

Gandillet Etienne, "Avec le porte-plume à réservoir, nous sommes loin de la plume d'oie", *la Science et la Vie*, March 1920.

Germano Stefano, *Signori, la Penna*, La Stilographica, Bologne.

Habert L., "Fountain Pen, les plumes d'or à réservoir", *la Nature* (no. 1 574), 1903.

Huber Jurg-Peter, *Griffel - Feder - Bildschirmstift, Eine Kulturgesicichte der Schreibgerate*, AT Verlag, Aarau, 1985.

Jackson Donald, *The Story of Writing*, Studio Vista, London. French translation, *Histoire de l'Écriture*, Denoel, Paris, 1982.

Lacroux Jean-Pierre and **VanCleem** Lionel, *la Mémoire des Sergent-Major*, Ramsay-Quintette, Paris, 1988. Italian translation, *Il Pennino*, Ulissediziona, Turin, 1988.

Lambrou Andreas, *Fountain Pen, Vintage and Modern*, Sotheby's Publications, London, 1989.

Lawrence Cliff, *Fountain Pens*, Paducah, Kentucky, Collector Books, 1977.

Lawrence Cliff, *Official P.F.C. Pen Guide*, Pen Fancier's Club, Dunedin, Florida, 1982.

Lawrence Cliff and **Lawrence** Judy, *An Illustrated Fountain Pen History*, Pen Fancier's Club, Dunedin, Florida, 1986.

Maginnis James P., "Reservoir, Fountain and Stylographic Pens", London, *Journal of the Society of Arts*, Nos. 2 761 to 2 764, Vol. LIII, October and November, 1905.

Nakasono Hiroshi, *les Porte-Plume réservoir dans le monde*, Tokyo, Kodanska, 1985.

Schneider Stuart L. and **Etter** Roberta B., *Collecting and Valuing Early Fountain Pens*, Hudson Valley Graphics, Teaneck, NJ, 1980.

Schneider Stewart and **Fischler** George, *The Book of Fountain Pens and Pencils*, Westchester, PA, 1992.

Sénéchal Georges, *l'Industrie des porte-plume réservoirs en France*, Éditions de la Revue dactylographique, Paris.

Tavanti Sergio, *La Penna silografica, origini, funzionamento e collezione*, Alberti & C., Arezzo, 1987.

Whalley Joyce Irene, *Writing Implements and Accessories*, Newton Abbot, David & Charles, 1975.

Collectors Clubs

(Between parentheses: year of founding and frequency of bulletin)

Belgium. Belgian Pen Collectors' Association (1986), *La Plume d'Oie/De Ganzepen* (x4)

Canada. Collectors' Club of Canada (1984), *Writing Instrument* (x4)

United States. American Pencil Club Collectors (1957), *Pencil Collector* (x12)
Pen Fancier's Club (1977), *The Pen Fancier's Magazine* (x6)
Pen Collectors of America, Inc. *The Pennant* (x4)
Pen World (non-affiliated)

France. Club des collectionneurs de plumes, porte-plume réservoir et objets d'écriture (1979) *Au fil de la plume* (x4)

Great Britain. Writing Equipment Society (1980), *Journal of the W.E.S.* (x3)

Germany. Internationales Forum Historische Burowe (1981) *Historische Burowelt* (x4), *HBW Aktuell* (x8)

Italy. Accademia Italiana della Penna Stilografica *Stilomania* (x4)

Acknowledgments

Roland Bergue, Roland Germain,
Bernard Jouve, Patrick Kuperfis, Kimiyasu Tatsuno,
Patrick van Hoof, Lionel Van Cleem.

Printed in Italy

by G. Canale & C. S.p.A.

Borgaro T.se - Turin